MW00465823

EARLY AMERICAN STUDIES

SERIES EDITORS:
Daniel K. Richter, Kathleen M. Brown, Max Cavitch, and David Waldstreicher

Exploring neglected aspects of our colonial, revolutionary, and early national history
and culture, Early American Studies reinterprets familiar themes and events in fresh
ways. Interdisciplinary in character, and with a special emphasis on the period
from about 1600 to 1850, the series is published in partnership with
the McNeil Center for Early American Studies.

A complete list of books in the series is available from the publisher.

# THE COMMERCE OF
# VISION

*Optical Culture and Perception in Antebellum America*

## PETER JOHN BROWNLEE

**PENN**

UNIVERSITY OF PENNSYLVANIA PRESS

Philadelphia

Published by
University of Pennsylvania Press
Philadelphia, Pennsylvania 19104-4112
www.upenn.edu/pennpress

Printed in the United States of America on acid-free paper
10 9 8 7 6 5 4 3 2 1

Library of Congress Cataloging-in-Publication Data
Names: Brownlee, Peter John, author.
Title: The commerce of vision: optical culture and perception in antebellum America / Peter John Brownlee.
Other titles: Early American studies.
Description: 1st edition. | Philadelphia: University of Pennsylvania Press, [2018] | Series: Early American studies | Includes bibliographical references and index.
Identifiers: LCCN 2018020816 | ISBN 9780812250428 (hardcover)
Subjects: LCSH: Visual communication—United States—History—19th century. | Visual perception—Economic aspects—United States—History—19th century. | United States—Commerce—History—19th century. | United States—Economic conditions—To 1865. | Vision.
Classification: LCC P93.5 .B739 2018 | DDC 302.2/22—dc23
LC record available at https://lccn.loc.gov/2018020816

# ⊱ CONTENTS ⊰

Phillips & honored our house with a call. But sages of the crowd are like kings foeenvironed with deference & ceremony, that a call like this gives no true word for the mind & heart.

The true medicine for hard times seems to be sleep. Use so much bodily labor as shall ensure sleep, then you arise refreshed and in good spirits and in Hope. That have I this morn. Yesterday afternoon I stirred the earth about my shrubs & trees & quarreled with the piper-grass, and now I have slept, no longer am morose nor feel twitchings in the muscles of my face when a visiter is by. The humblebee & the pine warbler seem to me the proper objects of attention in these disastrous times*. I am less inclined to Ethics, to history to aught wise & grave & practick, & feel a new joy in nature. I am glad it is not my duty to preach these few sundays & I would invite the sufferers by this screwing panic to recover peace through these fantastic amusements during the tornado.

Our age is ocular.

* The hollowness so sad we feel after too much talking is an expressive hint

## ⇥ INTRODUCTION ⇤

# An Ocular Age: Vision
# in a World of Surfaces

In a journal entry dated May 14, 1837, Ralph Waldo Emerson wrote: "Harder times. Two days since, the suspension of specie payments by the New York and Boston banks."[1] Emerson, like many of his generation, was attuned to one of the most pressing financial issues of the day. The chain of events leading to the suspension of specie payments that Emerson lamented was initiated by President Andrew Jackson's destruction of the Second Bank of the United States in the mid-1830s. As he departed office, Jackson vetoed the bank's recharter and issued the Specie Circular, a primary engine for westward expansion, which required purchases of government land be made in gold or silver, not in paper banknotes. As a result of President Andrew Jackson's scorn for the Second Bank, which served as a fiscal agent for the government, its charter had been allowed to expire in 1836. Amid the financial and cultural catastrophes of the Panic of 1837, Emerson's entry went on to praise sleep as the only palliative against the ills and ailments of the day. But the nation was now "wide awake" as it faced the prospect of further deregulation of banking in an era of western expansion and national development. Banknotes, which fluctuated wildly in value, underscored the watchfulness, the vigilance necessary to keep oneself solvent and self-sufficient. These worn pieces of paper circulated widely, emblematizing the exchange, and corresponding perception, of printed information and its continually fluctuating value that had come to define the era's cultural *optics*. Below the entry, Emerson scratched the elliptic but prophetic phrase "Our age is ocular" (Figure 1). The inscription is as vague and inscrutable as it is provocative. That he pairs it with the Panic of 1837 and the paper money economics of the period is one of the key subjects of this book.

Well before the collapse of the Second Bank of the United States, paper had become a central medium of exchange in antebellum America, circulating in the form of banknotes, handbills, broadsides, and newspapers.[2] These cultural forms and the practices they facilitated were part of a broader set of developments that historians have hailed as "revolutions" in transportation, communication, and the capitalist marketplace. Such changes altered the fabric of daily life during the second quarter of the nineteenth century. New forms of production and distribution fashioned new modes of consumption, as more Americans, urban and rural, were drawn into the market economy's system of wage labor and increasingly mechanized forms of commodity production. A growing infrastructure for transportation—manifested in the expansion of the nation's network of roads and canals and in the development of steam-powered railroads and boats—enlarged the market's reach, while new modes of communication—facilitated by new technologies such as the electromagnetic telegraph and steam-powered, mechanized printing presses—transformed the ways in which Americans related to one another, assessed their expanding nation, and understood the world around them.[3] The age was ocular, to borrow Emerson's elliptic phrase, because so much of its proliferating culture targeted the eyes: newspapers, pamphlets, books, posters, signs, popular prints, painting exhibitions, and spectacular entertainments. As something to be viewed, scanned, skimmed, or read, paper also functioned increasingly as a medium of perception, as a vehicle for a new kind of seeing. And just as these objects were intended to circulate, they were produced for people on the move, and thus remind us of the motility and mobility of observers and how these affected their perception. Amid this thriving print and visual culture, the eyes both saw and were seen. Eyes were considered the primary organ for visual experience and the accumulation of knowledge; yet, they were also, like so many other surfaces, to be scanned as one might gloss over a page of print. They were thought capable of penetrating discernment or indicative of a person's inner character, virtual windows onto the soul, and yet, they themselves often failed in fits of fatigue and overstimulation.

*The Commerce of Vision* attends to how vision was understood and experienced during this tumultuous period. To do so, it investigates how vision was rendered in the crowded visual field of antebellum America. The new visual experiences of the antebellum city produced new knowledge about vision's capabilities and consequentially cultivated new perceptual practices, habits, and aptitudes. But these new experiences also highlighted vision's shortcomings within a visual field increasingly defined by a print culture premised on mobility, ephemerality, and unbridled commerce. Shifting the focus of one's sight from the tiny print of newspapers, pamphlets, and periodicals to the boldest display types deployed on broadsides, posters, and signboards underscored for observers the necessity of maintaining the widest possible range of visual acuity. These forms stressed the importance of vision and emphasized its "normal" functioning as well as its thresholds and its limits. This thriving visual culture physically stressed the eyesight of observing subjects, while several of its many objects bore traces of the culture's reckoning with vision's physiological processes and problems. Emerson, who suffered from a failure of his own vision in the mid-1820s yet posited sight as a key trope in his transcendental philosophy, knew this first hand.

Early in the essay *Nature* (1836), Emerson expounds on what has since become one of the most enduring symbols of his day: "In the woods, we return to reason and faith. There I feel that nothing can befall me in life,—no disgrace, no calamity (leaving me my eyes), which nature cannot repair. Standing on the bare ground,— my head bathed by the blithe air and uplifted into infinite space,—all mean egotism vanishes. I become a transparent eyeball; I am nothing; I see all; the currents of the Universal Being circulate through me; I am part or parcel of God."[4] All seeing yet lacking substance, the disembodied, transparent eye floats in an infinite space. Capable of a clarity of vision often associated with the eye of God, this eyeball bespeaks a romantic seer for whom perception is all-encompassing.[5] It was but one of several images of the all-seeing, monocular eye that graced the cornerstones of buildings, the mastheads of newspapers, and the national seal in the antebellum visual field.[6] It was also the key component of the optical instrument known as the camera obscura, which since antiquity had served as a model for human eyesight.[7] Widely regarded as a seminal statement of American transcendentalism, the philosopher's lofty pronouncement is preceded, however, by an earthly concern. For the transparent eye crucially depends on properly functioning eyesight, which involves not one but both eyes working together, as Emerson acknowledges in the previous sentence. "There is no calamity that nature cannot repair except for the debilitation of the eyes." Emerson's trope fuses the ideal of a dematerialized, objective, and transcendent vision with a model of eyesight physiologically embedded in the mechanisms of the human body, subject to fluxes of time, space, and shifts in lighting or atmospheric conditions as well as to debility and disease. A pencil sketch by the little-known artist and Emerson accolyte Christopher Pearse Cranch playfully captures the hybridity of the philosopher's vision (Figure 2).[8] Embodied, though still monocular, Cranch's eyeball sits atop an armless body with long legs. Sporting a hat and coat with tails, the figure's long stride bespeaks a roving gaze and posits a thoroughly mobile, ambulatory vision. With top-hatted eyeball "bathed by the blithe air and uplifted into infinite space," Cranch's gangly figure demonstrates how Emerson's "transcendent" sight was weighted by the limitations of the body, here clothed in the fashion of the day. With coat and tails signifying his stake in the market economy, Cranch's figure vividly acknowledges that vision, as constituent of an age that is "ocular," was ultimately grounded in broader intellectual, scientific, and commercial currents. As he wanders, the clouds above his head allude to the difficulty of seeing clearly amid the market's obfuscating surfaces and dense networks of exchange.

Similar to most Americans whose eyes failed them, Emerson's own troubled eyesight provided the most instructive lessons in physiological optics. It is well known that Emerson suffered in the 1820s and early '30s from a partial loss of sight resulting from a bout with tuberculosis.[9] Suffering from an inflammation of the eye, he received treatment from Boston's preeminent ophthalmologist, Dr. Edward Reynolds. Reynolds represented the advanced guard of ophthalmic surgeons whose efforts helped to professionalize the field during the second quarter of the nineteenth century. A student of British surgeon James Wardrop, Reynolds brought back from his training in England Wardrop's methods for treating cataract and inflammation of the eye. In 1824, one year before he treated Emerson, Reynolds founded the Massachusetts Charitable Eye and Ear Infirmary. A decade of work there proved to Reynolds, writing in 1835, "that an unusual prevalence of diseases of the eye marks the period in which we live. Indeed, they are so prevalent, that they may be considered one of its common and peculiar trials."[10] It is likely that Reynolds diagnosed Emerson with a condition that Wardrop had identified as "rheumatic inflammation of the eye," or ophthalmia rheumatica, accompanied by arthritic pains in other parts of the body. Treatment involved puncturing the cornea and evacuating the aqueous humor collected behind it. This delicate operation required specialized knowledge of the eyes' anatomy and their morbid physiology as well as familiarity with the latest surgical techniques.[11] Reynolds's treatment was successful, allowing Emerson to continue writing and lecturing. His plight reveals that as the market system increasingly targeted the sensory capacities of human bodies in order to attract or interpellate and position them as consumers, Americans came to locate the properties, processes, and problems of vision in their own bodies, as well as in their fiscal ability to correct and maintain it.

With the emergence of physiological optics in the 1830s and '40s, and interrelated developments in the growing field of applied ophthalmogy, the mechanics of vision could no longer be explained without reference to the physiological functions of the human body. Thus the dematerialized model of vision demonstrated by the monocular camera obscura was largely abandoned, first in scientific circles and later by the public at large. Experimental physiology and applied ophthalmology revealed instead that the eye's aqueous humors functioned in tandem with the

"Standing on the bare ground, — my head bathed by the blithe air, & uplifted into infinite space, — all mean egotism vanishes. I become a transparent Eyeball." *Nature. p. 13.*

**FIGURE 2.** Christopher Pearse Cranch, *Illustrations of the New Philosophy:* "*Standing on the bare ground,—my head bathed by the blithe air, & uplifted into infinite space,—all mean egotism vanished. I become a Transparent Eyeball*" (seq. 4), c. 1837–1839. Houghton Library, Harvard University, Cambridge, MA.

retina in producing and maintaining sensation. Studies of binocular vision, which would eventually assume the popular form of the stereoscope, revealed that the eyes functioned as a pair, rather than separately, to enable a wider field of view and greater depth perception, as well as an array of other eye movements critical to "properly" functioning vision. So while the monocular, all-seeing eye continued to circulate widely in the visual field, its symbolic currency and cultural relevance faded as the model of vision it promulgated lost its utility in the imagination of a public whose eyes were diseased, malformed, or otherwise disfunctional. Abandoning the theoretical conceit that eyes, whether symbolic or actual, could enable an objective or godlike view, Americans became active stewards of their own vision and came to understand vision as *subjective*, that is, subject to the size and distance of the objects of vision, to varying light conditions, to movement, and to fluctuations in mental and bodily health. In response, they sought measures to correct and enhance their eyesight, as well as ways to train it, to entertain, or "please," it.

Moving outward from the embodied experience of seeing, the first steps in doing so—the process of what I will call the *culturing* of vision—often involved engaging first with printed, carved, or painted representations of eyes, some represented singly, but increasingly in pairs and bespectacled (Figure 3). Whether viewers consulted an ophthalmic treatise, looked up an ophthalmic surgeon in the local newspaper, or walked the city streets in search of an optician's shop, they were likely to confront such imagery, and in a multitude of forms. Along with their impact on the mechanics of sight, such imagery shaped expectations for vision itself.

In the urban visual field, depictions of eyes or the spectacles that came to represent them multiplied the roving eyes of people in parlors, stores, and streets. These orbs, bespectacled or bare, lurked in graphic form in type founders' and printers' specimens and in the various forms of ephemera their stock cuts, engraved in wood or steel, populated. Such representations of eyes in print or on signboards often advertised ophthalmologists and opticians; they peered out from the mastheads of newspapers, from posters and banners, and from the surfaces of paintings. In congested city streets, eyes, literal and figural, were to be apprehended at every turn. Architectural details, especially windows, were likened to eyes, as in George Lippard's description of *The Quaker City*'s TON Hotel, "which arises along Chestnut street, a monster-building, with some hundred windows varying its red-brick face, in the way of eyes, goggles intended to preserve the sight of the visual organs aforesaid; while the verandah, on the ground floor, affording an entrance to the bar-room, might be likened to the mouth of the grand-edifice,

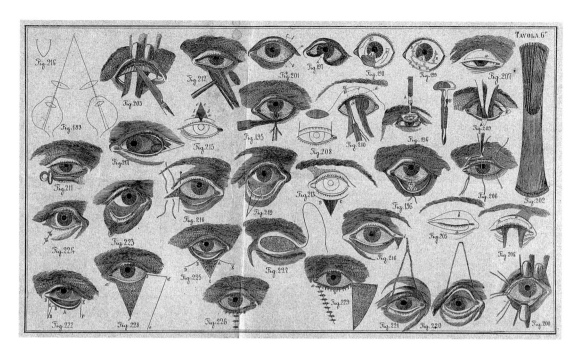

**FIGURE 3.** A sheet showing optical instruments, eye examinations, and anatomical diagrams of the eye with a numbered key, n.d., wood engraving, 20.5 × 36.2 cm. Wellcome Library, London.

always wide open and ready to swallow a customer."[12] Likewise, the windows of stagecoaches, omnibuses, and railroad cars also formed makeshift apertures, while awnings, buntings, sidewalks, market sheds, and signposts—eyelids of sorts—framed temporary views. In the suddenly fluid and fulsome exchange of words and images that came to characterize antebellum urban experience, these eyes circulated as a kind of currency amid the rapidly expanding *commerce* of vision, mirroring the binocular makeup of observing subjects left to reckon with vision in all of its philosophical and physiological as well as financial and fiscal dimensions. More so than their monocular predecessors had, these disembodied pairs of eyes had much more to say about the nature of embodied vision in an era of transformative social, economic, and technological change.

As part of the circulation of this widely disparate, widely dispersed iconography, the eyes and the vision they enabled became the subjects of both popular and specialized interest that examined the eyes' "philosophy" and "language" as well as their anatomy and physiology.[13] The blend of philosophical, physiological, and practical conceptions of the eyes invoked by Emerson in *Nature* was in fact characteristic of a broader cluster of discourses regarding vision and visuality in the antebellum decades. Rarely viewed solely as an abstract philosophical phenomenon, human vision was conceptualized and considered from a multiplicity of personal and professional perspectives during this period.[14] Early ophthalmic tracts blended philosophical musings with thinly veiled temperance messages and homespun remedies. Treatises explored the philosophy of the eyes, examined their physiognomic "language," and elaborated the physiological aberations of vision—retinal afterimages, subjective haloes, and physiological colors—which fascinated readers and enabled specialists to better define the range of "normal" vision. For others, these aspects of sight suggested techniques for seeing the unseeable, while still others traded in vision's metaphoric qualities to promote methods for figuratively seeing over the horizon and beyond. Outside the purview of clinical and applied ophthalmology, yet intuitively attuned to key discoveries in this emerging field, typefounders and job printers designed typefaces and orchestrated broadsides, respectively, each with the goal of attracting and appealing to human eyes. Writers and painters employed tropes and motifs from philosophical works as well as physiological and practical ophthalmic tracts to muse on the properties and problems of vision as well as the epistemological perils it posed. In a variety of forms—conceptual, theoretical, practical—vision itself circulated as a metaphor as well as a method, as a physical system premised on the transmission of light as well as a set of physiological processes grounded in the fluctuations of the body, and as a commercial product and as a productive phenomenon in a cultural moment in which experience itself was increasingly commodified and new forms of work and play restructured sensory activities.[15] At the intersection of these various discourses and practices, an entirely new understanding of vision and its limits emerged.

Navigating this constantly expanding field of visuality, a term I will use to describe the circulation of images or texts intended for visual interpretation or "consumption," required Americans to "watch their eyes" in President Jackson's parting words. Echoing broader currents, Emerson considered the eye "the best of artists." But even by the "mutual action of its structure" and of the "laws of light," he admitted, the eye failed to compose a unified picture of the surrounding world.[16] For Emerson, American cultural life, especially in urban centers, was increasingly defined by its surfaces rather than its depths. "In New York lately," he wrote in his journal in early 1842, "as in cities generally, one seems to lose all substance, & become surface in a world of surfaces. Everything is external and I remember my hat & coat, and all my other surfaces, & nothing else. . . . I visited twice & parted with a most polite lady without giving her reason to believe that she had met any other in me than a worshipper of surfaces, like all Broadway. It stings me yet."[17] Refuting period discourses of physiognomy and phrenology that claimed that surfaces could, in fact, be read or decoded to ascertain and reveal inner truths, Emerson's lament likely came in response to the proliferation of consumer goods as well as the newspapers, posters, and signage deployed to advertise them, the paper banknotes used to purchase them, even the lenses of spectacles that enabled clear sight of them. Such surfaces, as they referenced products, services, news of elsewhere, parcels of land available for purchase, or monetary value in the form of gold on demand, mediated their objects, offering refracted views of the "inner truths" of objects that bordered on the opaque. Leaving the sensibilities in shambles, the proliferation of surfaces in the 1840s decentered viewers and destabilized their perceptions of a rapidly changing landscape. "The ruin or blank, that we see when we look at nature," Emerson wrote, "is in our own eye. The axis of vision is not coincident with the axis of things, and so they appear not transparent but opake [sic]." Emerson's counter to surfaces was spirit, the so-called axis of things.[18] For the increasingly mobile culture of antebellum America, however, stable viewpoints and perspectives on the objects and the things they referenced often failed to align with the "realities" they referenced. Paper notes failed to align with the values they represented; land speculation maps alluded to but often failed to equate with the land they purported to represent. Apparently a transparent rendering of the physical world, a world increasingly given to the obfuscating mechanisms of consumer capitalism, was ultimately impossible. For Emerson, the rift that had opened between perception and transparence stemmed from the simple fact that man had become "disunited with himself." As a result, Emerson felt that the world of the mid-1830s—riddled with bank failures, rampant market expansion, unprecedented geographic and social mobility, and the vast circulation of paper in various forms—lacked "unity," which as he felt, left the world "broken and in heaps." For Emerson, perception was clouded by physiology just as a "unified" world was torn asunder by the ways that the market reconfigured social relations to account for and accommodate the fluid identities of persons and products. For Emerson and countless others, a theoretically transparent but properly functioning human vision was central to the equation.

To illuminate the practice of seeing during the antebellum decades, this book concerns itself with the materiality of vision through an analysis of both the objects *of* vision, such as signs and advertisement, as well as objects such as spectacles that facilitated it and objects such as newspapers and banknotes that as virtual surrogates figuratively extended its reach. Building on art historian Jonathan Crary's recovery of "an observer who also takes shape in other, grayer practices and discourses," *The Commerce of Vision* traces the formation of the observer in those "grayer practices and discourses" of both ophthalmology and popular physiology. But it also examines this observer's formation, and occasional disintegration, in objects including paintings, engravings, and signboards; in the construction, advertisement, and use of spectacles and other aids to vision; and in pictures of people studying the fine print of newspapers, banknotes, contracts, and maps.[19] Conceptions of vision and formulations of observing subjects do, in fact, cohere and reside in the line of an engraving, in the shaded areas of bold new letterforms, or in the meticulous rendering of transparent glass in prints and paintings. In these objects are to be found those traces of the viewer and notions of what constituted vision at a particular juncture in the cultural history of the United States.

Efforts to redefine vision reflected growing concerns about the body's fitness to withstand the increased demands placed on it by market life.[20] Through publication and practice, ophthalmology and its more popular forms helped to make vision *visible* for antebellum Americans, whose eyesight faced new challenges in a cultural landscape undergoing rapid transformation. Ophthalmology, like other forms and practices, evolved with the burgeoning market system and participated in the formation of "market" subjects, a general cultural process in which the marketplace reoriented its constitutents' perceptual habits, patterns of thought, and behaviors to the purposes of maintaining one's health and sobriety, earning a living wage, and consuming. Notions of embodied subjectivity, premised on ideas of possessive individualism and integral to democratic citizenship, relied on and were facilitated, in large part, by the theoretical and practical embodiment of vision in the opening decades of the nineteenth century. As demonstrated by the art historian Wendy Bellion, an earlier, crucial stage in this process had called upon spectators to hone their ocular abilities and skills to enable the degree of discernment necessary for navigating the new political realities of citizenship in the early national period.[21] As the market economy came to more fully constitute and structure the mechanics of daily life, such visual aptitudes and abilities became even more critical for political as well as professional and personal well-being. For the increasing number of clerks, copyists, and others of the so-called white-collar class during the second quarter of the nineteenth century, the profit of one's labor, the property it earned, and the propriety it ensured, increasingly depended on the "economy" of one's eyes, a period phrase that alluded both to the efficiency and efficacy of their mechanisms and the increasingly cost-based maintenance of their general fitness.[22] The contributions of ophthalmology and reform physiology to public notions of the capacities and character of vision incorporated these white-collar workers into the increasingly information-based, *visual* culture that facilitated the market's vast expansion in the years between the opening of the Erie Canal and the Civil War. But while emerging formulations of vision's embodiment facilitated a more thorough integration of the self into the machinery of the market economy, they also pointed out how individuals with poor eyesight might be denied access to or excluded from the manner of exchange that so prevalently defined and animated antebellum consumer culture.

With the aim of acuity and general ocular health, a growing and increasingly specialized group of ophthalmic surgeons sought to better understand the critical functions of acuity and accommodation in order to correct or ameliorate the key ocular problems of their day: cataract, astigmatism, myopia, hyperopia, and strabismus. In the course of investigating these conditions and devising methods for their correction, the emerging field of physiological optics developed a more sophisticated lexicon to describe the eye's complexities and its numerous pathologies. Filling the pages of scientific treatises, this increasingly specialized language also found its way into the common parlance of popular print, thus broadening the discourse of vision while highlighting its aptitudes and especially its failures. As clinical investigation and practical treatment of these problems advanced, however, the cultural conversation surrounding vision continued to hinge on issues of transparency and opacity, on the veracity of representation, and on perception's abilities to apprehend knowledge and truth. Indeed, as Emerson warned early in *Nature*, "empirical science is apt to cloud the sight, and, by the very knowledge of functions and processes, to bereave the student of the manly contemplation of the whole."[23] As nascent forms of professional ophthalmology and optometry strove to qualify and quantify vision, antebellum culture, more broadly, pondered from a variety of angles vision's complications and inadequacies. Because indistinct vision, or the inability to see, makes us look harder, it is only when vision breaks down that it becomes noticeable at all. Such ocular impairment raises questions regarding the knowledge that vision helps to produce, what it enables and allows us to know, even what it obfuscates and misconstrues. As such, this study fastens onto the cloudy, the unclear, the ambiguous as it calls attention to vision's inabilities and underscores cultural concern regarding its maintenance and meanings. Cartoons and genre paintings framed such questions in period syntax, probing vision's propensities and problems in engaging and entertaining ways. Stories lampooned the employment of spectacles or the foibles of faulty vision. Sight and seeing, or the inability to do so clearly, were also inscribed in the bold, ink-saturated surfaces, the new and revised shapes, and the enlarged scale of period typography. Together, these forms posed vision as subject to uncertainty, to fluxes of time and space, and to outright failure. Looking to conceptions and practices of vision circulating in scientific and philosophical discourse as well as the broader cultural field, *The Commerce of Vision* analyzes how ophthalmic and optometric practices, popular pamphlets and newspapers, literary stories and novels, prints and paintings, along with discourses of paper money economics, national expansion, urban planning, and spiritualism helped to fashion the shifting status of observing subjects, and the contours and experience of vision itself.

Though the term "visual culture" has been employed in a number of ways since its inception in the early 1970s, including as a shorthand reference to an expanded field of images and objects for analysis, I use it generally to refer both to visuality, or the datum of what we see, and to vision, or how we see it. But I employ the term specifically in this book to refer to the *culturing* of vision, that is, the cultivation of sight, including the mechanics of its physiological operations as well as the accumulation of visual experiences, predilections, memories, or references, what has been called the viewer's "cognitive stock," or "period eye."[24] The interrelated print and visual cultures of the period participated in the broader redefinition of visual perception in scientific and philosophical discourses circulating in the first half of the nineteenth century.[25] Printed forms and paintings both embodied and illustrated an emergent model of vision that resulted from an accumulation of knowledge concerning the eye's physiological functioning and the emergence of a new range of visual aptitudes and experiences constitutive of cultural and economic modernity. In shaping the experience of vision, these new cultural forms and practices also gradually modulated the perceptual habits of observers and the aptitudes of vision itself. This culturing of vision involved various, yet interrelated aspects of the visual field working in tandem in the production of observers and viable formulations of vision itself.[26] In this way, the imbricated spheres of antebellum culture mentioned above enveloped and overlapped with the sensibilities of antebellum observers, determining both intellectual and practical frameworks for assessing the nature of their eyesight and acclimating them to altogether new modes of practice.

Conceptions of eyesight emerging from the burgeoning fields of physiological optics and ophthalmology posited a model of vision that was subject to the fluxes of everyday life. Experimenters Johann Wolfgang von Goethe, Jan Purkinje, and Johannes Müller no longer considered vision objectively "universal," static, or completely dependent on exterior stimuli for its functioning.[27] Their experiments with retinal afterimages and other visual phenomena revealed that vision was, like the newspaper, the signboard, the banknote—fleeting and ephemeral, subject to fluctuations in time and space, and by extension, to fluctuations of the market and paper money economics. By the 1840s, vision was no longer theoretically situated in the apparatus of the camera obscura.[28] Nor was it securely contained within the laboratories and clinical spaces of physiological optics or the emergent practice of ophthalmology. Embedded in the physicality of the body, a body newly animated by the fluctuations of capital, eyesight was now considered subject to physical movement and vulnerable to an array of diseases, to the harmful effects of bright or dim light, or to the strain of focusing on a growing array of printed materials and other legible objects. Through the application of new ophthalmic techniques or the purchase and employment of spectacles, which aided the consumption of the daily paper and the discernment of broadsides, banknotes, and real estate maps, the mechanics of vision became integrated with the machinery of commodity production and the daily rhythms of a nascent industrial capitalism. The characteristically self-reflexive mode of seeing that emerged as a result, I will suggest, is a chief feature of antebellum visual culture and is indicative of the period's overarching concern with human vision.

# PART I

## The Problem of Vision

# CHAPTER ONE

# Ophthalmology, Popular Physiology, and the Market Revolution in Vision

Although extremely common, defective or degenerative eyesight was poorly understood and hence poorly treated in early America. Cataract and other ocular conditions, largely the result of poor nutrition and insalubrious sanitary conditions, plagued the eyes of early Americans. In the first half of the nineteenth century, however, a burgeoning field of clinical ophthalmology strove to take the guesswork out of diagnosis and treatment and experienced modest success. "It cannot have escaped the notice of every medical observer," wrote Boston's Edward Reynolds, an early specialist in ophthalmology, "that an unusual prevalence of diseases of the eye marks the period in which we live. Indeed," he continued, "they are so prevalent, that they may be considered one of its common and peculiar trials."[1] Reynolds's assessment echoes Emerson's observation of the period's obsession with ocularity. By 1835, the age-old problems of vision, increasingly treatable and correctable, were supplanted and occasionally exacerbated by conditions encouraged by a proliferation of print-based media and related viewing practices that emerged as part of broader economic and cultural transformations that together altered the antebellum visual field. Indeed, market modernization took an enormous toll on the eyes of Americans, especially those living in towns and cities. Amid vast technological, economic, and social change, new trades sprang up around the exchange of printed information—typesetters and printers, newspaper editors and journalists, clerks and copyists. White-collar work and labor practices reshaped by mechanization and the division of labor placed new demands on the human body and its sensory abilities. The so-called close work of labors involving the creation, manipulation, or use of minute parts, tools, or fine print performed in manufactories, countinghouses, legal offices, engravers' studios, and printing firms required healthy, temperate workers with dexterous hands, sharp minds, and even sharper eyes.

Market culture, characterized by intense urbanization and a proliferation of available goods and services, by vast flows of visual and typographic information to mediate and facilitate their distribution and consumption, and by new modes of impersonal social and economic exchange that developed as a result, required perceptual as well as cultural acuity. The proliferation of broadsides, handbills, signboards, and newspapers—all techniques for advertising an abundance of consumer goods—relied on the cognitive skills of viewing subjects as much as they cultivated, codified, and managed them. These new forms simultaneously increased visual aptitudes and appetites while attenuating the vision of those who suffered from "weakness" of sight. As this expanded culture of print proliferated, the importance of properly functioning eyesight grew considerably while new perceptual problems loomed. "In this age of progress, of letters and of multiform occupations," wrote New York physician James Henry Clark, "from the time that education is commenced to that period when active engagement ceases, earnest and practical people are ever taxing the eye to its utmost capabilities."[2] At both work and play, eyesight was subjected to a new range of visible objects, visual tasks, and viewing practices that, as Clark and others noted, "taxed" the eyes by exposing them to a profusion of pleasurable, profitable, and potentially perilous phenomena. Engulfed by this profusion of texts—printed ledgers and billheads, cheap newspapers and broadsides—and the dense visual nature of their myriad forms, antebellum culture registered the early stages of overstimulation, a phenomenon typically associated with the urban culture of the later nineteenth and early twentieth centuries. This resulted in widespread complaints of "weak eyes," reports of ocular ailments, and an outpouring of prescriptive techniques for avoiding or alleviating eyestrain.

New modes of production and consumption instigated widespread investigation of the body's productive and sensory capabilities. This remapping of the body and its senses enabled the rapid evolution of industrial capitalism during the nineteenth century. Like other medical or scientific fields devoted to the human body, the practice of ophthalmology experienced tremendous growth in the first half of the nineteenth century. A striking number of eye hospitals and infirmaries opened in American cities between 1820 and 1850, offering venues for the practice of a burgeoning field of surgeons increasingly devoted to ophthalmic pursuits, which included medicinal and surgical treatment, publication, and the education of others. Through dissection, surgery, and experimentation, ophthalmologists and physiologists began mapping the surfaces and interiors of the human eye, thus revealing the eye's internal "economy." A second category of optical specialists, working largely outside the increasingly codified arena of medical ophthalmology, recognized the economic implications of increasing the public's understanding of the eye. Specialists of all stripes published treatises explaining in lay terms the eye's basic mechanisms. Tracts written in an easy-to-understand vernacular instructed readers how to preserve and maintain eyesight through a commonsense program urging cleanliness, moderation, and temperance. Appropriating elements of physiologically based ophthalmic theories concerning the eye's properties, and combining them with homespun remedies and elements of reform literature, opticians and other popularizers of ocular principles explored the "economic" aspects and "productive" capacities of vision itself. Such treatises suggested ways to defend the eyes against disease and debilitation and posited a model of vision that coalesced around the needs of production and consumption in the antebellum decades.[3] In short, vision was both produced and consumed.

While vision remained subject to disease, damage, and debilitation, it was also subject to "improvement" through maintenance and training and, when these methods failed, to a range of corrective procedures and treatments. Techniques for the protection and preservation of the eyes disseminated in practical handbooks and popular tracts underscored the fragility as well as the profitability of healthy eyes. By providing remedies for ocular ailments, ophthalmology posited vision as an object of observation and treatment, and established "correct" vision as a commodity available on the open market. Recipients of ophthalmic treatment were in turn subjected to the flux of a capitalist marketplace that determined the availability of surgeons, facilities, medicines, spectacles, and other methods for correcting or caring for vision. In the process, both scientific and vernacular formulations of vision—as an object of ophthalmic investigation, as a productive tool in the workplace, or as an instrument for education or entertainment in the library or parlor—converged in their attention to the bodies of observers, both frail and fit, to offer conceptions of vision as alternately fixed and fleeting. As part of this complex matrix of social trends, advances in scientific thinking, and economic and technological developments, ophthalmology gradually evolved into an economically viable and socially valued practice. Vision, likewise, emerged as a valued and highly sought-after commodity.[4]

But despite enormous strides, ophthalmology, as a fully regulated and institutionally developed profession, did not emerge until after the Civil War. "Ophthalmologists" in the early republic were, in reality, general surgeons who specialized in certain ophthalmic techniques and practices. Some designated themselves ophthalmologists, while others retained the more general title. Regardless of the degree of individual specialization, however, the years between 1800 and 1850 were formative for the practice. Although ophthalmologists eventually succeeded in establishing their profession through an institutional network of eye hospitals and infirmaries, antebellum popular literature on eyesight and eyeglasses indicates that ophthalmology, in theory and practice, experienced the same ambivalence the general public held toward medicine and medical practitioners. Combining folk wisdom and an array of medical and surgical procedures in various stages of evolution and standardization, ophthalmology in this era was not a codified professional network of doctors and institutions. Although surgical and medicinal methods for correcting eyesight increasingly became the domain of well-trained surgeons working in officially sanctioned eye hospitals, they continued to be practiced and applied in patients' homes by family doctors or even itinerants with little to no medical training. Professionally trained ophthalmologists in the antebellum period struggled to establish themselves as authorities in the treatment of ocular diseases and disorders and strove to legitimize themselves and their practice through professional licensing. In their publications and advertisements they pitted themselves against itinerant "surgeons" or quackish "oculists," whose treatments lacked the precision and the sanction of "proper" medical training.[5]

The establishment of medical authority often necessitated the use of new media in the form of book and pamphlet publications and printed advertisements that with increasing frequency also featured graphic illustrations. To bolster their "professional" authority on optical matters, practitioners utilized treatises to explain complex ocular and optical principles, never losing an opportunity to publicly counter, expose, and devalue the quacks and pseudoscientists with whom they competed in the marketplace. Word of mouth and printed testimonials regarding their surgical and medical prowess also cemented their reputations. However, even as specialists devised and mastered techniques for the removal of cataracts and the correction of several other deformities and conditions, their efforts could not entirely *clarify* an antebellum visual field clouded by dense networks of market exchange, mass-produced commodities, and myriad forms of new media. In an elaborate period wood engraving (Figure 4), an ocular specialist authoritatively examines his patient, an activity pictured to explicate one step in an ophthalmic examination, showcase the pratitioner's knowledge, and emphasize his consumate skill. Notably, he is lighted while his patient remains in shadow. The latter's slightly smaller head and shaded face pairs on a more equal footing with

FIGURE 4. *Eye Doctor*, c. 1840, wood engraving. Granger, New York.

the filtered gaslight fixture, which casts a raking light across the surface of the patient's left eye, illuminating its interior for inspection. Both examiner and patient are fitted with lenses. Relatively simple in application, yet sophisticated in instrumental technique and theoretical armature, the practitioner examines a patient who clearly mirrors his own class status. With corresponding beard and genteel collared shirt and coat, the two figures share a certain understanding and appreciation for the scientific knowledge that undergirds the examination and guides the examiner. Their close, even intimate proximity demonstrates the tight circuit of practitioner and patient required for proper ophthalmic scrutiny, accurate assessment, and successful treatment. Along with disseminating knowledge of the practice and promise of clinical ophthalmology, the expertise and skill on display in this illustration reflect specialists' concerted efforts to create a culture of confidence needed to support and facilitate their expanding profession.

As this illustration attests, the professional literature published by practicing ophthalmologists steadily developed its own theoretical as well as technological sophistication, but an entire subset of ocular treatises prescribed methods for self-treatment and care. In fact, during this period of nascent development, standardization, and professionalization, the lines between these two literatures often blurred. Ophthalmic treatises published by physicians and surgeons both argued against and adapted elements from popular tracts, while self-help treatises incorporated elements of ophthalmic science. Vision and its treatment had become a contested arena where scientific, philosophical, economic, and vernacular formulations clashed and subsequently converged, as the work of "mainstream" and "sectarian" practitioners produced a body of knowledge on what constituted vision and what procedures offered the best ways to maintain it.[6]

During the early republic, ophthalmology in the United States experienced tremendous growth in the number of practitioners and institutions devoted to treatment of the eyes as well as the volume of dissertations and other treatises on vision-related topics. As knowledge of the eye spread, along with surgical methods and techniques to correct its problems, general surgeons incorporated ocular surgery into their range of surgical techniques. Phillip Syng Physick, William Gibson, and Samuel Gross, all of Philadelphia, made significant, albeit occasional contributions to ophthalmic surgery without necessarily specializing in its practice. Over time, however, a steadily growing number of surgeons worked exclusively on the eye, increasingly carrying out their work in hospitals and infirmaries based on European models. American students who had studied ophthalmology in London, Edinburgh, Utrecht, and Vienna returned to the United States to practice, publish, and teach. In Philadelphia, New York, and Boston, ophthalmic surgeons offered and attended lectures, demonstrations, and workshops, published in medical journals, popular magazines, pamphlets, and books, and opened hospitals and infirmaries devoted to the treatment of the eye and its surrounding muscular and neural frameworks. Practitioners treated an array of maladies such as cataracts, conjunctivitis, ophthalmia, inflammations of the eye, spots or ulcers on the cornea, and other ocular ailments, as the number of patients treated grew to the hundreds of thousands by century's end, and reports published in America's medical journals described treatments and recorded successes and failures.[7]

A smaller constellation of doctors and surgeons devoted their work exclusively to ophthalmology and were more directly involved in the development of the field and its institutional apparatuses. George Frick of Baltimore was the first American to restrict his professional work almost exclusively to ophthalmology. Completing his medical study at the University of Pennsylvania in 1815, he obtained a license to practice in his native city in 1817. That year, he visited Europe and studied with Viennese ophthalmologist Georg Beer. His year of study under Beer revealed to Frick the limited knowledge of eye diseases in America and the shortcomings of his American training. On his return to his native Baltimore, he immediately organized a special eye clinic connected to the Baltimore Dispensary and established a lecture series on the eye at the University of Maryland. He published his *Treatise on the Diseases of the Eye* in 1823, the first work of its kind to be produced in the United States.[8] Isaac Hays was born in Philadelphia in 1796 and spent his entire career there. Graduating in medicine from the University of Pennsylvania, his interest in ophthalmology led him to take a surgeon's post in the Pennsylvania Infirmary for Diseases of the Eye and Ear, founded in 1822. When the Wills Eye Hospital was founded in 1834, Hays became one of its chief surgeons, where he earned a reputation as a skilled and progressive ophthalmologist. He also contributed a number of articles to the *Journal of Medical and Physical Sciences* (soon after to become the *American Journal of the Medical Sciences*) and gave public lectures at schools and at the eye hospitals where he worked. Hays also edited American editions of Thomas Wharton Jones's *Principles and Practice of Ophthalmic Surgery* and William Lawrence's *Treatise on the Diseases of the Eye* and improved the design of ophthalmic instruments.[9] Squier Littell, whose brother founded the popular magazine *Littell's Living Age* in 1844, was born in 1803 and graduated from the University of Pennsylvania in 1824. After practicing briefly in South America, Littell returned to Philadelphia in 1826, where he joined the staff of the newly opened Wills Eye Hospital and remained there for thirty years. He published his *Manual on the Diseases of the Eye* in 1837, and in 1853 he edited the first American edition of H. H. Walton's *Treatise on Operative Ophthalmic Surgery*. Near the end of his career, he was an American pioneer in the application of the ophthalmoscope that Herman von Helmholtz invented and introduced into practice in the 1850s. Other American practitioners made significant contributions to the field of ophthalmology. In 1812, for example, Williams Ingalls of Boston published important suggestions regarding the operation for strabismus, and in 1821, surgeon William Gibson developed scissors for "cutting to pieces the crystalline lens in all cases of cataract." Other advances included surgical methods for operating on the eyelids, the cornea, blepharospasm, or spasms of the eyelids and insightful work on the theory of visual accommodation, or the process by which the eye adjusts and is able to focus at various distances.[10]

As protospecialists these practitioners, along with other general surgeons who performed eye surgery, eventually sought a centralized venue for their practice. Growing public need, philanthropically minded social reform, and the professionalization of an assortment of ocular specialists converged to establish a new institution: the eye hospital. Between 1817 and 1834 six major centers for the treatment of the eye and its maladies opened in New London, Connecticut, New York, Philadephia, Baltimore, and Boston. Based on European models, these facilities concentrated on surgical and medical treatment of diseases of the eye, where ophthalmologists treated both paying customers and charity cases. But while the establishment of eye hospitals advanced the quest of professional practitioners for medical hegemony, their presence by no means eliminated traditional homeopathic or "popular" cures. In 1817, Elisha North established the United States' first dedicated eye infirmary in New London, Connecticut. Describing the opening in his book, *Outlines of the Science of Life*, North discusses the interconnections between advertising his hospital to attract cases, disseminating knowledge concerning ocular conditions, and filling the purses of struggling practitioners. His comments indicate the overlap between scientific and economic investment in the body in the antebellum period and highlight the productive aspects of professionalized practice. But while the infirmary was successful in medical terms, the revenue it generated failed to meet its founders' pecuniary expectations. The opening (and closing) of North's facility did, however, hasten the development of other similar institutions.[11]

In 1820, the New York Eye and Ear Infirmary opened on the second story of a building at 45 Chatham Street (Figure 5). According to one estimate, 436 patients received care and treatment in the first seven months. The Institution for Diseases of the Eye and Ear opened the following year in Philadelphia, in large part through the efforts of George McClellan, then twenty-five years old and just beginning his career as a surgeon. But despite the financial support of prominent citizens and the endorsement of the Supreme Court, this small institution, which operated out of McClellan's office on Swanwick Street, near Walnut and Sixth, closed in 1824. That year, McClellan shifted his attentions to the founding of Jefferson Medical College, which opened in 1825. Meanwhile, the Pennsylvania In-

FIGURE 5. Frederick Augustus Pettit & (possibly William) Field, *New York Eye and Ear Infirmary*, n.d., print with text. Picture Collection, New York Public Library, Astor, Lenox and Tilden Foundations.

firmary for Diseases of the Eye and Ear had been established in Philadelphia in 1822. John Bell, one of the infirmary's surgeons disclosed an underlying motivation for eye care in his "address to the public," published as a pamphlet that year. "In calling the attention and soliciting the patronage of the public to an institution which is to embrace the relief of a class of diseases having so important a bearing on individual happiness and social comfort," Bell declared, "we need but advert to the success which has attended similar ones in Europe." There, he claimed, "thousands have been annually relieved and cured of diseases of the eye and ear, who otherwise would have lost the use of these all-important organs, and proved a burthen to themselves and to society." To further alleviate such burdens, others such as George Frick founded a similar institution in Baltimore in 1823, while Edward Reynolds and John Jeffries set up the Massachusetts Charitable Eye and Ear Infirmary in Boston in 1824.[12]

Wills Eye Hospital, which opened in Philadelphia in 1834, exemplifies the specialized ophthalmic or "eye" hospitals being established in cities across the

FIGURE 6. *Philadelphia-Wills Eye Hospital*, 1905–1935, photomechanical print, 3½ × 5½ in. George M. Brightbill Collection, Library Company of Philadelphia.

United States by the 1830s and '40s (Figure 6). Founded by a bequest from James Wills, the hospital allowed surgeons to practice ophthalmology exclusively, thus helping to establish it as a recognized specialty in the field of medicine. For its first five years only patients admitted to the hospital received treatment, and those who sought admission had to bring evidence of their reputable character or their indigent circumstances. During the hospital's first year, only 24 patients were admitted and treated, but in the thirty-five years up to 1869, a total of 59,011 patients received in-patient treatment. Wills began treating outpatients in 1839, and over the course of the next thirty years, some 29,000 of them had been counseled or treated.[13] Concern for the vision of the indigent blind also inspired the eye hospital's formation. On March 3, 1834, Joseph Ingersoll delivered an address at the hospital's opening that altruistically identified charity as a hallmark of modernity. Ingersoll discussed the place of vision in human experience and the importance of assisting those who lacked sight, and especially those who could not afford treatment. As one of the era's "monuments of active benevolence," the Wills Eye Hospital was founded and operated on the principle that the blind were just and rightful recipients of Christian charity. Curing blindness, Ingersoll averred, was one of the highest of aims: "Say, what *can* beset humanity with more intense severity, and yet be susceptible of relief, than a combination of poverty, lameness, and want of sight. These are ills, which, if left to themselves, imply the absence of all the external comforts, and many of the absolute necessities of life in present and painful reality." For Ingersoll, the worst conditions circumscribed people's ability to afford goods and services, prevented them from moving around freely of their own accord, and particularly hindered their ability to see. Reducing the burden of those dependent on the charitable projects of antebellum society equated in the minds of reformers and their corporate sponsors with increasing the collective body's economic productivity and social cohesion. The charitable aspect of the eye hospital's program of public outreach highlights ophthalmology's participation in the broader reform impulse that animated much of antebellum society. Like other infirmaries that provided for the care of the indigent or schools that provided for their instruction, the eye hospital, focused on the maintenance of the individual's sensory capacities, exercised its authority over the body in the disciplinary fashion of the prison, the factory, or the schoolhouse. But important visual work continued to take place outside the eye hospital. In spite of the concentration of ophthalmic practice inside the halls of these new facilities, a significant portion of ocular treatment persisted outside their walls in the form of quackish prescriptions and self-applications.[14]

Institutionalized ophthalmology was but one venue through which ideas about vision, both theoretical and practical, were disseminated among a disparate citizenry on whose eyes the early republic's market culture was taking an increasing toll. Mistrust of science and medicine was prevalent throughout early America, especially when being administered to ailing patients. Many placed their trust instead in the vernacular art of self-diagnosis and treatment. Recipes for eyewashes, for instance, were passed like cooking recipes and sewing tips between family members, friends, and neighbors. With formulae comprised of ingredients such as salt, white vitriol, hot sage tea, or teas made from elder flowers, laudanum, white copperas (crystallized ferrous sulfate), and sassafras, their effects would have been unpredictable, their effectiveness questionable.[15] With vernacular forms of diagnosis and treatment so prevalent, ophthalmology, like other branches of the medical sciences, had to acknowledge this cultural taste for the commonsensical. To establish itself in a position of authority, medical science in practice and prescription had to accommodate the people's predilection for what was essentially an amalgam of the folk remedies, self-determined treatments, and "scientific" medical knowledge that had assumed the status of "common sense." Ophthalmologists, opticians, and oculists had to couch the technical and scientific aspects of their practice in everyday language in order to maintain their social respectability and, as importantly, ensure the economic viability of their endeavors. Publishing treatises written in ordinary language could provide a smoother path to professional and institutional development. As historian Joan Burbick has pointed out, early republic Americans favored medical treatments that involved the patient's own wisdom and methods of treatment. Ophthalmic treatises of the era reveal the enormous influence of this valuation of patients' ability to cure themselves, or to know how to recognize or prevent certain ailments. Meanwhile the publications had to be marketable to a clientele already skeptical in their regard for medicine and unversed in the language of contemporary medicoscientific theories, but who valued greater visual acuity and clarity as part of a general sense of ocular well-being.[16]

As antebellum eyes smarted from the effects of a rapidly expanding visual culture, a proliferation of cautionary literature offered solutions to the problems accompanying this sudden and widespread need for keen sight. These works depicted vision as highly susceptible to damage, disease, and debility. Admonitory in tone, they reveal a debt to the reform physiology promoted by Sylvester Graham, Orson S. Fowler, and William Alcott, whose speeches and tracts describing various bodily systems and ways to maintain and even improve their efficiency laid the theoretical groundwork for linking sight with other bodily processes in the popular imagination. Graham appropriated François-Joseph-Victor Broussais's theories of "vitalism" to frame the body as an assemblage of systems that could be monitored, trained, and controlled through moderation and temperance. For Graham, overstimulation and overexertion of any of the body's parts— stomach, hands, eyes—led to their debility. Ophthalmic tracts of the period embraced this principle that overexerting or unduly straining the eyes would debilitate them and thus incorporated calculations and prescriptions of how best to safeguard them from overuse and self-inflicted damage. They counseled against the stress and strain of overexertion and exposure to the extremes of bright or dim light and warned of the dangers of selecting the wrong spectacles or donning them too early (or too late). They articulated these prescriptions in the most rudimentary of vernaculars so as to convey their message to a skeptical public.[17]

Georg Josef Beer's 1815 treatise *The Art of Preserving the Sight Unimpaired to Extreme Old Age* offered a template of sorts for subsequent treatises. Establishing the general tone of the work, Beer inveighs against the "superficial boasting" of his largely untrained competitors, "every day quacks" as he calls them, with their "pompous" advertisements. Yet he also distances his treatise from other works in his own branch of the medical arts that he deemed "too abstruse for general readers." In his "little manual of general utility written expressly for professional men" who may read the work "with advantage," Beer depicts the eyes as highly susceptible to self-inflicted damage and vulnerable to what he deems the detrimental effects of lavishly gilded or ornately decorated home furnishings and brightly painted or decorated rooms.[18] Among numerous "trifling abuses" to which the observer "daily exposes the visual organ," Beer points out the danger of rubbing one's eyes immediately on waking, especially with unclean hands and fingers. He stresses the importance of regularly cleansing the eye with cool spring water—"this, indeed," he argues, "ought to be a universal rule, particularly in large cities, where the quantity of dust is often the cause of repeated cases of ophthalmia." Indeed, air pollution, poor ventilation, and other aspects of dense urban living caused numerous maladies and exacerbated ocular ailments in eyes already stressed and strained too much.[19] Even interior decoration and fashion posed hazards. Beer also warns against exposing the eyes to direct sunlight on waking or to other brightly colored surfaces, including gilded ceilings, wainscots, mirrors, or picture frames. Doors and window shutters should be of some "softened color," he writes, while articles of furniture should be "rather of a brownish tinge than of a broad white." These and other potentially overstimulating interior decorations including wallpapers, tapestries, or other "brilliant ornaments" are, according to Beer, particularly "more hurtful than salutary to the eyes." Tight-fitting clothing also, he suggests, could have detrimental effects by placing strain on the flow of blood and oxygen to the head, and therefore to the eyes.[20]

Beer's treatise then transitions from the parlor to the laboratory, the atelier, and the workshop to warn readers of the potential harm awaiting the eyes there. "Whoever finds himself obliged to direct his sight almost constantly to small objects, all lovers of natural history, all painters, and, in short, many artizans [*sic*], both male and female, will do well to choose a habitation from whence a long perspective of different objects may be viewed at intervals; for nothing is more proper than this to relax the contraction of the eye, and as it were, to recreate it by the change." Highlighting the dangers to the eye present at work and play, in production and consumption, at home and abroad, Beer's writing and teaching exerted tremendous influence on a younger generation of ophthalmologists, including his most devoted pupil, George Frick of Baltimore. The publications of other authors, however, more closely resemble Beer's text than those of his student.[21]

A comparison of two texts, one by a quasi-professional practitioner often labeled a "quack" and the other by a professionally trained and institutionally based practitioner, reveals a shared orientation to the subject and a similar array of recommended techniques for avoiding or ameliorating common ailments. In the two works, science and common sense merge to guide their readers in the temperate ways of modest and polite behavior. John Harrison Curtis's *On the Preservation of Sight, the Diseases of the Eye, and the Use, Abuse, and Choice of Spectacles, Reading Glasses, &c, being Practical Observations for Popular Use* (1848) and James Henry Clark's *Sight and Hearing, How Preserved and How Lost* (1856) are just two of numerous works that prescribed methods for preserving the eyes through the exercise of reason and restraint. Curtis, who had already developed some specialization in the treatment of the ear, counseled against making sudden shifts from darkly to brightly lit rooms (a circumstance he considered particularly common to countinghouses) and exposing the eyes to an excess of gilding or whitewashed rooms.[22] Veils and colored spectacles, he thought, should be avoided, as well as tight-fitting clothing whose constricting quality were, he claimed, "manifestly hurtful to the sight" because of the "too copious flow of humours being thereby induced to the head." According to Curtis, reading immediately after dinner also placed an undue strain on the eyes, as did reading in a dim light. Meanwhile, "among the common causes of diseases of the eye," he wrote, " may be noticed derangement of the digestive functions—high living—excess in vinous and spirituous liquors—cold, fever, suckling too long protracted—an immoderate use of tobacco and cigars, which often produces debility in young persons—sitting up late at night, and being much excited by card-playing, &c.—straining and fatiguing the eyes by staying several hours in a theatre, as many persons of weak sight do, instead of retiring as soon as they feel any symptoms of dimness of vision, or pain in the eyes."[23] James Henry Clark, a practitioner associated with the New York Eye and Ear Infirmary and the Newark Eye and Ear Infirmary, which he founded in 1856, added the potential dangers of reading novels (especially in bed) and certain lamps and lampshades to the list. And writing in the mid-1850s with industrialization more firmly established, he also warned against exposure to noxious fumes, locomotive sparks, melted lead, and flying metal shards. Temperate moderation in all things and the purchase of vision aids comprised the course of treatment outlined in these treatises. When such measures failed, or when dangerous situations could not be avoided, "weakness of sight" ensued, with a concomitant decline in worker productivity and consumer efficiency.[24]

The detrimental effects of the new visual culture, as well as the application of published remedies are evident in the diary of Edward N. Tailer Jr., a hardworking Manhattan-born clerk employed by several downtown New York importing firms between 1848 and 1855. Like thousands of other young men, he was attracted by the city's enticements, but like many of them, he fell victim to its perceptual perils.[25] One Saturday evening the young clerk wrote, "this afternoon my eyes felt when the labors of the day were finished as if I was to become blind, a cloud appeared to hover over them, which prevented my seeing distinctly those minute objects, which would be presented for admission, to be portrayed upon the retina. The reason which I assigned to account for this singular occurrence was, that they had been strained and sorely tried by the miserable light which finds its way into our counting room."[26] Tailer's studied use of "optical" language in diary entries regarding his suffering eyesight attests to the influence of ophthalmic tracts and the relevance and applicability of their remedies. His plight also reveals the importance of good eyesight to productivity and the value of vision in relation to labor profitability. Though fully cognizant of his condition and engaged by the prospect of overcoming his ailment, over the next six months, Tailer's eyes worsened. In his diary entry for Thursday, May 30, 1850, he complained,

> My eyes still continue to give me, a sufficient cause, for uneasiness. They feel at times, as if filled with fine particles of dust, and smart in consequence of there being, a something present foreign, to what that delicate organ requires. Then again I am troubled, with sharp, shooting pains through the ball of the eye, and have good reason to believe that these unpleasant sensations, are caused by the optic nerve being strained & tasked too much by the miserable & blinding light, which finds its way into our counting room, and I am fearful that the time is not far distant, when I shall be obliged to consult an optician. In consequence of my eyes being in the state described above, I wrote but little, endeavoring to husband them up, if possible for future service.[27]

This "future service," of course, included Tailer's leisure activities. On leaving the store one afternoon, Tailer mentioned that threatening clouds of an approaching storm precluded an "opportunity of criticising, a greater variety of the fair &

beautiful daughters of the Empire City," in reference to the popular pastime of promenading along New York's fashionable avenues, an activity premised on seeing and being seen. Tailer places himself as both observer and object within the spectacle of the modern city. However, the ominous clouds threatening rain that preclude Tailer's ocular entertainments echo the specter of the blinding "cloud" that hovered over his weakened eyes in the counting room.[28]

Eager to "go ahead" through promotion, Tailer availed himself of New York's many resources for ophthalmic knowledge and expertise to forestall the deleterious effects of his writing and copying. His goal was to maintain his visual powers and thus the value of his labor, thereby remaining both physiologically healthy *and* financially solvent. On Thursday, September 9, 1850, he wrote, "I renewed my subscription for another half year to the Mercantile Library at Clinton Hall" where he obtained Johann Christoph August Franz's *The Eye; a Treatise on the Art of Preserving This Organ in a Healthy Condition, and of Improving the Sight; to which is Prefixed, a View of the Anatomy and Physiology of the Eye, with Observations on its Expression as Indicative of the Character and Emotions of the Mind* (Figure 7). Studying the book's diagramed frontispiece and a sampling of its chapters on "The Physiology of the Eye," "The Eye in Manhood," or "General Regimen with Reference to the Eye," Tailer likely identified his malady in what Franz described as "weakness of sight," a condition marked by ocular fatigue, blurred vision, and shooting pain. According to Franz, nothing is to be more strongly recommended for the prevention of weakness of sight

> than the strict observance of such rules as tend to preserve the general health of the body. . . . It may be mentioned that the eyes should not be over-exerted, and should be kept perfectly clean. Care must be taken to provide a mild and suitable light for every occupation. Excitement of the brain, especially long-continued study, and all violent emotions are to be avoided. Great attention must be paid to the state of the stomach and bowels. Residence in the country, exercise in wholesome air, indulging the eye upon verdant scenery, and the use of tepid, or still better, of cold baths, are highly to be recommended.[29]

But the free time Tailer needed for a therapeutic visit to the country was hard to obtain as work poured in. "I have so much writing to perform at the store now days," he wrote on December 18, 1849, "that it strains my eyes exceedingly, and I am afraid that I shall be obliged to decline the situation of assistant book-keeper unless they

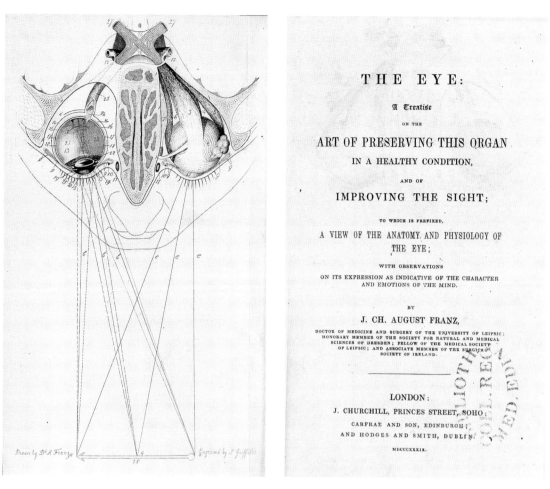

FIGURE 7. Johann Christoph August Franz, *The Eye; a Treatise on the Art of Preserving This Organ in a Healthy Condition, and of Improving the Sight; to which is Prefixed, a View of the Anatomy and Physiology of the Eye, with Observations on its Expression as Indicative of the Character and Emotions of the Mind* (London: J. Churchill, 1839), frontispiece and title page. Wellcome Library, London/Royal College of Physicians Edinburgh.

become stronger." His failing eyesight was affecting his productivity and prospects for promotion; about a month later he observed that "My eyes have troubled me considerably for several days past, so much so that I was compelled to desist from copying up the Sale, and from posting up the Invoice Books this morning, owing I think to cold and near sightedness combined." Reading Franz's treatise, it is little wonder that Tailer took a whole body approach to the repair of his eyes.[30]

Indeed, Tailer's failing eyesight so debilitated him that he lost his chance for promotion to the status of merchant: in mid-August 1850, he recorded, "Mr. Dunbar [a junior partner in the firm of Little, Alden & Co.] afforded me a fine opportunity of judging of how much he cared for my welfare, by telling me that 'I could never make a merchant, owing to my being near sighted,' and advising me in a most fatherly manner, to 'study a profession.'" Desperate to halt his degenerative vision and preserve his livelihood, indeed his sense of self, Tailer eventually sought out an optician to procure a pair of eyeglasses for himself.[31] "The person desiring the aid of spectacles will always do well to apply to an experienced and intelligent optician," wrote Franz, and should be prepared to communicate to the latter "the degree of myopy, that is, at what distance he can still see clearly and whether it is the same in each eye" and "the distance at which he wishes to be enabled to see clearly." Franz suggested that for "reading or writing, twelve to fifteen inches may be assumed as a proper distance." The customer must also explain "whether the spectacles are required only for some particular occupation, and if so, of what nature the occupation is, or whether they are intended to be worn constantly; and finally, whether he intends to use the spectacles chiefly in the day-time, or in artificial light."[32] Here, Franz's treatise offers instruction to the patient seeking the optician's help.

To determine this focal range, Franz recommended a self-applied vision test that utilized the very tools of Tailer's clerical practice. Using a piece of "printed paper with clear legible type," Franz advocated testing each of the eyes separately then together to determine the distance for reading "most easily and distinctly." "By means of such information," Franz asserts, "any good optician is enabled to lay before, or send to the applicant several glasses, more or less suitable, from which he may make his selection." But with range determined, lens power remained unevenly matched. In a footnote, Franz warns, "the numbering of glasses is unfortunately not everywhere according to the same standard. The glass which with one optician is No. 1, is by another No. 2."[33] In the face of such uncertainty, the time needed for "careful trial"—which included testing several pairs "carefully and leisurely" with significant pauses in between, "as the eyes by the frequent change would become strained and fatigued," would, under ideal conditions, last "some days or even weeks," according to Franz. "Spectacles, to be suitable," he wrote, "must represent the object clearly and correctly as to its size, form, colour, and distance. If the concave diminish, or the convex magnify the size of the objects; if they excite an unpleasant sensation, or feeling of exertion, weariness, pressure or pain in the eyes or head; or occasion giddiness; they are absolutely unsuitable." Eyeglasses should, he asserted, "create a sensation of comfort and benefit, so that on taking them off a desire is felt for the repetition of their use." If improperly selected, though, or donned too early or late, spectacles might exacerbate already persistent vision problems, distorting and further damaging already debilitated sight.[34] The indeterminate and therefore precarious nature of antebellum optical measuring systems, the imprecision of lens grinding, the inaccuracies of test lenses, and the approximate focal lengths used for determining near- and farsightedness made the prospect of wearing spectacles perhaps more perilous than promising for Tailer. But armed with his newly attained knowledge of the eye, its working parts, and the measures for remedying its maladies, maybe even with a page of the fine print of his ledgers, and probably guided in his selection by Franz's prescriptions, Tailer went to the firm of Benjamin Pike & Sons at 166 Broadway on October 3, 1850, where he purchased his first pair of spectacles, "No. Six Concave glasses," a measurement that gives a good indication of his near-sightedness.[35]

From his store on lower Broadway, Pike served a diverse though genteel clientele and wisely disseminated advertising woodcuts in broadsides and handbills, in the pages of illustrated city directories, and as the frontispiece for firm's famed illustrated catalogue (Figure 8), which revolutionized the trade by introducing nationwide distribution of eyeglasses and other instruments. Born in London in 1777, Benjamin Pike Sr. apprenticed for a short time there before migrating to America in 1798. By 1804, he had established his own business in New York. His three sons had taken over the business by midcentury, when the eldest, Benjamin Pike Jr., left to establish his own firm. The firms of Benjamin Pike & Sons and Benjamin Pike Jr., were located at 166 and 294 Broadway, respectively. Benjamin Pike Jr.'s enterprise was more innovative; he received numerous awards for inventions and improvements, but perhaps his greatest achievement was the *Illustrated Descriptive Catalogue of Optical, Mathematical and Philosophical Instruments*, which he published in 1848 and again in 1856. Encyclopedic in scope, the catalogue offered concise illustrations and detailed explanations of the features and functions of spectacles and other philosophical and mathematical instruments. The catalogue's nationwide success attested to the widespread demand for acute vision and the instruments to obtain, maintain, preserve, and even, in the case of microscopes, telescopes, and other such devices, extend it.[36] But as Tailer painfully came to realize, the problems of vision and the promise of vision aids were local and specific. Two years later, on his twenty-second birthday, Tailer noted, "my near-sightedness seems to be upon the increase, and I wear glasses constantly, using

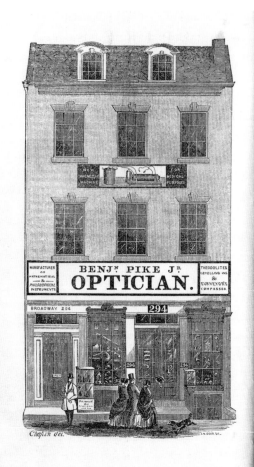

**PIKE'S**

ILLUSTRATED

**DESCRIPTIVE CATALOGUE**

OF

**OPTICAL, MATHEMATICAL,**

AND

**PHILOSOPHICAL INSTRUMENTS,**

MANUFACTURED, IMPORTED, AND SOLD BY THE AUTHOR; WITH
THE PRICES AFFIXED AT WHICH THEY ARE OFFERED IN 1848.

**WITH UPWARDS OF 750 ENGRAVINGS,**

MOSTLY ORIGINAL DESIGNS FROM THE INSTRUMENTS OF HIS ESTABLISHMENT
IN THE VARIOUS DEPARTMENTS OF

| | |
|---|---|
| ELECTRICITY, | MECHANICS, |
| GALVANISM, | OPTICS, |
| MAGNETISM, | ASTRONOMY, |
| ELECTRO-MAGNETISM, | SURVEYING, |
| PNEUMATICS, | NAVIGATION, |
| HYDROSTATICS, | METEOROLOGY, |

CHEMISTRY, &c., &c.

Designed to aid Professors of Colleges, Teachers, and others,
in the Selection and Use of Illustrative Apparatus,
in every Department of Science.

BY BENJAMIN PIKE, JR., OPTICIAN.

IN TWO VOLUMES.
VOL. I.

**NEW YORK:**
PUBLISHED AND SOLD BY THE AUTHOR,
AT HIS OPTICAL, MATHEMATICAL, AND PHILOSOPHICAL
INSTRUMENT MANUFACTORY,
294 BROADWAY,
A FEW DOORS ABOVE THE PARK.
1848.

FIGURE 8. Benjamin Pike, *Pike's Illustrated Descriptive Catalogue of Optical, Mathematical, and Philosophical Instruments* (New York: Published and Sold by the Author, 1848), frontispiece and title page. Library Company of Philadelphia.

three or four different powers, depending upon whether I want to see near by or far off objects." As his debts to the optician increased, so too did his productivity. Though temporarily imperiled by his poor eyesight, his prospects for promotion also rebounded.[37]

Tailer's self-education on the properties of the eyes and the mechanics of vision, his experimentation with the limits of his own sight, and his failure to correct his myopia by purchasing a succession of spectacles illuminate, at the level of the individual, the physiological, economic, and cultural ramifications of vision in the first half of the nineteenth century. The stages of his plight, his courses of action, and their results disclose the toll that market culture took on the eyes of one antebellum individual. These factors suggest the parameters of what I have called the market revolution in vision that imposed on "the noblest sense" an enlarged range of responsibilities and an expanded array of required aptitudes. Like Emerson, Tailer felt this acutely, though presumably less from a philosophical perspective than from a purely pecuniary point of view. With the use of spectacles Tailer eventually rose through the ranks to achieve considerable prominence in the New York business community. Others, as we will see in subsequent chapters, were not so fortunate.

The expansion of clinical ophthalmology and the concomitant proliferation of treatises instructing readers how to preserve their eyes signal the emergence of a set of cultural concerns instigated by the unsettling effects of rapid technological, scientific, commercial, and cultural change. As these developments suggest, the exponential growth of widely available printed matter, significant increases in the number of trades involving "close work" or white-collar labor, and the increasing availability of poorly made spectacles adversely affected eyesight. So too did the cramped, overcrowded spaces of the antebellum city, with its bad water, poor lighting, and lack of proper ventilation.

Taken together, these conditions explain the outpouring of concern about having good eyes and sharp vision. Directed at both lay and learned readers, ophthalmic literature of both popular and professional varieties publicized pathologies and maladies. They elucidated the problems of vision and the corrective procedures of opthalmologists. They explained the restorative possibilities of professionally administered surgical treatments or the selection and purchase of properly made and prescribed spectacles. Of course, home remedies and self-care persisted, though increasingly these were augmented by the consumption of published treatises, employment of the techniques they promoted, and the use of vision aids of one kind or another. As professional practice and popular literature supplemented or supplanted age-old remedies and common sense, vision's physiological function was articulated as an effect of market forces. Showcasing the structural "economy" of the eyes, treatises by Curtis and Clark linked acute vision to the temperate body and its attainment to self-cultivation and the accumulation of commercial and cultural capital. Together with Franz, they considered self-care of the eyes integral to a temperate and disciplined body. As they intimated, and as Tailer's plight attests, efficient and productive participation in the market economy necessitated visual acuity and required careful maintenance of the eyes. Akin to Tailer's temperate and skilled labor, good eyesight became a widely sought and briskly traded commodity; as vision was being bought and sold, sight increasingly defined the contours for living in a modern consumer culture.

## CHAPTER TWO

# Vision, Eyewear, and the Art
# of Refraction

The use of lenses dates back to antiquity, but the invention of spectacles did not occur until the late thirteenth century. Through a series of permutations, spectacles finally assumed their present form in the eighteenth century. Consisting of two lenses, connected by frames that saddle the nose and arms that rest on the ears, spectacles freed the hands for certain tasks that required acute vision: working with small parts, writing, and, of course, reading. Indeed, from the Renaissance, when output from Gutenberg's printing press helped to foster a rebirth of learning, through the age of Enlightenment, when the press disseminated knowledge and fueled revolutions, improvements in eyewear and print developed in tandem. When commercial printing took another enormous leap forward in the early nineteenth century, fostering an unprecedented "democratization" of printed information, the manufacture and use of spectacles grew apace.[1] In this way, an optics-based *visual* culture and print culture have been historically intertwined. Their symbiosis in the antebellum period can be seen in this handbill advertisement for Livingston's Book and Spectacle Office, circa 1850 (Figure 9). Featuring a pair of bespectacled eyes, the ad offers spectacles "good and cheap, accurately adjusted," to ready them, presumably, for viewers to wear while perusing and purchasing the books, pamphlets, and prints also for sale. Undoubtedly, these assisted eyes searchingly peer out from the page to meet those of other eager readers, readers whose vision, too, might be sharpened through the employment of the spectacles advertised.

Until the early decades of the nineteenth century, the majority of spectacles sold in America were imported ready-made from Europe.[2] Costly and difficult to obtain, the use of quality spectacles was largely restricted to a relative few. Their rarity in the early days of the republic helped to reinforce elite connotations of "correct" vision and the cultural power inhering in and stemming from the activ-

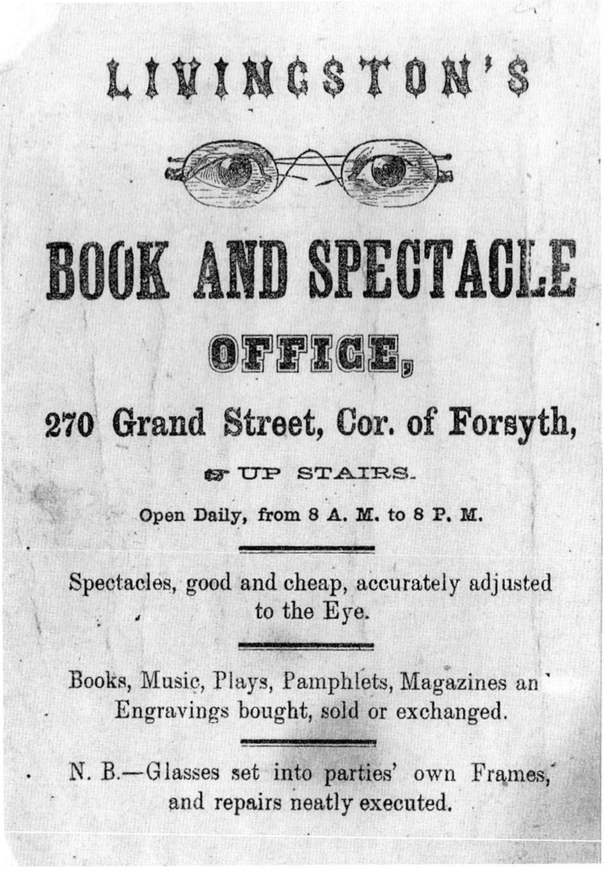

## LIVINGSTON'S

## BOOK AND SPECTACLE

## OFFICE,

### 270 Grand Street, Cor. of Forsyth,

☞ UP STAIRS.

Open Daily, from 8 A. M. to 8 P. M.

Spectacles, good and cheap, accurately adjusted
to the Eye.

Books, Music, Plays, Pamphlets, Magazines an
Engravings bought, sold or exchanged.

N. B.—Glasses set into parties' own Frames,
and repairs neatly executed.

FIGURE 9. *Livingston's Book and Spectacle Office*, c. 1850, handbill. Collection of the New-York Historical Society.

ities it facilitated. But gradually, the development of improved lenses and frames, and greater understanding of vision and its defects converged to form a thriving market for the production and consumption of better-fitting, increasingly standardized spectacles.[3] During the first half of the nineteenth century, spectacle production and distribution in the United States grew in magnitude to meet the demands of an increasingly urban, literate, and market-oriented population. Artisans who performed various forms of "close work" such as watch- and clockmakers, engravers, typefounders, and seamstresses also placed greater demand on spectacle makers as their need for acute vision rose with demand for their own goods and services. More widely available than in previous decades, spectacles came to embody the intersection of conceptual and practical aspects of human eyesight in the cultural imagination of antebellum America.

The increased production, promotion, and dissemination of spectacles, however, instigated a wide-ranging debate over their use value and their symbolic power. Opticians promoted vision aids as corrective instruments for improving and maintaining sight. But for a variety of reasons, the culture at large approached the use of spectacles with varying degrees of reservation, even trepidation. Some embraced these instruments as tools to increase and enhance the quality of their productivity and leisure. Others, heeding the advice of popular prescriptive tracts, mistrusted spectacles for the potential damage they might cause the eyes if incorrectly crafted or applied. Those more concerned with fashionable appearance than with "correct" vision feared that eyeglasses broadcast their infirmity or age and refused to use them. For skeptics, eyewear was more remarkable for the *spectacles* that wearing them (or not wearing them) might cause. But others employed vision aids to signify the opposite, wearing spectacles as an emblem of their refinement, literacy, or other skills that required a certain degree of visual acuity. For all their promises, for all they communicated, or failed to communicate, about their wearers, aids to vision also posed a number of potential dangers. As Johann Franz suggested in his treatise *The Eye*, these perils stemmed from selecting the wrong spectacles, donning them too early or too late. As much as it raised alarm, this cautionary literature, and the discourse it stirred, also raised the stakes for the purchase of corrective eyewear. Prior to scientific standardization in the study and treatment of vision, the process through which one obtained the visual acuity that spectacles promised was riddled with ambiguity and confusion. How was acuity measured and how did such a measurement enable observers to select the correct lenses? From whom should one procure eyeglasses? Could they be trusted with what many, after second-century Greek physician Galen of Pergamon, considered the most divine organ?[4] These questions and the potential perils of making the wrong selection were both very real and very persistent in the antebellum imagination. Long before Dutch ophthalmologist Herman Snellen developed an eye test chart premised on twenty-twenty vision in the early 1860s, the exact measure of what constituted "normal" vision or of what made for a proper match between a pair of spectacles and the ocular shortcomings of a particular wearer remained far from precise. Still, the efficacy of spectacles evolved with the growing professionalism of opticians who specialized in manufacturing and distributing them. Yet as their availability increased, every pair of spectacles properly prescribed by a professional optician was doubled or even tripled by eyewear traded by wholesalers, retailers, and street vendors. Spectacles effectively commodified "normal" vision, but when circulated in the absence of specialists who designed and deployed them, their unregulated production, distribution, and application complicated efforts to establish and maintain visual standards across vast spaces, varied local conditions, and individual needs. To reach an ever widening audience, several firms, such as that of Benjamin Pike & Sons who pioneered and exemplified the practice, utilized new forms of print to expand the marketplace for their wares as well as the knowledge of acute vision they purported to provide.

The visual culture that supported the nascent industry of spectacle production and distribution illustrated and explained the properties of vision aids and elaborated notions of correct vision enabled by eyewear properly applied. Engravings, printed texts, and advertisements helped to cultivate in viewers an appreciation for vision's significance in successfully navigating the market economy. However, as representations of spectacles proliferated, the modes and meanings of the vision they signified fluctuated. Oil paintings in which figures sported eyeglasses, wood and steel engravings of eyewear and optical instruments in trade catalogs, and exquisite cartoon etchings made "visible" the vision that spectacles afforded. Like spectacles themselves these visual forms demonstrated for antebellum audiences an accumulation of knowledge about the eye's mechanisms; the technological development of materials and technical expertise; and the acculturation of literate, productive, market-oriented populations who suddenly found them necessary in pursuits both profitable and pleasurable. Such representations of eyewear and their application defined a commercialized, commodified form of vision and outlined a set of material practices for the creation and maintenance of an optically enabled self. But images of spectacles also raised new questions concerning the effficacy, reliability, and potential danger of eyewear when wrongly applied.

As part of broader debates over the nature of vision and the ability of spectacles to successfully procure it, the representation of spectacles conveyed important information about their construction, application, and use. Such depictions also commented on the nature and extent of the clear, unobstructed vision that spectacles and other vision aids purported to provide. Though spectacle lenses were transparent in their material form, an effect rendered convincingly in oil painting, they were anything but in graphic reproduction. Philadelphia painter Rembrandt Peale, for instance, obsessed over the issue of transparency in portraits he made between 1800 and 1820, rendering "transparent" the glass of spectacle lenses with the translucent and opaque materials of pigments and their binders. In print, however, engraved lines or tints designated the surfaces and contours of spectacle lenses. Intended to lend the graphic representation of transparent glass pictorial definition, the engraver's tightly arranged, horizontal lines also suggested, without precision, the lens's refractive power. In cartoons, often made in haste for timely publication, however, spectacle lenses were articulated simply with circular lines to indicate their circumferences against the blank of the page. Such renderings appear with great frequency in the trade catalogues and advertisements of opticians, in popular engravings, in the handbills and broadsides of job printers, as well as in the specimen books of typefounders that sourced these various forms of print. Wide variation in the representation of lenses expanded significantly the range of their possible meanings. Ironically, methods for articulating the optics of transparent mediums such as eyes or lenses relied on the opacity of engravers' tints or painters' pigments. Thus the illustration of refractive media both underscored and troubled period conceptions of properly functioning eyesight. For embedded in the unregulated and varied syntax of engravers' tints employed to articulate the refractive power of lenses is an overriding sense of the imprecision with which such lenses were ground and applied in the antebellum period. It is nearly impossible to overstate the value of their metaphoric import for a culture whose questions about correct vision and the eyes' health and proper functioning toggled between transparency and opacity, between promise and peril, between fashion and faux pas, between clarity and outright confusion.

In 1824, William Kitchiner, celebrated author of *The Cook's Oracle*, *The Art of Invigorating and Prolonging Life*, and *The Pleasure of Making a Will*, among other titles, published *The Economy of the Eyes: Precepts for the Improvement and Preservation of the Sight* (Figure 10). In this volume, the multitalented author explains only those properties of human vision enabled or enhanced by spectacles or an array of other vision aids.[5] The book dispenses with the explanation of the eye and the mechanics of sight typical of books devoted to optical and ophthalmic topics published during this period. Kitchiner opts instead to open by making a few "general observations" on spectacles. This striking omission, especially given the bent of similar treatises, seems to suggest that there are no eyes, and therefore no vision, without spectacles. Without them he writes, "all the other working tools, of most Artists, soon after their 40th year"—artists whose "Eyes are their estate" and the "mainspring of their Fame and Fortune"—would be "almost useless."[6] Indeed, the only eyes illustrated in the tract are the bespectacled pair printed on the book's flyleaf. For nearly every ocular ailment, in Kitchiner's view,

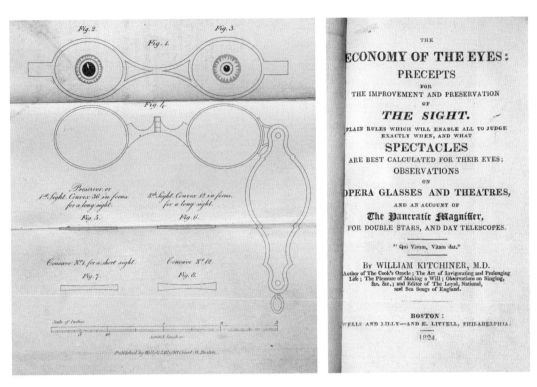

FIGURE 10. William Kitchiner, *The Economy of the Eyes: Precepts for the Improvement and Preservation of the Sight. Plain Rules which will Enable All to Judge Exactly When, and What Spectacles are Best Calculated for their Eyes, Observations on Opera Glasses and Theaters, and an Account of the Pancratic Magnifier, for Double Stars, and Day Telescopes* (London: Printed for Hurst, Robinson, & Co. Cheapside, 1824), frontispiece and title page. Library Company of Philadelphia.

there is an optical device to ameliorate or correct it, for every ocular function or task, a corresponding instrument to enhance or economize it. From concave and convex lenses for spectacles to the most intricate opera glasses, telescopes, or the author's own Pancratic Eye Tube, Kitchiner prescribes instruments for the various tasks of visual consumption: reading, attending the opera, viewing paintings and prints, or stargazing through telescopes. He also cites the need for spectacles in carrying out various modes of production including but not limited to needle-work, miniature painting, engraving, clock- and watchmaking, typesetting, and printing.

Kitchiner's text grounds visual experience, however spectacled, in the reality as well as the flux of the everyday. He situates the above activities in particular interior spaces—parlors, bedrooms, artisanal workshops—spaces that function in the text as virtual laboratories to test the collaboration of vision and vision aids in the production of acuity, or clear sight. The opera, however, stands out in Kitchiner's treatise as a complex yet relatively quantifiable scenario in which to test relationships between vision, light, and lenses. Where other writers alerted readers to the opera's "ocular" dangers, Kitchiner deemed it an apt laboratory.[7] Experiencing the theater's multiple viewing positions, elaborate stage sets, and dramatic candle or gas lighting often necessitated the use of spectacles or opera glasses (or perhaps both) to accommodate a considerable range of viewing distances and bring into sharp focus the movements of the actors moving about on stage. Vision aids also helped to more clearly differentiate foreground and background elements and enhanced the eyes' continual adaptation to fluctuating levels of darkness and light.[8] Of course, Kitchiner's own opera glasses take center stage in these activities. As he describes the matrix of ocular, optical, and spatial interplay that constitutes the operatic viewing experience—in his "economy of the eyes" the opera's aural aspect is notably absent—Kitchiner posits a formulation of vision that is simultaneously scientific, commercial, and aesthetic.[9] No longer posited as an abstract philosophical certainty, or as a problem solely for clinical science, Kitchiner's conception of vision situates it as a component of the human body activated, enhanced, maintained, and preserved by the application of vision aids. In Kitchiner's view, sight is less a set of muscular and neural processes maintained through exercise, proper behavior, and overall bodily health than it is a phenomenon subject to the selection and employment of spectacles and other lensed instruments. But his account is not exclusively "optical" in nature. The author manages to undergird a few of his own prescriptions with elements of physiological science in a series of vignettes describing cases of individual ailment. Nevertheless, it remains quite clear in Kitchiner's text that optical instruments, not physiological principles, are the products for sale. Instructing his readers in matching apparatus to ailment, the author expounds the mechanical components and intrinsic value of each. Through a series of "plain rules which will enable all to judge exactly when, and what spectacles are best calculated for their eyes," Kitchiner repeatedly stresses the importance of knowing exactly when to begin wearing spectacles and how and where to use them most effectively. As he professes, "*The choice of Spectacles* is one of those acts which cannot be properly performed by proxy—the Sight cannot be perfectly suited, unless 'Every Eye negociate for itself.'"[10]

Such negotiations were the speciality of the optician, a term, writes Edward Hazen in *The Panorama of Professions and Trades*, "applicable to persons who are

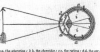

FIGURE 11. Edward Hazen, "The Optician," in *The Panorama of Professions and Trade; or Everyman's Book* (Philadelphia: Uriah Hunt, 1837), 246–247. Library Company of Philadelphia.

particularly skilled in the science of vision, but especially to those who devote their attention to the manufacture of optical instruments; such as—the spectacles, the camera obscura, the magic lantern, the telescope, the microscope, and the quadrant" (Figure 11). Associating commercial products with the laws of science, Hazen then links their optics with eyes. "The art of constructing optical instruments," he writes, "is founded upon the anatomical structure, and physiological action of the eye, and on the laws of light. They are designed to increase the powers of the eye, or to remedy some defect in its structure."[11] The optician's augmentation of human sensory capacity through the application of lenticular instruments grew in both precision and profitability during these years. The prominent Philadelphia firm of John McAllister & Son (and its later iterations) for instance, specialized in the kind of personal attention that Kitchiner promoted through the importation, grinding, and fitting of lenses. Already a successful manufacturer and

FIGURE 12. Thomas Sully, *John McAllister, Jr. (1786–1877)*, 1831, oil on canvas, 76.8 × 63.8 cm (30¼ × 25⅛ in.). Harvard Art Museums/Fogg Museum, Cambridge, MA, Bequest of Grenville L. Winthrop, 1943.157, Photo: Imaging Department © President and Fellows of Harvard College.

importer of canes and whips, McAllister Sr. acquired a stock of spectacles in 1799 from William Richardson, the first Philadelphian, according to historian Deborah Warner, to specialize in optical goods.[12] Over the next decade, spectacles gradually displaced whips and canes in McAllister's storeroom. In 1811, John McAllister Jr., recently graduated from the University of Pennsylvania, joined his father in business (Figure 12). As McAllister & Son (1811–1830)—and later as John McAllister Jr. & Co. (1830–1836), McAllister & Co. (1836–1853), and McAllister & Brother (1853–1865)—the firm manufactured frames and fitted them with imported lenses. Between 1815 and 1837, they produced and sold thousands of pairs of gold-framed spectacles to prominent and wealthy Americans across the country.[13] The firm also manufactured less expensive silver frames, which it sold both wholesale and retail along with imported frames of tortoise shell and steel[14] (Figure 13). McAllister's customers included presidents Thomas Jefferson and Andrew Jack-

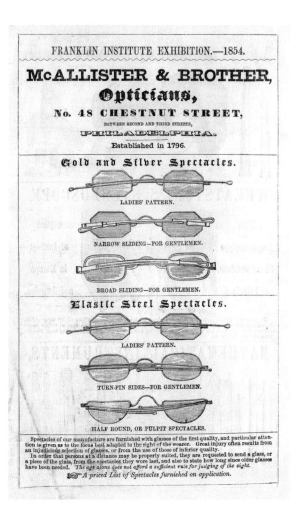

FIGURE 13. McAllister & Brother, *Franklin Institute Exhibition—1854*, trade catalogue. Library Company of Philadelphia.

son, the Philadephia-based daguerreotypists Robert Cornelius and William and Frederick Langenheim who purchased their camera lenses from the firm, and several members of the family of artist, naturalist, and museum impresario Charles Willson Peale. On turning over the daily operation of his optical instrument firm to his sons in 1834, John McAllister Jr. served as the manager of the Wills Eye Hospital from 1848 to 1854, and again from 1857 to 1859. As even this abbreviated clientele would suggest, John McAllister Jr. and his firm linked the nascent fields of ophthalmology and optometry and cultivated a patron network that included both producers and consumers of the period's intertwined print and visual cultures. The McAllister firm and others like it, most notably that of Benjamin Pike in New York, assembled, manufactured, and disseminated an entire range of vision aids, including spectacles and a broad array of optical and mathematical in-

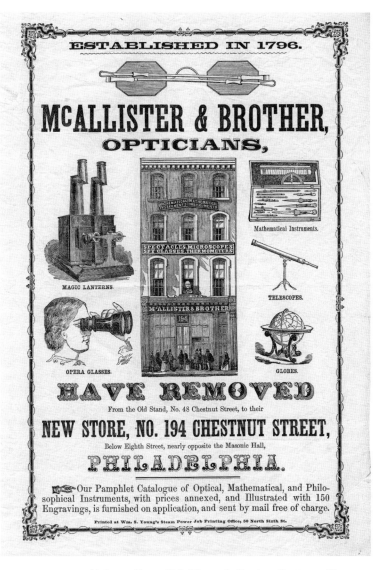

FIGURE 14. Alphonse Bigot, "McAllister & Brother, Opticians Have Removed from the Old Stand, No. 48 Chestnut Street, to Their New Store, 1855" (Philadelphia: Printed By Wm. S. Young's Steam Power Job Printing Office, 1855), broadside. Library Company of Philadelphia.

struments. Advertisements for the firm picture the building as an iconic landmark of Philadelphia's bustling commercial and visual cultures (Figure 14). Printed in city directories, in illustrated catalogues, and on handbills and broadsides, this engraving of the shop's façade, as evidenced by period daguerreotypes, nearly replicates its actual appearance. Along with signboards that read "mathematical in-struments, spectacles, microscopes, spy glasses, thermometers," a pair of gold spectacles embossed on the plate-glass windows look outward while a larger pair, carved from wood and hung perpindicular to the building's facade, watchfully protrude over those passing by. Above the crowd that has gathered along the sidewalk in front of the store, the gilded bust of Benjamin Franklin, father of American bifocals and patron of science and learning, looks out from the central second-story window.

It is likely that the two pair of spectacles prominently worn and held in Rem-brandt Peale's 1801 portrait, *Rubens Peale with a Geranium*, came from McAllis-ter's shop (Figure 15, Plate 1).[15] The Peale family's ties to the McAllister firm were extensive and illustrative of the intimately personal relationships opticians pro-moted in their practice and advertisement. Rubens's weak eyes precluded him from becoming a visual artist like his father and his brothers Raphaelle and Rem-brandt. Instead, he managed his father's museum in Philadelphia and Baltimore before becoming director of the museum on its removal to New York, where he eventually oversaw the transfer of its contents to P. T. Barnum's American Mu-seum. Later in life, he returned to painting and undertook and developed an in-terest in magnetism. Toward the end of his life, Rubens retrospectively recounted a visit to McAllister he made as a young man. Of what for him was the novel experience of seeing objects clearly from a considerable distance, Rubens Peale wrote in his "Memorandum" of 1856: "It was always thought that I required con-cave glasses and every degree of concavity was tried in vain, at last I happened to take a large burning-glass and placed it to my eye and to my great astonishment I saw at a distance every thing distinctly. My father then went with me to Mr. John McAlister's store in Chestnut near 2nd St. He had no spectacles of so high a power, and he then set in a frame glasses of 4½ inch focus, with these spectacles I could see to read and even to read the signs across the street."[16] McAllister's prescription expanded Rubens's visual sphere considerably and enabled the close looking Rubens undertakes in Rembrandt's portrait. The painting's crystalline facture and well-ordered composition visually accord with the transparency and objectivity characteristic of Enlightenment thought, which both relied on and promulgated vision's unobstructed capacity to enable and facilitate perception, and thus understanding, of the natural world. Scholars have noted how this worldview framed the extensive range of artistic activities, scientific pursuits, and commercial endeavors undertaken by Charles Willson Peale and several of his many children.[17] The intertwining of acute vision and scientific inquiry—an echo

FIGURE 15. Rembrandt Peale, *Rubens Peale with a Geranium*, 1801, oil on
canvas, 28 ⅛ × 24 in. National Gallery of Art, Washington, DC, Patrons'
Permanent Fund/Bridgeman Images. (See Plate 1.)

of the relations between the McAllister and Peale families—is reflected in the rhyme of the geranium's serpentine tendrils with the twists and turns of Peale's gleaming eyeglasses. Botany, or the identification and classification of plants, relied on acute perception and close looking of the kind in which Rubens engages. Like the painting's tight pairing of botanist and specimen, Rubens is conjoined with his two pairs of spectacles. As pictured, they are fashionably congruent with his attire and appropriate to his pursuit. Part and parcel of his identity as a learned and inquisitive member of the esteemed Peale family, his spectacles, with their gleaming silver frames, bespeak precision of manufacture, their compact lenses and tight fit, precision of application. Rubens exemplifies the optically enabled self situated within an uncluttered space conducive to study and the unimpeded transmission of light and knowledge. But the clarity with which Rembrandt delineated this nondescript interior belies the blurred vision characteristic of Rubens's ocular condition of hyperopia, or farsightedness.

As a painting centered on the act of close looking, its engagement with the issue of visual acuity is articulated most coherently in Rembrandt's delicate handling of the spectacles' lenses. Though rendered in opaque pigments mixed and applied with transluscent glazes—unlike the more popular printed depictions of spectacles to which I will attend in a moment—the lenses of Rubens's spectacles, under Rembrandt's hand, read not only as transparent, but illusionistically *refractive*. As described by Edward Hazen in the *Panorama of Professions*, "Any pellucid or transparent body, as air, water, and glass which admits the free passage of light, is called a *medium*. When rays, after having passed through one medium, are bent out of their original course by entering another of different density, they are said to be *refracted*; and when they strike against a surface, and are sent back from it, they are said to be *reflected*."[18] Both are on display in Rembrandt's portrait. Light rays appear to bend as they pass refracted through the lenses of Rubens's eyeglasses as Rembrandt masterfully approximates in paint their magnifying power. In particular, scholars have noted the size, shape, and density of the "bright pools of refracted light" that appear behind the lenses as evidence of their focal power.[19] Eyeglasses enabled for Rubens a range of clear sight extending from the close inspection of geranium leaves to letterform signboards across the space of a city street. But such a range, given the technology of the time and the extreme degree of Rubens's hyperopia, might have required not one, but two pairs. Scholars have debated the various reasons for their inclusion in the painting. One such study introduces the theory that Rembrandt added the spectacles Rubens wears at a later date.[20] The tiny circumference of their lenses, and the proximity of Rubens's head to the leaves of the plant to which he attends—a distance of about four and half inches—suggests, at least at quick glance, that their focal power enables the close inspection in which he is engaged. But regardless of the accuracy of their depiction, they stake out the parameters of an unimpeded visual field enabled by eyewear. By suggestion, they designate the extent of Rubens's acuity. And while the appearance of two pairs of spectacles in *Rubens Peale with a Geranium* further emphasizes precision by referencing the eye's natural capacity for near and distant focusing, the property known as visual accommodation, they also reference the proliferation of commercially available spectacles during this period. Here, as if taking a cue from Kitchiner, we look to the purportedly refractive qualities of the lenticular glass that fills his silver spectacle frames instead of reading the surfaces of Rubens's eyes for clues to his ocular condition.

While the lenses in *Rubens Peale with a Geranium* read as translucent media that refractively concentrate rays of light, the metal and glass of both pairs of spectacles catoptrically reflect glints of light delicately rendered in impastoed white highlights. In the left lens of the pair Rubens holds, viewers can discern the reflection of window panes—a motif that appears with some frequency in the still-life paintings of Raphaelle Peale—which hints at an outer world of commerce and exchange.[21] Eradicating the confusion of blurred vision, Rubens's spectacles bring sharp focus to the visual field he beholds with their aid—the space of the botanical laboratory—just as the stasis of Rembrandt's picture holds at bay the chaotic freneticism of the marketplace outside. Regardless of its depiction of Rubens's gentlemanly pursuit and quiet, reflective space of study and solitude, Rembrandt's picture is also implicated in Kitchiner's commercial "economy of the eyes."

The issues of transparency, translucency, and refraction, it seems, were of especial concern for Rembrandt. Around the time he painted *Rubens Peale with a Geranium*, he made three other portraits in which he masterfully rendered transparent or translucent media, including optical glasses, the gauze of a veil, and a soap bubble, with great sensitivity to their material and optical properties. In a second portrait of Rubens in profile, Rembrandt rendered his eyeglasses with great care to incorporate them seamlessly into this refined yet austere image (Figure 16). As if working against the blurry and ineffectual sight of its subject, the portrait is rendered with mathematical precision. Situated in an undefined space and viewed in profile, Rubens looks out to the viewer's left. The shape and positioning of his head recalls the eggs that formed the basis for exercises in shading and profile drawing that would later appear in Rembrandt's highly influential instructional treatise, *Graphics: A Manual of Drawing and Writing, for the Use of Schools and Families* (1835).

FIGURE 16. Rembrandt Peale, *Rubens Peale*, 1807, oil on canvas. National
Portrait Gallery, Smithsonian Institution, Washington, DC, Partial gift
of Mrs. James Burd Peale Green.

In another intimate portrait of around the same time, *Eleanor May Short*, Rembrandt lovingly depicts with extraordinary sophistication his veiled spouse (Figure 17). In fact, the portrait demonstrates the artist's illusionistic handling of several materials, fabrics, and surfaces in one composition. Translucent rather than fully transparent, her sheer, diaphanous veil registers the barest transmission of light. Even the lightweight fabric of her gauzy blouse stands out against her fur and her eyes. Along with the table and the sash behind her, these materials are fully opaque, yet her eyes, in two subtle glints of white pigment, reflect the light pouring in from an adjacent window. In *Portrait of Franklin Peale—Boy Blowing a Bubble* (1808), Rembrandt pictures the young subject in the act of inflating a soap bubble. The

FIGURE 17. Rembrandt Peale, *Artist's First Wife, Eleanor May Short*, c. 1811, oil on canvas, 28⅜ × 23¼ in. Mead Art Museum, Amherst College, Amherst, MA, Gift of Edward S. Whitney, Esq. (Class of 1890)/Bridgeman Images.

prismatic effects of this refractive medium appear in the reflection of light from a window seen in the outward-facing bulge of the bubble's delicate surface.[22] Painted during Rembrandt's time of study in Paris, one must wonder if the artist's experiments with the rendering of transparency in painting coincided with the the early signs of failure stemming from the gradual erosion of his own vision.[23] Within two decades, Rembrandt would paint the first of a number of self-portraits that depict him wearing eyeglasses (Figure 18).

Rembrandt's preoccupation with lenticular refraction—and the related issues of acuity and accommodation—was far from isolated. His paintings allude to the efforts of opticians and optometrists to define focal ranges and properly measure and safely apply test lenses in their examinations, both of which benefited from a more thorough understanding of visual accommodation. The study of this aspect

FIGURE 18. Rembrandt Peale, *Self-Portrait*, 1828, oil on canvas, 19 × 14½ in.
Detroit Institute of Arts, Founders Society Purchase and Dexter M. Ferry Jr.
Fund/Bridgeman Images.

of vision excited much discussion during the first half of the nineteenth century.
As William Clay Wallace, a New York physician, described in his 1850 pamphlet,
*The Accommodation of the Eye to Distances*, "the adjustment of the eye has been as-
cribed—to alteration of the form of the organ; to alteration of the diameter of the
pupil; to muscularity of the crystalline lens; and to alteration in the position of
that lens."[24] The complex of muscles, tissues, and lenses responsible for accommodation relied on the elasticity of the eye's component parts. Exercising the eyes by
fixing them alternately on near and distant objects helped observers to maintain
the widest possible range of focal lengths and helped to avoid the extreme limits

of sight.[25] But even as specialists refined their knowledge of the mechanisms of accommodation and better understood the extent of vision's focal range, imprecision remained. Practitioners had long understood the conditions that produce presbyopia (farsightedness) and myopia (nearsightedness) in human eyes. In the former, the eye loses its elasticity after middle age. Its lens is not sufficiently convex, so light rays entering the eye are concentrated too far back. In the latter, the lens is too convex, and the rays converge anterior to the retina. Nevertheless, as French ophthalmologist Jules Sichel pointed out in his 1850 treatise, *Spectacles: Their Uses and Abuses in Long and Short Sightedness,* "the differences comprised bewteen these two extremes, are so numerous that it is difficult to determine a precise standard of normal vision" and "establish the precise limits where presbyopia and myopia commence to manifest themselves."[26]

To better determine these "precise limits," practitioners devised a wide array of instruments and techniques to reduce the guesswork involved in the measurement of visual accommodation and ocular refraction. In 1823, Czech physiologist Jan Evangelista Purkinje described an "acuity apparatus," which he urged be used routinely in the physiological examination of the eye. British optician William Porterfield defined the optometer as an instrument used for "measuring the limits of distinct vision," and "determining with great exactness the strength and weakness of sight." During the 1820s, Thomas Young redesigned the optometer, improving on Porterfield's earlier and less sophisticated instrument. By estimating the magnitude of the eye's spherical and chromatic aberration, the instrument enabled the examiner to determine the strength of lenses needed to correct varying degrees of presbyopia or myopia.[27] One of the more significant advances in the field of optometry occurred in the United States in 1828. That year, as Philadelphia surgeon Isaac Hays describes in his 1854 American edition of William Lawrence's *Treatise on the Diseases of the Eye,* the Reverend Mr. Goodrich consulted Philadelphia optician John McAllister Jr. concerning a deficiency of sight Goodrich called "near sighted." McAllister used a version of the optometer to determine Goodrich's condition, which led the optician to develop a pair of cylindrical glasses to correct what he determined was astigmatism, marking the first successful treatment of this condition in the United States. Soon after, Hays, surgeon to the Wills Eye Hospital, and other ophthalmologists were prescribing these spectacles for patients exhibiting astigmatic symptoms.[28] Such improvements were plentiful during this period, but a lack of regularity and standardization continued to plague the nascent practice of optometry.

Measuring systems, for instance still varied from country to country.[30] Hence the persistence of Sichel's "sliding scale." Indeed, as McAllister, Kitchiner, and their colleagues in the field were well aware, matching spectacle lenses to a particular individual's needs represented the most difficult and imprecise step in their prescription. Although opticians were able to grind lenses with a relative degree of precision, numbering them according to their focal length or the degree of their concavity or convexity, the measurement of the eye's focal capacities was far more difficult. As Kitchiner and his contemporary, the English optican and spectacle maker John Thomas Hudson, observed, only the collaboration between optician and customer could determine the proper match. In his pamphlet, *Spectaclaenia; or the Sight Restored, Assisted, and Preserved by the Use of Spectacles*, Hudson argued that an adequate amount of time must be spent in selecting spectacles. As he suggests, at least half an hour is necessary to fit the head with frames and to ascertain "the sight of the glasses." But, as Hudson admits, "no optician, however great his natural genius, or acquired skill, can be half so good a judge of all these matters, as the intelligent wearer himself."[31] For Hudson and his colleagues, the optician's professionalism is only effective when matched by the intelligence of the well-informed buyer, the optically enabled self. Together, producers and consumers collaborated in the "manufacture" and maintenance of what Hudson calls "continuous, distinct and perfect vision."[32]

An elaborate broadside published on behalf of Boston optician Daniel B. Widdifield reinforces the point, illustrating at the same time the imprecise nature of measuring visual acuity, a task that would later fall to the specialized practice of optometry (Figure 19). The broadside also underscores the importance of print for the enterprise of obtaining distinct sight. In the midst of a long discourse on the eyes and the values of spectacles, the optician acknowledges that while "in the choice of spectacles, every one must finally determine for himself, which are the glasses through which he obtains the most distinct vision," but he is quick to point out that "some confidence should be placed in the judgment of the artist, of whom they are purchased, and some attention paid to his directions." These often involved the application of a sequence of trial or test lenses of varying focal length to determine the patient's visual acuity. However, when applied too hastily, or for too extended a period, this technique posed a threat to ocular health: "By trying many spectacles the eye is fatigued as the pupil varies in size with every change that is produced," the broadside continues. "Hence, the purchaser often fixes upon a pair of spectacles, not the best adapted to his sight, but those which seem to relieve him most while his eyes are in a forced and unnatural state; and consequently,

# DANIEL B. WIDDIFIELD,

## SIGN OF THE

### No. 141, *Washington Street,* (*Nearly Opposite the Old South,*) *Boston,*

**MANUFACTURES, AND KEEPS CONSTANTLY ON HAND,**

## A GENERAL ASSORTMENT OF

# GOLD, SILVER, SHELL AND STEEL MOUNTED

# SPECTACLES,

WITH GLASSES ADAPTED TO ALL THE VARIOUS DEFECTS OF THE EYE WITHIN THE REACH OF OPTICAL ASSISTANCE.

ALSO....SILVER AND GOLD MOUNTED EYE GLASSES, READING GLASSES, GOGGLES, SUN GLASSES, MICROSCOPES, &c. &c., WHICH HE OFFERS FOR SALE AS LOW AS THEY CAN BE PURCHASED IN THE CITY.

### ☞ *SPECTACLES REPAIRED AT SHORT NOTICE.*

---

THE discovery of optical instruments may be esteemed among the most noble, as well as among the most useful gifts, which the Supreme Artist hath conferred on man. For all admirable as the eye came out of the hands of him who made it, yet he has permitted this organ to be more assisted by human contrivance, than any other of the animal frame, and that not only for the uses and comforts of common life, but for the advancement of natural science; whether by giving form and proportion to the minute parts of bodies, that were imperceptible to the unassisted sight, or by contracting space, and as by magic art, bringing to view the grander objects of the universe, which were rendered invisible by their immense distance from us. Noble as these inventions are, the discovery of Spectacles may still claim the superiority, as being of more universal benefit, and more extensive use. They restore and preserve to us one of the most noble and valuable of our senses; they enable the mechanic to continue his labour, and earn a subsistence by the work of his hand, till the extreme of old age. By their aid the scholar pursues his studies, and recreates his mind with intellectual pleasures, and thus passes away days and years with delight and satisfaction, that might otherwise have been devoured by melancholy, or wasted by idleness.

### GENERAL RULES FOR THE CHOICE OF SPECTACLES.

The most general, and perhaps the best rule that can be given, to those who are in want of assistance from glasses, in order so to choose their spectacles, that they may suit the state of their eyes, is to prefer those which shew objects nearest their natural state, neither enlarged nor diminished, the glasses being near the eye, and that give a blackness and distinctness to the letters of a book, neither straining the eye, nor causing any unnatural exertion of the pupil.

For no spectacles can be said to be properly accommodated to the eyes, which do not procure them ease and rest; if they fatigue the eyes, we may safely conclude, either that we have no occasion for them, or that they are ill made, or not proportioned to our sight.

Though, in the choice of spectacles, every one must finally determine for himself, which are the glasses through which he obtains the most distinct vision; yet some confidence should be placed in the judgment of the artist, of whom they are purchased, and some attention paid to his directions. By trying many spectacles the eye is fatigued, as the pupil varies in size with every different glass, and the eye endeavours to accommodate itself to every change that is produced. Hence, the purchaser often fixes upon a pair of spectacles, not the best adapted to his sight, but those which seem to relieve him most, while his eyes are in a forced and unnatural state; and consequently, when he gets home, and they are returned to their natural state, he finds what he had chosen, fatiguing and injurious to his sight.

Let it, therefore, be carefully remembered, that magnifying power is not the point that is most to be considered in the choice of spectacles, but their conformity to our sight, their enabling us to see distinctly, and with ease, at the distance we were accustomed to read or work, before the use of spectacles became necessary: or, in other words, glasses should so alter the disposition of the rays, at their entrance into the eyes, as will be most suitable to procure distinct vision at a proper distance; an end of the highest import, as in this respect it places the aged nearly on a level with the young, and enables him to read a common print with ease, at a period when, without assistance, he could hardly distinguish one letter from another.

An attentive consideration of the following rules, will enable every one to judge for himself, when his sight may be assisted or preserved by the use of spectacles.

1. When we are obliged to remove small objects to a considerable distance from the eye, in order to see them distinctly.

2. If we find it necessary to get more light than formerly; as for instance, to place the candle between the eye and the object.

3. If on looking at, and attentively considering a near object, it becomes confused, and appears to have a kind of mist before it.

4. When the letters of a book run one into the other, and hence appear double and treble.

5. If the eyes are so fatigued by a little exercise, that we are obliged to shut them from time to time, and relieve them by looking at different objects.

When all these circumstances concur, or any of them separately take place, it will be necessary to seek assistance from glasses, which will now ease the eyes, and in some degree check their tendency to grow flatter; whereas if they be not assisted in time, the flatness will be considerably increased, and the eyes be weakened by the efforts they are compelled to exert.

We are now able to decide upon a very important question, and say how far spectacles may be said to be *preservers of the sight.* It is plain they can only be recommended as such, to those whose eyes are beginning to fail; and it would be as absurd, to advise the use of spectacles to those who feel none of the foregoing inconveniences, as it would be for a man in health to use crutches to save his legs. But those who feel those inconveniences, should immediately take to spectacles, which, by enabling them to see objects nearer, and by facilitating the union of the rays of light on the retina, will support and preserve the sight.

When the eye sensibly flattens, all delay is dangerous; and the longer those who feel the want of assistance, defer the use of spectacles, the more they will increase the failure of the eye; there are too many who procrastinate the use of them, till at last they are obliged to use glasses of ten or twelve inches focus, instead of those of 36 or 40, which would otherwise have suited them; thus preferring a real evil, to avoid one that is imaginary. Mr. Thomin mentions several deplorable cases of this kind, particularly one of a lady, who, through false shame, had abstained from wearing spectacles so long a time, that at last it was impossible to suit her, but with those adapted to eyes that have been couched. Whereas the instances are numerous of those who, by using glasses of a long focus at the first approaches of long-sightedness, have brought back their eyes to their natural sight, and been able to lay aside their spectacles for years.

These considerations point out clearly the advantages that may be obtained by a proper choice of spectacles on first wearing them, and the importance of making such a choice; as the eye will endeavour to conform itself to any improper focus, and thus be brought into a state of extreme age, at a much earlier period than would have happened, had they been suited with judgment. There are very few opticians but what must have seen instances of those, who, by habituating their eyes to too short a focus, or too great a magnifying power, have so injured those tender organs, as to deprive them of future assistance from glasses. This frequently happens to those who purchase their spectacles of persons who are unacquainted with them, men equally ignorant of the science of optics, and the fabric of the eye.

☞ *Long or short-sighted persons, residing at a distance, wishing for Spectacles, are requested to observe the following directions:*

Only send the exact distance, in inches, at which they can see to read *this print* best without glasses, and the distance at which they wish to see it with them, (the common distance is about 15 inches,) or at any distance within the latitude of naked vision.

*Note.*—In case it is not possible to see distinctly at any distance without glasses, they are then requested to send a pair, (or their focus,) with the distance at which they can see with them best, as before directed.

Likewise, persons having glasses which do not suit, can have them exchanged, as well absent as present, by strictly observing the above particulars.

---

☞ BEALS & HOMER, PRINTERS....BOSTON.☜

FIGURE 19. Beals & Homer, printers, *Broadside of Daniel B. Widdifield*, No. 141 Washington Street, Boston, c. 1850. Courtesy of The Winterthur Library, Wilmington, DE: Joseph Downs Collection of Manuscripts and Printed Ephemera

when he gets home, and they are returned to their natural state, he finds what he had chosen, fatiguing and injurious to his sight."[33] In Widdifield's broadside, the text that delivers his admonitions and prescriptions is printed in two columns and headed by a stock woodcut engraving of a pair of spectacles that float above a few centered lines of display types arranged to accentuate the broadsheet's central object. The sheet's symmetrically balanced layout echoes and thus reinforces the binocularity of its viewer. The illustrated spectacles, a stock cut seen in numerous advertisements and specimen books, face away from the viewer. With their arms folded before the lenses and nearest to us, they invite beholders to try them on for size in order to gauge their effectiveness in enabling them to read the sheet's fine print. In fact, Widdifield utilizes the broadside's small type as a test for the vision of those "long or short-sighted persons" residing at too great a distance to visit his shop. Those "wishing for Spectacles" are requested to observe the following directions: "Only send the exact distance, in inches, at which they can see to read *this print* best without glasses, and the distance at which they wish to see it with them, (the common distance is about 15 inches,) or at any distance within the latitude of naked vision." Another optician, William White Cooper writing in 1847, suggests that the distance at which ordinary print is legible "varies from twelve to twenty inches."[34] Though in specifying such focal lengths the broadside purports proximity and alignment between observers and the techniques of the optician in measuring the powers of observers' eyesight, it actually underscores the physical distance between the two, and suggests, by its very existence, the physical and conceptual disconnects that often separated optical specialists from those who required their assistance.

Only a relative few lived within easy reach of urban-based opticians such as McAllister and Pike. Thus, various techniques, often in the vein of Widdifield's broadside, were devised for measuring and communicating one's acuity with only the optician's instructions as a guide. In an advertisement published in *Poulson's Daily Advertiser* on September 1, 1825, for example, the McAllister firm promised "attention is always given in advising to the focus most suitable to the sight." But when the store could not easily be reached, the optician had further instructions: "Persons at a distance, ordering Spectacles are requested to send a glass or a piece of glass from the Spectacles last used, as the age alone does not afford a sufficient rule. . . ."[35] Critical here is McAllister's dismissal of the notion that one's age automatically determined the powers of one's sight. Clearly, the firms of McAllister and Pike, among others, effected the commercialization of vision by making a commodity of acuity via the manufacture and distribution of eyeglasses. With the extended reach of their advertisements in city directories, and their mail order catalogues, their commodification of the "noblest sense" expanded considerably through the deployment of print. Hence, in cases in which the opportunity for, in Kitchiner's words, "every eye to negotiate for itself" could not be obtained, those who wished to purchase spectacles had to do so through mail order catalogues.[36]

Trade catalogues, handbills, city directory listings, and other forms of advertisement often featured multiple pairs of spectacles illustrative of the expansive variety of frame materials, styles, and focal lengths afforded by their lenses. In *O'Brien's Philadelphia Wholesale Business Directory*, advertisements for Paine's "Improved Perifocal or Patent Parabola Spectacles," sold in Philadelphia by Edward Borhek of Chestnut Street depict spectacled eyes peering outward while another pair with arms folded lower on the page faces away from the viewer (Figure 20). A page from Philadelphia typefounder Alexander Robb's *Specimen of Printing Types and Ornaments* of 1844 includes one pair of spectacles with delicate wire arms and earpieces with rectangular lenses (Figure 21). This pair floats on the page above a second pair with oval lenses and steel frames. In each, the lenses are shaded slightly differently. In the rectangular pair, the lenses are shaded along a diagonal axis with part of the lens left blank. In the pair below, lenses are densely shaded throughout in thread-like lines of black and white. Not coincidentally, I would argue, these spectacles share a page with two period printing presses, as well as a dresser, a carriage, and a funeral scene. In these stock cut engravings of spectacles, the design and execution of details such as the frames and lenses were paramount in order for such images to be recognizable and legible. The indexicality of this imagery depended on the engraver's calculated use of tints. Arrayed in parallel lines arranged horizontally or diagonally, or in intersecting lines that formed loosely crosshatched, offset grids, these marks served to make visible the magnifying power of optical glass. Intended only to suggest the physical presence of lenses within spectacle frames, such marks may have been erroneously interpreted by antebelleum observers as approximate indicators of their refractive power. These and other variations in the graphic treatment of lenses reinforced the "sliding scale" and imprecision of grinding techniques, lens systems, and prescription. When the sale of spectacles expanded beyond the polite network of word of mouth and the printed materials circulated by profesional opticians—that is, when such exchanges moved from retail to wholesale—their application became more complicated, and less effective. In the hands of "hawkers" and "quacks," the precision requisite to properly pre-

FIGURE 20. Edward Bohrek, "Paine's Improved Perifocal or Patent Parabola Spectacles, For Sale Only in Philadelphia by Edward Borheck, No. 93 Chestnut Street, Philadelphia," in *O'Brien's Philadelphia Wholesale Business Directory and United States, South America, West India, London, Liverpool and Paris Circular Wherein are Classed the Principal Mercantile Houses, Extensive Manufacturing Establishments, Eminent Artists, and Various Miscellaneous Departments, which Contribute to the General Business of the City of Philadelphia* (Philadelphia: King & Baird Printers, 1849), woodcut advertisement, 232. Library Company of Philadelphia.

FIGURE 21. Alexander Robb, *Specimen of Printing Types and Ornaments Cast by Alexander Robb* (Philadelphia: Alexander Robb, 1844), stock woodcut illustrations, n.p. Library Company of Philadelphia.

## PAINE'S
### Improved Perifocal or Patent Parabola
# SPECTACLES,

For Sale only in Philadelphia by
## EDWARD BORHEK,
**No. 52 Chesnut Street,**
PHILADELPHIA.

These Glasses have been examined and highly recommended by Dr. D. Lardner, of England; the late Dr. G. McClellan, of Philadelphia; Dr. G. S. Pattison, of New York; Dr. N. R. Smith, of Baltimore: Dr. R. D. Mussy, of Cincinnati, and many others who have practically tested them. They possess clearness and finish not equalled by any lenses of foreign or domestic manufacture, and never cause that giddiness of the head, or unpleasant sensation to the eyes that many experience from using the ordinary kind, but tend to strengthen and improve the sight, as is evidenced by numerous testimonials of their superiority over all other lenses, given by citizens of the highest respectability of this and other places.

The public are cautioned against purchasing Glasses termed PERIFOCAL or PARABOLA, except from the subscriber, as the English Periscopic and various bent imitations are offered for sale, which have an injurious effect upon the eye.

Difficult cases of deficient vision solicited.
Parabola Glasses inserted into other Spectacle Frames.
Also for sale, Self Regulating Thermometers and Barometers.

### Gold and Silver Spectacles Manufacturers.

Barber, Ralph, 109 Race st, above 3d, Manufac'r. Gold, Silver and German Silver Spectacles, Electro Plater, &c.
Borhek, Edward, 52 Chesnut st, Gold and Silver Spectacles Man'r, and sole Agent in Philadelphia, for H. M. Paine & Co.'s Patent Perifocal, or American Periscopic Spectacles, the best to help the human sight ever invented
Fisher, J., 58 Chesnut st
McAllister & Co., 48 Chesnut st
Morgan, Nathan E., Artisan's Buildings, Ranstead Place, 4th story, Gold and Silver Spectacles Manufacturer
Patton, Wm., s e cor 6th and Arch sts
Peters, James, & Co., 105 n 2d st, above Arch

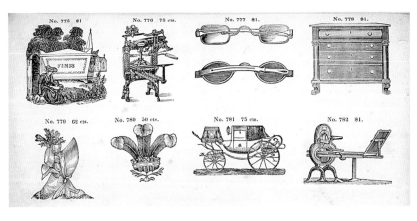

scribe spectacles by matching lenses with eyes diminished considerably. Spectacles hawked by city street vendors and itinerant peddlers threatened the sanctity of one's sight. When they circulated beyond opticians' polished glass cases and found application without the delicate yet imprecise prescription of practicing professionals, spectacles posed a hazard—enough to cause public spectacles. In one particular image clearly not commissioned or deployed by an optician, the engraver's lines typically used to indicate the refractive properties of lenses as a visual guaranty of their effectiveness are entirely absent.

*Modern Spectacles Easily Seen Through*, a satiric cartoon published in New York by engraver William Charles in 1806, figures spectacles in an entirely different way (Figure 22). Here, the transparency that Rembrandt Peale rendered so elegantly and effectively in his portraits and the engraved tints used to denote optical glass in stock cuts of the period are replaced by simple outlined circles. Neither transparent nor refractive, the cartoon's conception of bespectacled vision is unsettlingly opaque, eyeless, and blank. Best known as a cartoonist of the War of 1812, Charles depicts a street vendor selling spectacles by the score, calling out to his several customers "Buy spectakel, very goot, very sheap," an obvious ethnic slur. However, these spectacles clearly do not work. The five stumbling figures who wear them bump into one another and step on one another's toes. One caption reads, "Demme sir your spectacles are of no use could you not see my toes?" To which the perpetrator replies, "beg pardon sir rather short sighted." A man stands on the corner closest to the vendor, holding a sign that reads "To be disposed of / a quantity of puppies / may be viewed at / Pool's Hotel / corner of Princes street / every day from / 12 o'clock till 4." No one appears to gaze upon his sign, which stands in as a kind of makeshift eye test chart. Another man, possibly the figure near the corner with his back to the viewer, says "must take a turn to the billiard room / see if I can pluck a goose for my dinner" as he walks away. The etching's fluid style accentuates its suggestive title. The corner on which the action takes place is rather nondescript; clues to the scene's locations are few. Disproportionately drawn, the rippled lines of the figures' ill-fitted coats and pantaloons accentuates their foppery. Charles's loose handling throughout the composition also invokes the experience of shortsightedness or other variants of indistinct vision.

*Modern Spectacles Easily Seen Through* condenses several of the warnings of professional opticians in a single image. It vividly illustrates the dangers and ill effects that often resulted from the dangerous combination of poorly made, mass-produced spectacles; uninformed customers and itinerant peddlers untrained in the optical arts. So prevalent was this trade becoming that London optician John

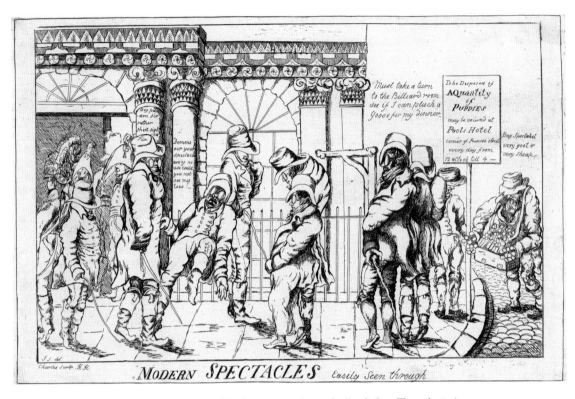

Text in the engraving:

They have seen sir rather their sight

Demme our your Spectacles are ye no usii could you not see my toes!

Must take a turn to the Billiard room see if I can pluck a Goose for my dinner—

To be Disposed of A Quantity of PUDDIES may be veiwed at Poots Hotel corner of Francis street every day from 12 o'clock till 4—

Buy Spectahel very good & very Sheap.

J.J. del

Charles Sculp. N.Y.

MODERN SPECTACLES *Easily Seen through*

**FIGURE 22.** William Charles, *Modern Spectacles Easily Seen Through*, 1806, engraving. Library Company of Philadelphia.

Thomas Hudson felt compelled in his 1833 treatise *Spectaclaenia* "to exhibit the abuses and impositions which have been practised by spectacle venders [*sic*] . . . to the great scandal of our most useful and honourable occupation." Inveighing against these roving salesman, he continues, "There is no profession in which the system of puffing and extortion by specious advertisements in the country newspapers, has been more generally or more successfully practiced, nor one in which the injury inflicted on the eyes or in the pockets of the public has been greater."[37] Hudson then sharpens his attack, explaining the vendor's specious products and techniques and elaborating in detaill how the "fair-dealing" optician differs. He describes the best materials for the construction of spectacles and offers instruction in the method of obtaining a proper fit in order to enable customers to detect and avoid "the spurious spectacles of the itinerant puffer."[38] In establishing his own authority, he also emphasizes that of his readers, clearly assumed to be potential customers. Repeatedly, he stresses that they themselves are the best judges in obtaining the proper fit. This carefully crafted sense of agency, however, is lost on Charles's bespectacled buffoons.

Most striking is the way in which Charles has delineated the lenses of the scene's several pairs of eyeglasses. The loose grids gracing the lenses of the spectacles depicted in McAllister's circulars have given way in Charles's etching to blankness. Within these white orbs, references to the presence of lenses or eyes are entirely absent. Grossly enlarged and markedly opaque, the spectacles nearly cover the wearers' faces and obscure the eyes, which, as physiognomic principles held, conveyed information about one's interior state, emotions, and intentions. As neither they nor we can "see through" their spectacles, the figures in Charles's cartoon are unable to fathom the inscrutable intentions of those around them. Their spectacles cloud rather than clarify meaning. Even the eyes of those lacking spectacles, a group that includes the vendor, his current client, and several others at left, are mostly obscured, by overhanging hats or turned heads. These omissions enlarge on the theme of inscrutability, especially in the context of commercial trade. As graphically depicted here and elsewhere in printed advertisements and catalogues, modern *spectacles* are, in fact, not so easily seen through. Indeed, as a result of wearing cheap, poorly crafted spectacles, the bespectacled figures in Charles's cartoon make *spectacles* of themselves. Hastily purchased as a fashion accessory and worn merely for show, an act of "blind" conformity, Charles's spectacles are silly in appearance and even sillier in application. The cartoon openly questions their efficacy and wittily probes the social affectation of their conspicuous consumption. The stumbling, bumbling scene makes faulty vision visible while comically overstating its typically understated ubiquity in the cultural field. Focusing attention on the figures' inability to see correctly, Charles's etching highlights the idiocy of both their vanity and misguided conformity.

In Charles's cartoon, spectacles of both optical and social varieties participate in the confusing and chaotic atmosphere of the capitalist marketplace. The emergence of this ramshackle "society of spectacles" tended to eclipse modes of unassisted sight and raised new questions about the epistemological nature of vision itself.[39] The lingering ambiguity of spectacles—the delights they offered and the dangers they posed—hinged on the critical question of whether they clarified or obfuscated reality. Edgar Allan Poe explores this conundrum more fully in his humorous tale of love at first sight, "The Spectacles." Poe wrote the story while living in Philadelphia during the early 1840s. It was first published in the March 27, 1844, issue of the *Dollar Newspaper* and occupied nearly the entire front page.[40] Published by A. H. Simmons & Co. at the southwest corner of Third and Chesnut

Streets, the paper's headquarters were just a few doors away from McAllister's on Chestnut. Along with seeing the shop on a somewhat regular basis while walking to and from the newspaper's offices (see Figure 38), Poe may have also drawn inspiration from another contemporary satire, "The Blunderer. Being a Few Passages in the Life of a Short-Sighted Man," published in *Knickerbocker Magazine* in February of 1837. That story, as Poe's would a few years later, opens with the narrator's confessional lament:

> Of all the evils to which mankind are subject, there is none more pitiable in its victim than an inordinary limitation of vision. I, alas, are one of those unfortunate individuals, whose nose is doomed to be "spectacle bestrid" during my mortal existence, and who can discern no object, unless it be thrust into my very face. This, it may readily be imagined, is at all times disagreeable, but particulary so when the article in question is obnoxious to the senses. Oh ye bipeds of oculars unimpaired!—ye all-seeing gentry.... Little do ye ken the numerous *faux pas* that we of the limited vision are almost constantly being pushed into, to the imminent jeopardy of our moral and physical sense, as men of feeling.[41]

Utilizing the same narrative conceit employed in "The Blunderer" to achieve its satire, Poe's tale portrays a humorous but instructive episode of "subjective" vision. Told in the first person, "The Spectacles" recounts the story of Simpson, a man whose poor vision and refusal to wear spectacles lead him to mistakenly fall in love with a woman who turns out to be his great-great-grandmother, Madame Lalande. As we later learn, she has come to America to find Simpson, whom she has selected as her heir. She immediately realizes the identity of her foolish admirer and conspires with a mutual friend to dupe her relative. After expounding the powers of "love at first sight," Simpson admits that although his eyes are "weak to a very inconvenient degree," he still feels that "the brightest and most enduring of the psychal fetters are those which are riveted by a glance."[42]

Several of Poe's stories, most notably "The Purloined Letter," "The Assignation," and "The Tell-Tale Heart," pose questions regarding the unstable nature of visual perception. But none do so as directly as "The Spectacles," a story that complicates notions of "correct" vision through a narrative framed by faulty sight and obsessed with ocular correction. With faulty vision as its central underlying premise, Poe's tale calculatingly deploys a narrator suffering from this condition. Though Simpson purports to see himself and others clearly, his self-admitted "infirmity of vision" at the outset establishes a point of view fraught by a lack of proper focus that "clouds" and confuses the narrative. Only in hindsight, which is here twenty-twenty, do we see the stumbling progress of his folly, as he strives unsuccessfully to make sense of a reality through visual faculties that deny him a clear and distinct rendering of that reality. Episodes of Simpson's narrative vivify in prose the visual effects of myopia or other ocular maladies such as astigmatism or strabismus, or perhaps worse, wearing ill-prescribed glasses. As a whole, the story stages a kind of optical puzzle in narrative form, one that probes the nature and limits of eyesight, what it is able to accommodate, the measures by which one obtains acuity for it, and the reliability of those measures once taken.

Written in Philadelphia, a city whose array of opticians' firms, eye infirmaries, and dedicated ophthalmic professionals made it a center for the study and treatment of vision, Poe's tale directly counters the published statements of McAllister, Kitchiner, and Hudson, inserting itself into the broader cultural debate over the efficacy and fashionableness of spectacles. Given Poe's interest in natural philosophy and other emerging forms of science, including optics, in which Poe was well versed,[43] it is plausible to assume that he would have been aware of the recent publication of any number of treatises regarding physiological optics. As an often-addled author and editor who worked in close proximity to the McAllisters' shop, Poe was surely familiar with the optical instrument firm, and perhaps even patronized it on occasion. Elements in the story also demonstrate more than a passing familiarity with the kinds of products the McAllisters sold and echo in tone and content the admonitory and prescriptive tracts that opticians circulated constantly throughout the 1840s. The story draws liberally on the language of both bodies of literature.

Simpson, whose real Christian name is Napoleon Bonaparte Froissart, opens by explaining his rather confusing ancestral lineage. Then with physiognomic precision, he describes his "personal endowments": "I believe that I am well made, and possess what nine tenths of the world would call a handsome face. In height I am five feet eleven. My hair is black and curling. My nose is sufficiently good." From a description of outward appearance, the narrator turns to a description of his eyes, which according to physiognomic principles purportedly spoke equally well for the exterior and the interior of the person to whom they belonged:

> My eyes are large and gray; although, in fact, they are weak to a very inconvenient degree, still no defect in this regard would be suspected from their appearance. The weakness itself, however, has always much annoyed

me, and I have resorted to every remedy—short of wearing glasses. Being youthful and good-looking, I naturally dislike these, and have resolutely refused to employ them. I know nothing, indeed, which so disfigures the countenance of a young person, or so impresses every feature with an air of demureness, if not altogether of sanctimoniousness and of age. An eyeglass, on the other hand, has a savor of downright foppery and affectation. I have hitherto managed, as well as I could without either.[44]

Simpson's vain refusal recalls Napolean Bonaparte's legendary reluctance to don spectacles in spite of his pronounced myopia and echoes Kitchiner's description of youthful pride as an obstacle to the use of eyeglasses: "When would-be-thought-young Persons first feel the necessity of giving their Eyes optical assistance, they are nevertheless shy of mounting Spectacles, which they seem to consider an inconvenient manner of advertising their age, upon their nose."[45] These admissions map the coordinates of Simpson's tragic fall from innocence into experience, which coincided with his transition from indistinct to perfect and continuous vision. Simpson represented for antebellum audiences the folly of refusing eyewear when needed. But the story's latent critique of spectacles insinuates that we can see and be duped at the same time, that perception and deception are perpetually intertwined. This dialectic plays out across a number of fictive spaces known to antebellum audiences for their inherent ambiguity. Significant scenes take place in the theater, in a small square at dusk, in the dimly lit parlor of a mansion, in a carriage traveling through the countryside in the middle of the night, and at a rural inn at daybreak. Dimly lit, interstitial, mobile, and transitory, these spaces derive their ambiguous character from the interplay of absolute darkness and varying degrees of light and shadow.[46] Of course, these conditions only heighten the sense of confusion produced by Simpson's already problematic vision. Noted for their potential danger to the eyes, the transitions of daybreak and dusk and evenings at the theater numbered among the situations that opticians and ophthalmologists warned readers to avoid. Poe's use of these locations suggests a passing familiarity with popular tenets of antebellum ophthalmology as disseminated in the temperance-inspired reform literature discussed in the previous chapter. Considered perilous to the eyes, the visual conditions of these spaces prompted Poe's readers to be on the lookout for the interplay of perception and deception.

Simpson first sees the object of his affection in the theater, William Kitchiner's favored laboratory for vision and vision aids. Bored with the performance, Simpson amuses himself by observing the audience. Eventually his eyes are "arrested and riveted" by a figure in one of the theater's private boxes. The angle of the narrator's vantage affords him only a partial view of the woman's face, enough to engulf his attention for the ensuing length of the performance. He asks his friend Talbot for an opera glass to obtain "a more distinct view of her beauty," but as "the stern decrees of Fashion had, of late, imperatively prohibited" their use, he replies in the negative. Without these aids to vision, Simpson mistakenly fastens his gaze on the elder of the two women seated in the box and pleads for his friend to confirm her beauty. Talbot responds affirmatively, mistakenly referring to the younger of the two women, also named Madame Lalande.[47] The coupling of young and old woman, and particularly the oscillating way in which Poe presents them here, bears a striking literary resemblance to the famous optical illusion known as "my wife and my mother-in-law." Optical puzzles of this kind circulated in newspapers and periodicals throughout the nineteenth century. They provided their viewers examples of what W. J. T. Mitchell has called "metapictures," for the ways they comment on the complex nature of images and thematize certain related acts of vision or aspects of perception. Dialectical images such as these challenge viewers to see one or the other against the impossibility of seeing both simultaneously, as philosopher Ludwig Wittgenstein described in his formulations regarding the famed duck-rabbit. This constant oscillation underscores the dialectical nature of the narrator's faulty optics.[48] When Madame Lalande notices Simpson's steady gaze, she pulls out her eyeglass to inspect and discern the identity of her admirer. Simpson, of course, interprets this as a bold assertion of her mutual attraction and continues to woo her from afar. Her eyeglasses enable her to identify him as the distant relative and potential heir whom she has come to the United States to meet. From his perspective, he notes what he thinks are the "visible effects" of their interlocking gazes on her countenance. His attempts to meet her after the performance are thwarted; likewise, the next time Simpson glimpses Madame Lalande, she is speeding by in an open carriage, forcing Simpson to make her acquaintance and his persistent appeal to her through an exchange of letters. Assured of Lalande's mutual attraction to him, Simpson liberally professes his feelings for her with pen and paper. To his delight, she sends a reaffirming reply. "Her eyes—her magnificent eyes," he glowingly notes, "had not belied her noble heart."[49]

A third encounter, though the first actually face-to-face, takes place in a quiet public square at twilight. Conversing in French, Simpson gives way to the "impetuous enthusiasm" of his nature and asks for Lalande's hand in marriage. She resists, urging "the old story of decorum," reminding her suitor that he knows little about her, her past, her prospects, even her age. Closer than he has ever been to her, Simpson still can not see her clearly: his poor vision is compounded by the dim light of dusk out of doors and by the low lighting inside the mansion into which she "smuggles" him in the "character of an old acquaintance" for an evening's entertainment. Chatting with Lalande later that evening, Simpson relates many of the earlier passages of his life, concealing nothing from his lover's "confiding affection." After listing a few of his minor ailments, he finally reveals the "disagreeable and inconvenient, but hitherto carefully concealed, weakness" of his eyes. Madame Lalande laughingly replies, "'you have been surely injudicious in coming to confession; for, without the confession, I take it for granted that no one would have accused you of the crime.'"[50] She then pulls from around her neck the pair of eyeglasses she used to gaze upon him in the theater. She asks if he remembers them as she hands the glasses over to her suitor. While Simpson inspects them, she indicates that she will yield to his entreaties should he do her but one favor. He anxiously agrees, even before hearing her request. Madame Lalande exhorts: "You shall conquer, for my sake, this affectation which leads you, as you yourself acknowledge, to the tacit or implied denial of your infirmity of vision. For this infirmity you virtually deny, in refusing to employ the customary means for its relief. You will understand me to say, then, that I wish you to wear spectacles." She then offers him her eyeglass for this purpose: "You perceive that, by a trifling modification thus—or thus—it can be adapted to the eyes in the form of spectacles, or worn in the waistcoat pocket as an eye-glass. It is in the former mode, however, and habitually, that you have already consented to wear it *for my sake*."[51] Simpson hastily agrees and promises to fulfill her request the next morning after they are married. They spend the rest of the evening together planning their wedding ceremony.

The following day, Simpson dons the newly crafted spectacles to face his beloved. To his horror, he finally sees before him the reality that has eluded him throughout the tale. Instead of the beautiful face he has foolishly adored, he sees the "corrected" image of an eighty-two-year-old woman. Simpson immediately faults the spectacles, not his own feeble vision, or his foolish behavior, and dashes them to the ground. In finally rendering his faulty vision acute, they have revealed an unexpected, undesired "truth." Once Simpson realizes his error, he explains: "The eye-glass was presented by way of adding reproof to the hoax—a sting to the epigram of the deception. Its presentation afforded an opportunity for the lecture upon affectation with which I was so especially edified. It is almost superfluous to add that the glasses of the instrument, as worn by the old lady, had been exchanged by her for a pair better adapted to my years. They suited me, in fact to a T."[52] That the narrator refers to a pair "adapted" to his years is expected, as this was commonly applied as a measure of one's ocular health.

But why do Simpson's spectacles suit him "to a T"? To what metric does Poe refer? What does it mean for a pair of spectacles to fit their wearer "to a T," that is, both optically and physically? In the arcane lexicon, or as print scholars call it, the "anatomy" of a typeface, lineaments of individual letters are described in bodily terms: head, shoulders, arms, legs, knees. Some letterforms even have "beards." As Poe was probably aware, given his intense interest in typography and printing, the source of the phrase "to a T" is "to a tittle," a reference in printers' terms to the small, very precise dot over the the lower case *i* or the minute cross of a *t*. The mark is an indicator of precision, deriving not just from the delicate casting of the type-face itself, but also, presumably, from one's ability to optically discern it once printed. Poe engaged his printers to utilize the unique communicative power of typography and print to punctuate the stories he placed in popular magazines such as *Graham's Magazine*, the *Southern Literary Messenger*, and his own *Broadway Journal*.[53] Here, in the story's original printing, Poe's insistence on the capital *T* in boldface underscores the visuality of his text, and his belief in the signifying capacities of type. The symmetric construction of the letter *T* also corresponds with the frame of the binocular human body. The letter derives its sense of balance from its two even arms stemming from a central axis. Note, for instance, how the *T* forms the axis of Widdifield's elaborate broadside. In "The Spectacles" the eyeglasses fit to a "T," that is, they align what is perceptible with what is real. Emerson described this axis "of things," in *Nature* and writes of man's coincidence with it. When this axis falls out of alignment, Emerson argued, man becomes "disunited with himself."[54] Simpson's refusal to wear spectacles enacts this misalignment; his blind love, itself the result of his near blindness, works against his own interests. The story suggests the folly, for the purposes of fashionable appearance, of rejecting the use of custom made eyewear and the pronounced need for acute vision in a culture of shifting appearances and spectacular entertainments. Despite the growing professionalism of opticians, and the scientific and technological advances in the manufacture and prescription of lenses, Poe's character resists at his own peril.

The distance from Peale to Poe represents the broad spectrum of responses to the emergence of profesionally crafted spectacles and the standardized field of optometry. These ranged from eager acceptance and use to outright rejection. This spectrum can also be read in the various ways spectacles were represented, from the painted portraits of Rembrandt Peale to the engraved spectacles included in their advertisements and catalogues or mocked in the cartoons of William Charles. In spite of the promotions of Kitchiner, Hudson, McAllister, and Widdifeld, the mistrust and skepticism with which many viewed the sliding scale of acuity and accommodation—approximated in painterly and graphic representations of spectacle lenses—formed the basis for skepticism and critique.

As the measurement of visual acuity became more precise and the dissemination and use of carefully calibrated test lenses and spectacles became more widespread, cultural perceptions of these and other vision aids gradually over the course of the nineteenth century assumed a more positive cast. This change did not result solely from the standardization of opticians' prescriptions and practices. Rather, spectacles became more widely accepted and valued for how they performed and what they communicated about the status of the observing subjects who wore them. As evidenced in period portraiture and in the success of certain optician's firms over the course of the nineteenth century, Americans with the means for procuring spectacles gradually developed a taste for wearing them. Their increased use over time suggests that correct vision became a central component of bourgeois selfhood in a market system that placed new demands on the eyes of its participants. In portraits in which sitters wear or hold spectacles, these instruments assume an iconographic currency as appropriate, even fashionable, accoutrements of bourgeois costume and modes of self-display. The conspicuous consumption of spectacles and other vision aids in portraiture, as well as in everyday life, projected an image of subjects as literate and profitably engaged in activities requiring acute vision. Along with announcing infirmity, as in Poe's tale, a pair of spectacles in the antebellum era also emblematized productivity, efficiency, mobility, and economy. Moreover, in the commodity form and the "commodified" form of vision that they facilitated, spectacles in the antebellum period invoked and lent shape to a binocular observer and a binocular model of vision. But the culture's oscillating mistrust and valorization of spectacles reveals the contested terrain of modernity's scopic regime, which in the early nineteenth century was increasingly dominated by notions of "correct vision," notions that circulated amid other commodities in the marketplace.[55] At each and every focal length, acute sight now had a corresponding number and price. This commodification of acute vision increased its availability as well as its market value. But, as we have seen, it also invited and encouraged a healthy dose of skepticism.

These conceptions of vision were inscribed in the transparency of ground glass lenses and articulated in the densities of applied pigment and printer's ink. The engraved lines and tints intended to designate refractive capacity deployed in open-ended mass communications such as cartoons, trade catalogues, broadsides, and newspaper ads complicated this relationship in the absence of visual standards for acuity and the production of lenses that aided observers in procuring it. This lack of standards, which for spectacles encouraged their proliferation and use, would also encourage the expansion and elaboration of display typography, which, once standardized, would provide opticians with a method for measuring, with a considerable degree of accuracy, the actual acuity of the eyes.

# PART II

## The Chaos of Print

FIGURE 23. Frederick Spencer, *The Newsboy*, oil on canvas.
Collection of Peter Rathbone. (See Plate 2.)

## CHAPTER THREE

# Broadsides, Display Types, and the Physiology of the Moving Eye

Frederick Spencer's 1849 painting *The Newsboy* poignantly testifies to the saturation of typographic forms in the urban visual field and vividly illustrates antebellum culture's insatiable desire for and eager consumption of printed matter (Figure 23, Plate 2). This snippet of a scene, snatched from the ebb and flow of the urban streets, delineates a world in which spectacles might be required, a world in which clear, unobstructed sight was difficult to attain much less maintain, a world in which visiblity and legibility were paramount, where confusion rather than clarity was the norm. The newsboy stares out toward the painting's viewers who in turn strain and squint to make out letters, words, and phrases plucked here and there from the worn, text-laden backdrop. Even by 1837, as the "agreeable and well informed" correspondent for the *Boston Daily Atlas*, aptly named "Wall Street," wrote in his "Sketches of Life in New York": "Everything here is done by printing. . . . Press is the be-all and end-all of every department of life. Newspapers, pamphlets, caricatures, handbills, and cards are the main machinery of existence here."[1] With a paper at the ready, Spencer's newsboy and the wall behind him bear this out. "Cards," or broadsides like those behind him in varying states of decay, constituted the most outwardly audacious of the "surfaces" Emerson lamented.[2] Others scorned the bill-stickers responsible for such cluttered displays.[3] Spencer's painting captures the chaos of print unleashed during the late 1830s and '40s, now bolder in tone, larger in scale, and deployed across nearly every available wall, post, or window. "Handbills are . . . to cards what Brobdingnag was to Lilliput," the correspondent continued. "They are generally too big for in-door visitations, though sometimes suspended upon door screens, and on hat pegs, in the bar-rooms of alehouses, gin-shops, and hotels. Their place is on dead walls, or on yellow pine boards prepared for the purpose, and dropped here and there at public corners, leaning up against post,—whence they are called posters by the pasters."[4] Of such "Dead Wall Literature," a writer for *Eliza Cook's Journal* explained: "These are truly the times when 'Wisdom cries aloud in the streets,'—we mean from dead walls. The most popular literature of the day is displayed there . . . to many, the dead wall is the only newspaper." Freely available to the masses, so-called "dead walls" hosted announcements both public and private, civic and commercial, sacred and secular. "Many an effective broad-side first sees the light on the dead wall." But far from "dead" or irrelevant, this "literature" was a telling indicator of cultural sentiment: "if you want to know what is stirring the mind and heart of the people, look to the dead wall."[5] Strategically placed at or near eye level, broadsides visually hailed voters and investors, diners and drinkers, travelers, shoppers, and soldiers. Their increasing magnitude and ubiquity, however, were but two features of their modernity.

Broadsides, cards, and posters provided vehicles for the new wood display types. Carved in malleable wood instead of brittle and cumbersome metal, typefaces of old and new letterforms not only grew in size. Their shapes and styles multiplied as founders exploited the surfaces and contours of lettters to increase their capacity for ink saturation and the inclusion of decorative elements and ornamental flourishes. Display letters evolved rapidly to better attract attention, announce events, and advertise goods and services in an increasingly crowded and congested visual field. The innovations of wood engraving in the early nineteenth century and the expanded use of steam power and mechanized production made possible the invention of a lateral router for their mass production. The brainchild of New York printer and typefounder Darius Wells, wood types took the world of commercial printing by storm. Unlike the more refined typefaces used for newspaper and book printing, display types, with their bold and chunky forms, their densely saturated expanses of ink, their inventive shapes and inflated scale, were devised to be anything but "invisible" or transparent conduits of information, a position favored by typefounders in the eighteenth century. Rather, their brash boldness, garish colors, and shaded or "perspective" rendering clamored for attention, hailing subjects more aggresively, and from all directions. Amid the effervescent economic climate of the 1830s and '40s, "it was no longer enough for the twenty-six letters of the alphabet to function only as phonetic symbols."[6] The market revolution necessitated a larger scale. But it also encouraged the development of new letterforms with different tactile and expressive characteristics that might give them a greater, and perhaps more lasting, visual impact. From the foundries of Darius Wells, L. Johnson, Alexander Robb, and other creative entre-

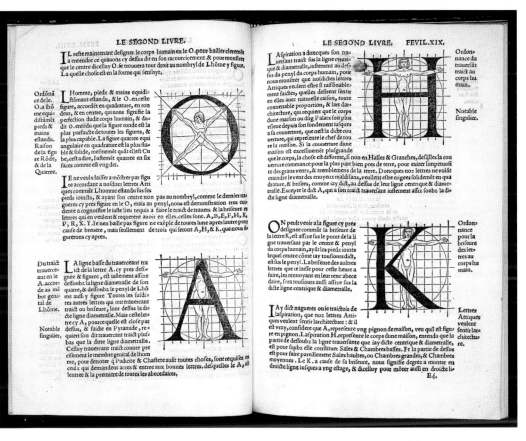

**FIGURE 24.** Illustration of Letters and Human Figures in Geoffroy Tory, *Champ Fleury*. 2nd Book (Paris: Gilles de Gourmont, 1529), 19. British Library, London, © British Library Board. All Rights Reserved/Bridgeman Images.

preneurs emerged letters nearly abstract in form, but capable, at quick glance, of attracting and exciting the eyes of passersby. Indeed, the deployment of typographically elaborate broadsides such as we see in Spencer's painting testify to the increased volume of print in the streets of the metropolis as well as to increased pedestrian traffic. The size of the letters suggest the presence of observers and indicate the viewing positions and distances at which they were expected to best see them. Though observers are visually absent in Spencer's picture, their traces are present throughout the composition.[7]

Constituitive of its structure and, thus, the basis of its visual appeal was a letter's correspondence to the human body itself. Modeled on the proportions of the human frame, the letters of the Roman alphabet had evolved over centuries to resonate with the bodies of those who cast, printed, and read them (Figure 24).

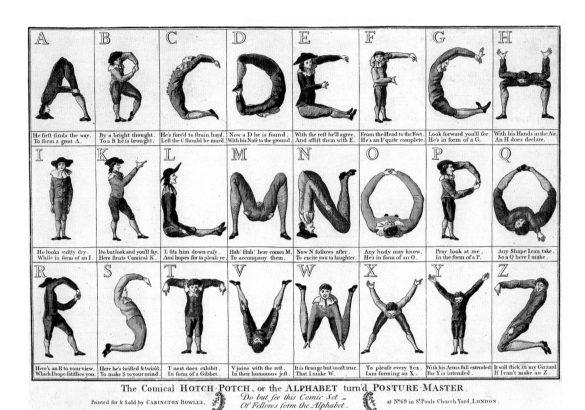

The various components of typefaces even came to be described in bodily terms: heads, shoulders, arms, legs, and feet. In his early sixteenth-century text, *De Divina Proportione*, Luca de Pacioli wrote, "From the human body are all measures and their names derived." He and other late Renaissance figures, including the French engraver Geoffroy Tory, utilized the human anatomy as scaffolding on which to form properly proportioned letters.[8] Modulated by the passage of time and shifting tastes, the orderly symmetry of the fifteenth-century alphabet was playfully manipulated in *The Comical Hotch-Potch, Or, the Alphabet Turned Posture-Master*, published in 1782 by the English engraver, drawing instructor, and cartographer Carrington Bowles (Figure 25). In this acrobatic alphabet, the bodies of twenty-six rather flexible individuals contort themselves into letterforms and give animated expression to the new stresses that would be placed on display types a few decades later in the 1830s and '40s. Bowles's alphabet simultaneously acknowledges the fluid expressivity of letterforms and their construction on the model of the human body, however pliant, thus lending new meaning to the threadbare protagonist of Frederick Spencer's painting.

As our eyes scan the wall's multicolored surface, sizing up this letter or that, our roving gaze comes time and again to rest on the rumpled figure of the news-boy hawking his wares. "The news-boy is emphatically a creation of the new world," a "necessity of the times," wrote George D. Strong in 1840. Like the rag paper he hustles, the newsboy is *woven* into the machinery of the antebellum market economy. "Bearing on his front the impress of that rapidity of motion, and absence of repose, which exist in perfection in no other quarter of the globe," wrote Strong, he "comes in the same order and progression of events as the railroad and telegraph, and raises in his corresponding sphere the self same questions. That he presents himself in a dirty face and jacket does not by any means diminish the claims of his case to a careful consideration."[9] In Spencer's painting, however, the newsboy's is not the only dirty "face" lurking out from this sordid corner of the metropolis. Here in the picture, figure and ground overlap. As an embodied extension of the visually arresting yet worn broadsides before which he is perched, this news-slinging urchin fastens and centers our attention, both arresting and diverting the viewer's gaze; his static position anchors the observer's multiple points of view. As the man of the hour, his momentary stasis still suggests motion.

The newly englarged, grotesquely "fattened" letterforms deployed on the broadsides behind him traced the paths and trajectories of ambulatory multitudes.[10] Indeed, the fat-faced display letters mapped the desires and directions of viewers continually positioned, and repositioned, as potential consumers. Along with attracting their notice, the bold, ink-saturated letters suggested warehouses overflowing with mechanically produced goods and signified the eagerness of manufacturers and middle men to move their stock from storehouses to showrooms. In their gargantuan forms, they often overstated the importance of what they signified, including the status of their purveyor. As a result, the expansion, elaboration, and exaggeration of letterforms drew criticism as a new and more grandiose form of "puffing," a colloquial term for inflating the value of things advertised. Just as exaggerated letterforms also spoke to a surfeit of consumer goods and streets saturated with consumers, they may also, in some cases, have encouraged in some an inflated sense of self premised on the ravenous consumption that advertisements endeavored to elicit. But within a fluctuating paper-money economy, wealth accrued and disappeared in an instant, a fact echoed in the ephemerality of advertising. Broadside stickers or pasters strove to post their sheets on the best walls in order to capitalize on the prime vistas, the most unobstructed sight lines, and the most attractive angles. But the city's contours were constantly changing as commercialized public spaces became increasingly defined by kinetic motion and the visual chaos encouraged by the proliferation of print. As evidenced in the painting's colorful array, posters were routinely tacked up and torn down, posted and pasted over one another, worn out and washed away. Obvious, even obstreperous, then obsolete.

Like the newspapers he sells and the handbills and posters behind him, the newsboy is ephemeral too. According to Strong, "With him [the newsboy] the past and the future are equally invisible." Both he and the broadsides remain in flux as events come and go and the paper he peddles physically wears away. "His sheet is indeed an epitome of the hour; a picture to be glanced at and forgotten; a moving diorama, ever exhibiting new features; a vision, like the dawn of morning, pleasant but evanescent."[11] In Spencer's painting, words referencing objects, persons, or events elsewhere perform their work and then are gone in an instant, left behind as apocryphal traces, faded signifiers rendered in the vibrant colors of the painter's fluid pigments (see Figure 23, Plate 2). In their ephemerality, printed sheets of multicolored paper, as delineated by Spencer, approximate the kaleidoscopic and fugitive effects of subjective vision—particularly those aspects of sight such as retinal afterimages that occur within the eyes of observers once removed from a stimulus. This feature of vision provided evidence of its *productive* qualities as well as its embeddedness in the human body. Together, the newsboy and the "dead wall literature" behind him constitute and collaborate in a kind of moving diorama, but the movement belongs solely to the wandering eyes and perambulating bodies of viewers both within the space of Spencer's composition and standing before the painting itself. The viewing experience staged in the painting metaphorizes through print's fugitive materality a vivid sense of vision's evanescent and fleeting qualities. The motley assortment of typefaces depicted in the painting also subtly delineates the motility of observing subjects as they invisibly perambulate back and forth, to and fro. Momentarily fixed in position yet suggestive of fluctuations in time and space, the newsboy's steadfast presence in the picture underscores the body's centrality to the creation, deployment, and consumption of the new display typography. These aspects of the painting suggest that the formation and placement of display types were beginning to be conceived in accordance with the body's binocular symmetry as well as the physiology of the moving eye. Their new target: the attentive yet mobile viewer.

Printed on one side of a sheet of paper ranging in size from handbill to mammoth placard poster by the mid-nineteenth century, broadsides covered the walls, fences, taverns, storefronts, and signposts of antebellum America. Until around 1800, "public notices generally followed book typography. Whether announcing lost cattle, a circus, or a town meeting, they were printed in letters that were essentially the same as those used for books and set in a format that echoed the symmetrical and polite arrangements of title pages."[12] With only subtle differences between thick and thin strokes, old style type, a form of Roman letter, had been refined over three centuries for the specific purpose of achieving maximum legibility in the small space of a page.[13] The refinements of the full modern face, a new letterform based on the sharp contrast of thick and thin, relied on improvements in the printing press and on the introduction of woven paper.[14] These improvements would also pave the way for the introduction of larger and more pronounced typefaces and facilitate the application of these types to larger and larger sheets of paper weighted to receive their emboldened impressions.

At the dawn of the nineteenth century, most type used in the United States was still imported from Europe. Publications of all sorts, including books, newspapers, and broadsides continued to be set in Caslon old style types, a small and austere letterform originally designed and cut in the 1720s and '30s by English founder William Caslon (Figure 26).[15] Benjamin Franklin's Philadelphia printing office, for instance, was equipped with mostly imported Caslon types.[16] During the century's final decade, several collections of imported materials from England, France, and elsewhere came into the possession of two Scotsmen, Archibald Binny and James Ronaldson, whose Philadelphia foundry was begun in 1796. With a penchant for innovation and enterprise, the firm improved on old style letterforms (such as pica, long primer, and brevier) and produced the first type cast dollar sign. Their types were used for a number of the most prominent books published during the early national period, including Joel Barlow's epic poem *The Columbiad* (1807), Alexander Wilson's *American Ornithology* (1808–1814), and Isaiah Thomas's *History of Printing in America*, published in 1810.[17]

In 1809 the foundry issued what is widely considered to be the first type specimen printed in the United States: *A Specimen of Metal Ornaments Cast at the Letter Foundry of Binny & Ronaldson*. The slender volume, measuring only five by eight and a half inches, consisted of twenty-three pages featuring 101 ornamental designs, borders, cartouches, eagles, and other animals cut in metal and wood. It was fol-

# A SPECIMEN

By W. CASLON, Letter-Founder, in Ironmonger-Row, Old-Street, LONDON.

ABCD
ABCDE
ABCDEFG
ABCDEFGHI
ABCDEFGHIJK
ABCDEFGHIJKL
ABCDEFGHIKLMN

French Cannon.

Quouſque tan-
dem abutere,
Catilina, pati-
*Quouſque tandem*

**DOUBLE PICA ROMAN.**
Quouſque tandem abutere, Catilina, patientia noſtra? quamdiu
nos etiam furor iſte tuus eludet?
quem ad finem ſeſe effrenata jac-
ABCDEFGHIJKLMNOP

**GREAT PRIMER ROMAN.**
Quouſque tandem abutere, Catilina, patientia noſtra? quamdiu nos etiam furor iſte tuus eludet? quem ad finem ſeſe effrenata jactabit audacia? nihilne te
nocturnum præſidium palatii, nihil urbis vigiliæ, nihil timor populi, nihil con-
ABCDEFGHIJKLMNOPQRS

**ENGLISH ROMAN.**
Quouſque tandem abutere, Catilina, patientia
noſtra? quamdiu nos etiam furor iſte tuus eludet?
quem ad finem ſeſe effrenata jactabit audacia?
nihilne te nocturnum præſidium palatii, nihil
urbis vigiliæ, nihil timor populi, nihil conſen-
fus bonorum omnium, nihil hic munitiſſimus
ABCDEFGHIJKLMNOPQRSTVUW

**PICA ROMAN.**
Melium, novis rebus ſtudentem, manu ſua occidit.
Fuit, fuit iſta quondam in hac repub. virtus, ut viri
fortes acrioribus ſuppliciis civem perniciofum, quam
acerbiſſimum hoſtem coërcerent. Habemus enim ſe-
natuſconſultum in te, Catilina, vehemens, & grave:
non deeſt reip. confilium, neque autoritas hujus ordinis: nos, nos, dico aperte, conſules defumus. De-
ABCDEFGHIJKLMNOPQRS 'VUWX

*Double P: .. Italick.*
*Quouſque tandem abutere, Catili-*
*na, patientia noſtra? quamdiu*
*nos etiam furor iſte tuus eludet?*
*quem ad finem ſeſe effrenata jac-*
*ABCDEFGHJIKLMNO*

*Great Primer Italick.*
*Quouſque tandem abutere, Catilina, pa-*
*tientia noſtra? quamdiu nos etiam fu-*
*ror iſte tuus eludet? quem ad finem ſeſe*
*effrenata jactabit audacia? nihilne te*
*nocturnum præſidium palatii, nihil ur-*
*bis vigiliæ, nihil timor populi, nihil con-*
*ABCDEFGHIJKLMNOPQR*

*English Italick.*
*Quouſque tandem abutere, Catilina, patientia noſ-*
*tra? quamdia nos etiam furor iſte tuus eludet?*
*quem ad finem ſeſe effrenata jactabit audacia?*
*nihilne te nocturnum præſidium palatii, nihil ur-*
*bis vigiliæ, nihil timor populi, nihil conſenſus bo-*
*norum omnium, nihil hic munitiſſimus habendi ſe-*
*ABCDEFGHIJKLMNOPQRSTVUW*

*Pica Italick.*
*Melium, novis rebus ſtudentem, manu ſua occidit.*
*Fuit, fuit iſta quondam in hac repub. virtus, ut viri*
*fortes acrioribus ſuppliciis civem perniciofum, quam a-*
*cerbiſſimum hoſtem coërcerent. Habemus enim ſenatuſ-*
*cer um in te, Catilina, vehemens, & grave: non deeſt*
*reip. confilium, neque autoritas hujus ordinis: nos, nos,*
*dico aperte, conſules defumus. Decrevit quondam ſenatus*
*ABCDEFGHIJKLMNOPQRSTVUWXYZ*

Pica Black.
And be it further enacted by the Authority
aforeſaid. That all and every of the ſaid Exchequer Bills to be made forth by virtue of
this Act, or ſo many of them as ſhall from
ABCDEFGHIKLMNOPQRST

Brevier Black.
And be it further enacted by the Authority aforeſaid. That all and every
of the ſaid Exchequer Bills to be made forth by virtue of this Act, or ſo
many of them as ſhall from time to time remain undiſcharged and uncan-
celled, and the diſcharging and cancelling the ſame purſuant to this Act.

Pica Coptick.

Pica Armenian.

English Syriack.

Pica Samaritan.

FIGURE 26. Willliam Caslon, *A Specimen*, 1734. Private Collection/
Bridgeman Images.

lowed in 1812 by a volume of forty-one pages, making it the first catalogue produced in this country that displayed type (Figure 27).[18] This specimen followed the pattern of earlier volumes produced by Caslon and others. The 1812 specimen adapts Caslon's Latin passage and sequencing from largest to smallest types, followed by borders and stock cuts.[19] The volume begins with the following announcement: "To the Printers of the United States: The very liberal encouragement the Proprietors of this Foundery have received, while it has stimulated their exertions to deserve it, has also put it in their power to extend and improve their establishment on the grand scale, of which this Specimen exhibits a proof. . . . The letters of a larger size than seven lines Pica (with which this Specimen commences) shall be finished as soon as possible; and they have now in hand several new and important articles which could not be got ready for it, but which shall be added to it from time to time."[20] The firm's expansion and professed eagerness to supply larger letters at a quickened pace are telling indicators of the new demands being placed on typography by the emerging market system. Such demands effectively transformed the look, feel, and overall applicability of typefaces. In Binny & Ronaldson's seven-lines pica (Figure 28), the bold, thick

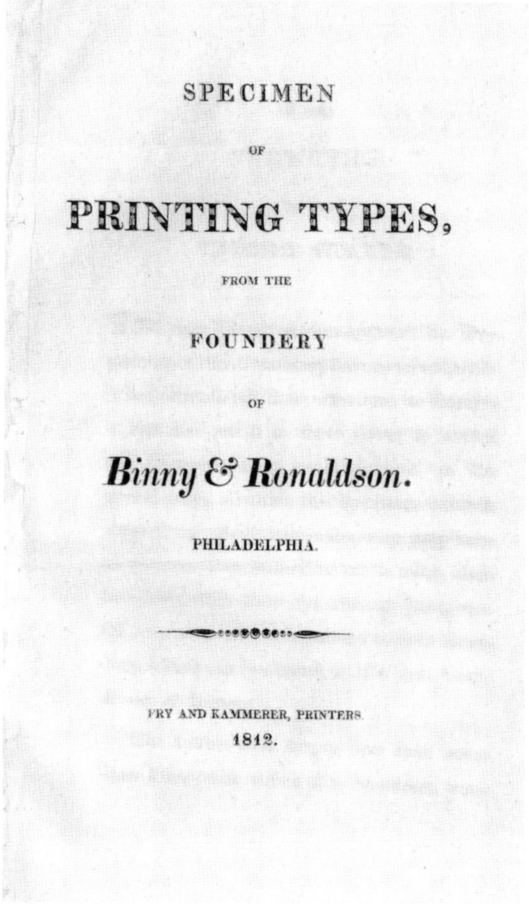

SPECIMEN

OF

# PRINTING TYPES,

FROM THE

FOUNDERY

OF

*Binny & Ronaldson.*

PHILADELPHIA.

FRY AND KAMMERER, PRINTERS.
1812.

FIGURE 27. Archibald Binny & James Ronaldson, *Specimen of Printing Types from the Foundery of Binny & Ronaldson, Philadelphia* (Philadelphia: Fry and Kammerer, Printers, 1812), title page. Library Company of Philadelphia.

FIGURE 28. Archibald Binny & James Ronaldson, "Seven Lines Pica," in *Specimen of Printing Types from the Foundery of Binny & Ronaldson, Philadelphia* (Philadelphia: Fry and Kammerer, Printers, 1812). Library Company of Philadelphia.

SEVEN LINES PICA.

# ATHENS
# Machine

strokes, connected by thin strokes, echo the basic lineaments of the letterforms that had generally served the needs of newspaper and book printing. However, while a significant contrast between thick and thin strokes of typefaces typically used in newspapers and books made them somewhat illegible for hurried reading and practically invisible from a distance, increasing the size of the letters and multiplying the visual magnitude of the thick strokes, in particular, helped to counter this phenomenon. In answer, the 1816 edition of the specimen featured a fourteen-line pica, which doubled the size of the largest type in the previous edition. Along with increases in size and scale, basic letterforms such as Roman, Antique, and Gothic were refashioned, as older typefaces were simply not assertive enough for nineteenth-century commercial printing. Clients requested and soon required the visual weight of fatter display types; a thriving commerce demanded it.

Essentially a "swollen version" of the modern face, so-called fat face types are large, exaggerated letters with a thick stroke whose width is nearly half as wide as the letter's height.[21] Versions of these letterforms were developed some time before 1820, but not without considerable difficulty.[22] The characteristics of the fat

FIGURE 29. Ten line Pica Roman, Antique, and Gothic fat face types, in Darius Wells & Ebenezer Russell Webb, *Specimens of Wood Type Manufactured by Wells & Webb for Sale at Their Printer's Warehouse No. 18 Dutch Street, corner of Fulton, New York, and the principal type founders in the United States and Canada* (New York: Wells & Webb, 1854). Courtesy of the Newberry Library, Chicago, Wing Folio Z 40583.962.

faces are for the most part the same as those of the classical modern face: thin, flat serifs, vertical stress, and abrupt contrast of thick and thin strokes.[23] Typically eight line or larger and consistently dark in color, fat face types, particularly exaggerations of basic letterforms like Roman, Antique, and Gothic, were instantly popular among job printers patronized by commercial interests looking for ways to better publicize their goods (Figure 29). On these basic letterforms hundreds of variants were produced. Considered grotesque or offensive by some, fat face, according to print historian Nicolete Gray, was "obviously intended to be neither normal nor obtrusive or beautiful," but "merely expressive."[24] However as the size of display types crept upward, problems with creating and using them also magnified. Costs ballooned. Large types were difficult to produce and once cast were not only costly but also heavy, brittle, and cumbersome to use. Because of the way liquid metal cools in the cast, it was nearly impossible to form large letters with even surfaces needed for full and consistent ink saturation.[25] Several techniques were employed in the search for a solution to this problem. On William Caslon's model, English typefounder Edmond Fry utilized sand casting techniques in the

1820s to create types ten line or larger. But such methods were time-consuming, costly, and only partially able to produce satisfying results. And because founders generally sold type by the pound, the cost of larger printing types mushroomed alongside the size of the individual faces for sale. Until the late 1820s, cost prohibitions, and structural limitations, limited their use.

Darius Wells, a job printer from upstate New York rectified this problem. In March 1828 he issued his first catalogue of wood type specimens from the back room of George Long's Book Store at 161 Broadway, just a few doors below Benjamin Pike & Sons, Optician and Instrument Makers at 166. As he wrote in the catalogue's introduction: "For want of large type, no larger posting bills than of medium size were then printed, and these exhibiting but a lean variety; while the metal type cost so much as to limit their use to a very few establishments. The manufacture of Wood Type formed a new era in job printing; and the use of them, although at first opposed by a strong prejudice, has now become general; and the universal satisfaction they have given, attests the high estimation in which they are held. In regard to their cheapness and durability, no argument is now necessary."[26]

Wells's innovations culminated roughly forty years of evolution in typographic design. But his comment points to debates concerning the price and durability of larger types, and perhaps their mammoth aesthetic as well. This was a period that witnessed the magnification of letterforms in the modern and later fat face types. It also saw extensive elaboration and embellishment of their surfaces, both to accord with their new enlarged scale, but also to perform the task assigned to them: visibility and legibility at the greatest possible distances and from the greatest number of angles. Setting aside centuries of technological evolution and practice, Wells traded molten metals for docile wood as the medium in which to carve rather than cast his types. Though wood had long been an integral part of the arts of printing, Wells's innovation derived from his method of carving and mass-producing letters. He carved on the end grain of the wood after the manner of wood engravers, rather than on side grain, which was customary for printers who typically carved large letters for their own use. Soon after, Wells devised the lateral router, which finally made the mass production of wood types not only practical but also highly profitable.[27] The lateral router, in combination with a pantograph mechanism added by George Leavenworth in 1834, constituted the essential machinery for making end-cut wood types on a mass scale. Almost instantly, these large types populated the pages of founders' and job printers' type specimens across the country.

Wells's return to wood in this instance marks one of the many effects of market revolution. It reflects the convergence of an explosive synthesis of historical revivals of older typographic forms, improved technology, increased commercial demand, and the creative energies of entrepreneurial men like Wells and his competitors George F. Nesbitt, William H. Page, and others.[28] Casting large types, as Wells pointed out, was costly, time-consuming, laborious, difficult, and ultimately ineffective. Wood with its tremendous flexibility for carving and its capacity for receiving and transferring ink was recovered for use in the creation of letterforms beginning in the second decade of the nineteenth century. Its flexibility, in particular, was exploited by a market system seeking inexpensive means for mass advertisement and display, for novelty, and variety. After the first of Wells's wood types came onto the market in 1828, it was only a short time before typefounders around the country were selling them. The 1834 catalogue of Johnson & Smith of Philadelphia stated on the price list, "Most of the six-line and larger types are cut on wood." The White, Hagar & Company price list for 1835 announced that the sixteen-line and larger types were cut on wood, and both Connor & Cooke and Robb & Ecklin (also of Philadelphia) in 1836 mention in their price lists that designs six-line and over were cut on wood.[29] Set in rhythmic and occasionally evocative arrangements approximating poetry, their specimens featured in abundance a great variety of the latest letters, in all available sizes (Figure 30). For an advertisement to achieve its primary goal of attracting the attention of passersby, scale, design, and density were paramount.

A new breed of jobbing printers such as Philadelphia's entrepreneurial Howell Evans employed specialized steam-powered presses able to accommodate the popular new letters. He and others spilled exponentially more ink and capitalized on the availability of larger and larger sheets of paper to convey bold statements of advertising fact and fiction. Indeed, the inflation of letterforms, and the increased emphasis with which they endowed certain words, gave audaciously visual form to the detested act of puffing, or aggrandizing a particular person, product, or service. Such criticisms might very well have been leveled against Evans, whose signage and advertisements depicted in numerous promotional wood-engraved images appear guilty of this very act. A portrait of Evans, painted in rather pedestrian fashion by Philadelphia artist Robert Street, attests to the printer's inflated sense of self as he dwarfs two of his employees who work nearby (Figure 31). An article titled "Puffing vs. Advertising" summarily untangles the two, associating the deplorable act of "puffing" with the use of display types instead of the ordinary "advertising types" to pronounce one commodity for sale over and above any others.

> An advertisement, where a man in his own name offers his goods to the public, is a fair, open, legitimate transaction. The party interested says what

TWO-LINE SMALL PICA ORNAMENTED, No. 10.

**SKILFUL HANDIWORK**

TWO-LINE SMALL PICA ORNAMENTED, No. 11.

**CURLY-HEADED**

TWO-LINE SMALL PICA ORNAMENTED, No. 12.

**TRANSLUCENT WATER**

TWO-LINE PICA CONDENSED TUSCAN SHADED.

**NASTURTION TENDRILS**

TWO-LINE PICA CONDENSED ORNAMENTED.

**DRIPPING ROCKS BELOW THE FALL**

TWO-LINE PICA ANTIQUE SHADED.

**CLOUDED**

TWO-LINE PICA ITALIAN SHADED.

**THOUGHTLESS**

TWO-LINE PICA GOTHIC SHADED.

**CHALK ROCKS**

DOUBLE PICA TUSCAN SHADED.

**SCOLLOPED**

TWO-LINE PICA ORNAMENTED, No. 2.

**ROCK CRYSTALS**

TWO-LINE PICA ORNAMENTED, No. 3.

**STAR-GIRDLED**

TWO-LINE PICA ORNAMENTED, No. 4.

**MORNING STAR**

TWO-LINE SMALL PICA ORNAMENTED, No. 13.

**FROLICKSOME**

TWO-LINE SMALL PICA ORNAMENTED, No. 14.

**COMING MORN**

TWO-LINE PICA GOTHIC CONDENSED SHADED.

**THE HOUSE OF GLASS**

DOUBLE PICA ANTIQUE OPEN.

**LUNAR Eclipse**

TWO-LINE PICA GOTHIC ORNAMENTED.

**PURE ELEGANCE**

TWO-LINE PICA IONIC.

**ECCENTRICITIES**

TWO-LINE PICA GOTHIC DOUBLE SHADED.

**SNOWCAPT MOUNTS**

TWO-LINE PICA TUSCAN ORNAMENTED.

**TOMATO-BED**

TWO-LINE PICA ORNAMENTED, No. 5.

**SEABEATEN SHORE**

TWO-LINE PICA ORNAMENTED, No. 6.

**SEED-DROPPING**

TWO-LINE PICA ORNAMENTED, No. 7.

**RUSTICAL SCULPTURES**

TWO-LINE PICA ORNAMENTED, No. 8.

**STARS AND STRIPES**

FOR PRICES OF FOUNTS, SEE CLASSIFIED PRICE LIST.

L. JOHNSON & CO.　　　　66　　　　PHILADELPHIA.

FIGURE 30. L. Johnson & Co., *Specimens of Printing Types, Plain, and Ornamental, Borders, Cuts, Rules, Dashes, &c, from the Foundry of L. Johnson & Co.* (Philadelphia: L. Johnson & Co., 1859), 66. Courtesy of the Newberry Library, Chicago, Case Wing Folio Z 40583.4541.

FIGURE 31. Robert Street, *Howell Evans and His Printing Shop*, 1844, oil on canvas. © Philadelphia History Museum at the Atwater Kent/ Bridgeman Images.

he has to say, or what others have said, in favor of his goods. No one is necessarily misled by it, even if it is over-colored or untrue; *because the very type gives him warning* that he is to be on his guard, to discriminate between the absurd exaggerations of flash "catch-pennies," and the sober man of business, who, in the consciousness that he has an article of substantial value for sale, is satisfied to say what he has to say, without designedly overstating or unduly exaggerating its merits. (italics mine)[30]

Exaggeration, as can be seen in a wood engraving of Evans's office located on Fourth Street below Chestnut, was apparently one of the printer's chief calling cards (Figure 32). With signs deployed on or protruding from nearly every available surface of his building, Evans clearly sought to make a bold impression in the minds of the potential customers who strolled along the sidewalk out front. Returning to "Puffing vs. Advertising," now with the example of Evans in mind: "But an advertiser who 'climbs up some other way' into notice, and gets the editor, either for pay or favor to say for him, what he thinks might not be believed or attended to as coming from himself, does, in our opinion, what he ought not to do. He intends to make a *false impression on the public mind*, that there are peculiar merits in his merchandize, which challenge the spontaneous notice of intelligent and disinterested parties. This we call 'puffing,' as distinguished from advertising" (italics mine).[31] For this writer, certain typefaces warned viewers to be on their guard by encouraging discrimination, scrutiny, and skepticism. While the use of large display types expanded, and often exceeded, the value of the objects they advertised, the "false impression" they produced "on the public mind" was considered more sinister. In his 1852 novel *Pierre; or the Ambiguities*, Herman Melville leveled such a critique at publishing houses eager to achieve commercial success from the voluminous output of their often overworked authors. The novel's narrator equated their title pages with placards and their publishers with billstickers, promoters of books with long, ponderous titles, "lumbering and laborious in movement and disproportionately thick and heavy."[32] For Melville and others, both titles and the typefaces in which they were printed conveyed value or lack thereof. Apparently, the larger the scale of both the sheet and the font, the more the event or product advertised effectively had to "prove," which put the viewer on his mettle to discern. For critics, the larger the font, the less culturally refined and lower on the cultural register. At the base of this sliding scale of cultural taste was the disconnect between bold type and the importance, relevance, or utility of a particular event, service, or product. This gap between boisterous advertisement

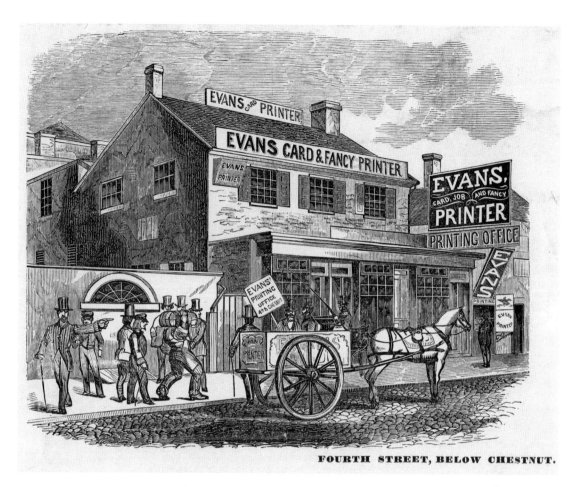

FOURTH STREET, BELOW CHESTNUT.

FIGURE 32. Unknown Artist, "Evans Card and Fancy Printer," c. 1856, woodcut illustration. Library Company of Philadelphia.

and product quality was exacerbated, according to one critic, by the tight correspondence between posters and the pocketbook. "Here we have placards in all shapes and sizes, and with all variety of typographical illustrations," wrote "Presbyterian" for the *Weekly Messenger* in 1844. "But we have nothing to do with the 'wonderful attractions,' 'astonishing feats,' 'great novelties,' &c. &c., which catch the eye of the passer-by, and not unfrequently affects his pockets." The very type itself gives him warning that he is to be on his guard.[33]

Broadsides typically utilized the largest and boldest types for the leading line and an assortment of variously elaborated types for key words or phrases in subsequent lines (Figure 33). These were often centered in the space traditionally oc-

# CHESTNUT STREET THEATRE!

STAGE MANAGER, MR. JOSEPH PARKER.   LESSEE, MR. J. QUINLAN

## PRICES OF ADMISSION.

Dress Circle and Parquet, - - Fifty Cents | Second Tier and Family Circle, Twenty-Five Cents
Third Tier, - - Twenty-Five Cents | Boxes for Colored Persons, Twenty-Five Cents
Proscenium Boxes, $5,00 | (Private Boxes, holding Twelve Persons, $9,00) | Single Seats in Private Boxes, 75 Cts.
PRIVATE BOX IN COLORED GALLERY, - - - - FIFTY CENTS;
Box Office open from half-past 9 o'clock, A. M. until 3 o'clock, P. M.
CHANGE OF TIME.--Doors open at half-past 7 o'clock.   Curtain will rise at 8 o'clock precisely

# LAST NIGHT

OF THE ENGAGEMENT OF MR. AND MRS.

# W. J. FLORENCE

## A Great Bill for Saturday Night!

### MR. & MRS. FLORENCE
WILL APPEAR IN

# FOUR NEW PIECES!

## SIAMESE TWINS!
## MISCHIEVOUS ANNIE!
## YANKEE GAL AND
## CATHARINE HAYES!

### SATURDAY EVENING, July 23d, 1853,
Will be presented

# THE YANKEE GAL

BARNEY O'CONNER, MR. W. J. FLORENCE.   PEG ANN MEHITABLE HIGGINFLUTER, MRS. W. J. FLORENCE
In which Mrs. FLORENCE will sing an Original Yankee Song, called BOBBIN AROUND.

Major Skinner, a retired nabob......Mr. LOMAS | Slave, a Sheriff's officer......Mr. DOW
Mr. White Post, a swindler......Mr. CLARKE | Fenella, a blooming Miss......Miss EBERLE
Fred Sommers, in love with Fenella......Mr. BRIGGS | Mrs. Skinner......Mrs. MANN

After which, the

# SIAMESE TWINS!

DENNIS, } The......Mr. FLORENCE | Vivid......Mr. BRIGGS
Simon, } Tw'ins......Mr. CLARKE | Sally......Miss F. DENHAM
Mr. Forceps......Mr. LOMAS | Marian......Miss EBERLE

DANCE, - - - - - - - MISS M. A. DENHAM

To be followed by a New Farce, written by Mr. W. J. Florence, entitled

# MISCHIEVOUS ANNIE

TIM SOUNS,   Mr. W. J. FLORENCE

Max Stanley......Mr. LOMAS | Annie Sprice, 
Charley Gale......Mr. BRIGGS | Frow-Sigitersypipesfunderknigelsquipinox,
Lawyer Holmes......Mr. BOSWELL | Bridget, an old woman of 90,
Laura Howard......Miss EBERLE | Miss Primp, a danceuse,   MRS. W. J. FLORENCE
Mrs. Croperanium......Miss F. DENHAM | Aramintha Dazenberry, a Yankee Gal,
DURING THE PIECE, MRS. FLORENCE WILL
SING AN "ORIGINAL DUTCH SONG," AND DANCE "LA FILLE DU REGIMENT!"

The whole to conclude with the new farce written by Mr. FLORENCE, entitled

# CATHARINE HAYES

MICKEY,   Mr. W. J. FLORENCE

Harry Norton......Mr. BRIGGS | Winifred......Miss EBERLE
Old Tonood......Mr. LOMAS | Mary......Miss F. DENHAM
James......Mr. DENHAM

'IN REHEARSAL,

# UNCLE MIKES CABIN,

NEVER BEFORE ACTED IN PHILADELPHIA
Scott's Steam Job-Press Printing Establishment, 12 Hudson's Alley below Chesnut, above Third Street, Philada

cupied by a book's title or a newspaper's masthead. According to J. Luther Ring-walt, editor of the *American Encyclopedia of Printing* published in Philadelphia in 1871, "almost every variety of displayed work should have one leading line, superior to all others in size, clearness, and effect. The leading line should consist only of the word or words which embrace the pith and marrow of the subject, the words most likely to arrest the eye and give an insight into the object of the work."[34] In the article "Placard-Printing in Vienna," author J. G. Kohl echoes Ringwalt's prescription in his description of a particularly successful printer of announcements for fetes, plays, and concerts. "The proprietor of this establishment, Mr. Hirsh-field," he writes, "has many people in his serve, who thoroughly understand the most striking way of announcing such matters to the street public, by the judicious arrangement of the alluring words 'Bal Brilliant,' 'Magic Illumination,' 'Rose-tinted Garments of Pleasure,' &c."[35] From an optical perspective, these key words and phrases, when set in fat face display types, helped to create a strong simple pattern against a fairly open background.[36]

But while this strong simple pattern stood out against the open background of the individual sheet, such open space, judging from the dense palimpsest of broadsides seen in Spencer's painting, was difficult to come by. In response, printers deployed bold or ornamented types set in striking words and phrases to stand out from the rest. In this regard, it was by no means coincidental that this leading line often corresponded with the general position of the human head. While the letters themselves conformed to the contours of the human frame, itself a "dynamic center" to borrow a phrase from perceptual psychologist Rudolf Arnheim, the visual, physical, and psychological appeal of symmetrical design, deriving its visual gravity from what Arnheim designates the "power of the center," corresponded with, and consequently appealed to, the binocular makeup of observing subjects.[37] Centrally arranged at the head of poster-sized sheets, the lead "headline" was designed to momentarily fasten connections between observers and the poster's subject. The multiplication of broadsides with their combinations of large leading words and phrases, centered in headlines set at eye level—captured most vividly in the newsboy paintings of Frederick Spencer—gradually honed in observers a new set of visual skills for retrieving information from dense visual fields.

Initiated by the "prick" of the broadsheet's leading line, such techniques enabled observers to perceptually distinguish items of special interest from a profusion of printed information. The overlapping broadsides papering the wall in Spencer's *Newsboy*, for instance, demonstrate in their profusion the "average effect" of the period's heavily typographic visual culture.[38] But the broadside's leading line has the obligation to break through, to catch the attention of passersby. These "sensitive" points that punctuate or disturb the general effect—whether it be the prick of a leading line of a single broadside amid others or the same effect elicited within a painting of a broadside-covered wall as seen in Spencer's *Newsboy*—elicit the kind of personal response that advertisers sought. Whether it be a "RIOT," as in Spencer's painting (see fig. 23) , or a "Dancing Soiree," the broadside's leading line "shoots" outward like an arrow traveling in multiple directions to prick the sensibilities of observers of the painting or the wall that it depicts.[39]

The newsboy in Spencer's painting occupies the center position before us, but his presence only momentarily fixes the viewer's gaze. His placement also marks the position, in reverse, of a bewildered spectator scanning the multifaceted surface of the wall behind him. Though alone, his singular presence suggests multitudes. Two neoclassical columns frame this aggregate of signs and signifiers. Further, the space before the wall is graduated by a series of four steps down into the space occupied by the painting's viewer. Regardless of these framing devices, however, the painting disperses the viewer's attention here and there. Which sheet, which words, which phrases attract and draw viewers' attention, and in what sequence? A few types and words certainly stand out. The word fragments "DIS CON" are set in Gothic perspective or "shadow" letters, as is the word "RIOT," set in a shaded version of fat face Egyptian, a font critical to both the enterprise of the eye test chart examined below and architectural signage, the subject of the next chapter. Jumping from one font to the next, crisscrossing the typographic history of the modern face and its bastard offspring the fat face, the act of looking at the painting and its subject enacts a sequence of saccadic movements, the fitful jumping of the eyes from one typeface to another, from one word or fragment to another, from one poster to another. The tendency to read from left to right is continually interupted by broken words, faded pronouncements, nonsensical phrases. Scanning across the canvas, the words "Notice genuine riot pills something comeing grand model artists rats notice California license" lead viewers' eyes laterally across the painting's surface, but to what viewers are left to wonder. Even the eye's tendency toward the center is confounded by a dense field made up of individual yet interwoven visual objects torn and frayed, physically degraded by light and exposure to the elements, and layered atop one another in random patterns and sequences. On what, beyond meeting the newsboy's outward gaze, are viewers' roving eyes to fasten upon?

Given the fractious experience of the street, the balanced symmetrical composition of most broadsides—a carryover from the printed book's title page—sought to counter but could not entirely correspond to the shifting vantage points of mobile observers subjected to the city's often disjunctive sight lines. While books and newspapers typically fixed viewers in space and focused their attention accordingly, broadsides could only hope to momentarily slow, not fix, the constantly shifting positions of upright and mobile observers. Such ambulatory movement, a chief feature of the pedestrian culture of antebellum cities, both highlighted and encouraged vision's tendency toward asymmetry and imbalance. Amid the frenzy of the bustling thoroughfares and byways that crisscrossed the commercial city, fixed viewing positions were as ephemeral as the broadside texts that beckoned them. Historically, typeface alphabets had been modeled to facilitate the standard reading practices of a static human body. But how was a founder to model letterforms on the basis of a moving spectator and for the extremely ephemeral format of the poster or placard? How did the creation of letterforms evolve to better accord with the physiological operations of eyes scanning and reading, operations just beginning to be better understood in the early nineteenth century? In seeking to capitalize on the increasingly congested lines of sight, and with the constant threat of having one's broadsheet covered or pasted over, how the eyes processed each letterform as it scanned the page became a point of particular focus.

The relationship between types and eyesight, or more specifcally the act of reading and the physiology of the moving eye, became topics of considerable interest and were addressed in various ways and from multiple perspectives. However, such musing still lacked a shared vocabulary to adequately articulate its subject. Meditating on the impact of the display types, J. G. Kohl wrote, "The monster types are all of wood; the effect of the great black letters upon men's eyes and fancies is always speculated on." Kohl then expands upon their complex compositions: "the pictorial announcements of estates for sale by lottery, when all the letters are composed of pictures of castles and rural views, and where every million is presented entwined with the elegant flowery wreaths of hope, are really masterpieces in a psychological as in a xylographic point of view."[40] Kohl here describes entire worlds within the twists and turns of artistically carved letters as he ponders their effects on eyes and minds. As Kohl speculated, typographic expression, as deployed on broad sheets and placards in particular, came to hinge on the location at which the sensation, the impression elicited by strategically deployed letterforms against a contrasting colored background, struck the retina. Ornamented and shaded display types such as

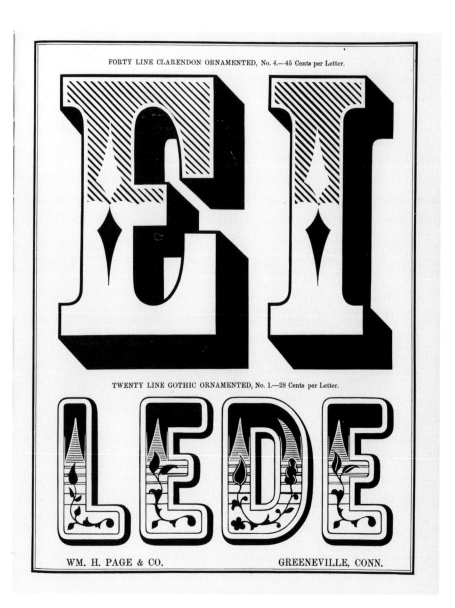

FIGURE 34. Wm. H. Page Wood Type Co., Forty Line Clarendon Ornamented, No. 4, in *Specimens of Wood Type, Borders, Rules, &c. Manufactured by Wm. H. Page & Co.* (Greenville, CT: Wm. H. Page & Co., 1859), n. p. Courtesy of the Newberry Library, Chicago, Case Wing Folio Z 250.P34 S64 1859.

those featured in the specimen of Wm. Page & Co. of Greeneville, Connecticut reveal a nascent interest in determining, with some precision, how the moving eye registered the shape and import of letterforms at distances near and far as well as at varying speeds and from a variety of angles (Figure 34). Enlargement was but one technique among many to better capture viewers' attention. Variety was another. Exploiting wood's malleability, and the precision and efficiency afforded by Wells's lateral router, wood-type manufacturers experimented widely. A new attention to shading, color, and tint all shaped the look and appeal of wood letters. The emergence of shaded letters, dimensional letters, letters set at an angle, and the use of dark letters on light grounds or light letters on dark grounds suggests widespread and decidedly nonclinical experimentation with the perceptual properties of letterforms (Figure 35). In enlarging the size, fattening the shape, or constructing ornate or flamboyant alphabets, founders demonstrated their growing interest in locating and targeting the precise spot where these visual forms "struck" the retina and their desire to increase the magnitude of the impressions they left.

Amid the great proliferation of print culture in the late 1830s and '40s, physiologists had good reason and numerous occasions to turn their attention to the mechanisms of the eye engaged in the act of reading. Therefore it is no wonder that certain passages of *The Philosophy of the Eye*, a treatise published in 1837 by John Walker, surgeon at the Manchester Eye Hospital, reads more like of a *physiology* of the eyes. His are some of the most astute observations of the period on the ocular processes involved in reading, which involved the muscular and neural mechanisms of eyes scanning printed pages. "In reading a page of letter-press," he wrote, "to how many points of its surface is the eye directed; every portion of each letter must be passed over in succession accurately and critically, in order that a due impression may be conveyed to the nervous structure and thence to the brain; and this could not be effected but by the agency of the muscles of the eye."[41] Though he acknowledged that while reading the eyes move in a roving fashion, he apparently had not yet reached the conclusions of later experimenters such as Louis Émile Javal (1839–1907) of the University of Paris concerning the eye's saccadic movements when reading letterforms on the page or sheet.[42] Both Walker's fluid succession of orderly perception and Javal's jumping eye movements are at play in the discontinuous and fragmented viewing experience staged in Spencer's *Newsboy*. Merely one sordid corner of a much larger urban visual field, Spencer's "dead wall" references in microcosm the multiple points of attention to which they eyes were continually directed. Writ large, such viewing experiences were redefining the culture's visual aptitudes, habits, and viewing practices, increasingly

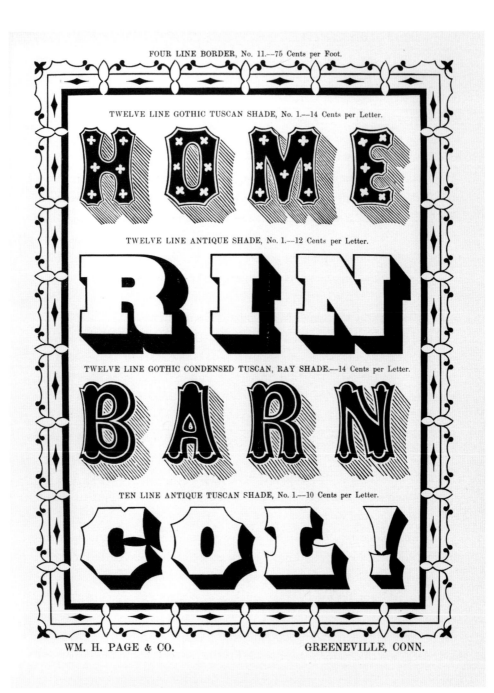

FOUR LINE BORDER, No. 11.—75 Cents per Foot.

TWELVE LINE GOTHIC TUSCAN SHADE, No. 1.—14 Cents per Letter.

HOME

TWELVE LINE ANTIQUE SHADE, No. 1.—12 Cents per Letter.

RIN

TWELVE LINE GOTHIC CONDENSED TUSCAN, RAY SHADE.—14 Cents per Letter.

BARN

TEN LINE ANTIQUE TUSCAN SHADE, No. 1.—10 Cents per Letter.

COL!

WM. H. PAGE & CO.          GREENEVILLE, CONN.

FIGURE 35. Various twelve-line shade letters, in Wm. H. Page Wood Type
Co., *Specimens of Wood Type, Borders, Rules, &c. Manufactured by Wm. H. Page
& Co.* (Greenville, CT: Wm. H. Page & Co., 1859), n. p. Courtesy of the
Newberry Library, Chicago, Case Wing Folio Z 250.P34 S64 1859.

premising these on models of dispersal and distraction as opposed to sustained attention and deep concentration.[43]

Countering the misalignments and asymmetries of reading letters in books or on the streets, Walker stressed the ocular need for alignment between the objects of vision and the eyes of observers. The impressions formed by letters or other objects on the retina, he argued "must always be made on that particular portion which we have described as corresponding to the axis of vision. And in order to bring the images there, it is essential that the axis of the eye be directed immediately to the object, which it is by the muscles."[44] Proper vision, then, resulted from the muscular attainment of alignment between the object of vision and the retinal surfaces. The book and the static body were easily integrated and profitably enmeshed in acts of reading. However, ambulating through narrow city streets and subjected to a proliferation of monster types in various sizes and shapes arranged on single or overlapping sheets of paper in various stages of wear and decay, these materials and conditions presented numerous opportunities for the eyes of observers to fall out of alignment with the letters and words they beheld. In a description that recalls the way that a piece of type set in the forme of the press strikes the page to makes its impression, Walker explains the need for the kind of centered focusing characteristic of a static observer and what results when this is not achieved. "When an impression is made upon the retina, in that unsatisfactory degree which is the effect of its striking any part but the centre, there is an effort made to direct the axis towards it, or, in other words, to receive the rays from it upon the more sensible centre. It is this sensibility," Walker claims, "conjoined with the action of the muscles of the eye-ball, which produces the constant searching motion of the eye."[45] To produce the "correct" impression, the eye's musculature must adjust through what Walker calls a "searching motion" to focus the letterform at the *center* of the retina. The ubiquitous deployment of display types on multiple sheets, as seen in Spencer's *Newsboy*, encouraged this constantly searching motion of the eyes, but resolutely refused to offer any particular "center" on which to fasten the gaze.

Ernst Gombrich would later qualify the visual experience of those impressions falling outside of the zone that Walker credits with having the capacity to form a "correct impression." In his analysis of a magazine advertisement photo of moving soldiers, Gombrich suggests that "things are not simply blurred outside the foveal area, they are indistinct in a much more elusive way."[46] Visual psychologist Rudolf Arnheim also wrote about this phenomenon, using the term "retinal orientation" to describe the angle of vision at which the stimulus shaped by the letter reaches the retinal surface.[47] All three writers addressed the eyes' continual searching moment, its "hunger" for alignment, and the hazy, indistinct aspects of visual stimuli that failed to reach retinal centers. This centered impression, though at times difficult to attain, forms an internalized version of the correspondence between symmetrically designed broadsides and binocular observers.

This correspondence was more than visual. Walker suggests as much in his claim that in some instances, small marks resembling letterforms were visible on the surfaces of the eye itself: "A very remarkable appearance is often noticed on the surface of the iris. An irregular kind of ring or band is seen to run round it, not far from the pupil, and which separates the inner from the outer portion. This band is much lighter, often white, and consists of a number of segments of circles united together. The shape of these coloured fibres which form this band is some-times such as to give an appearance remotely resembling the letters of the alpha-bet; and some very ingenious persons, and others very credulous, have persuaded themselves that they have been able to trace words written upon the iris."[48] Given the challenges of attracting the undivided attention of persons navigating the busy streets of the antebellum metropolis, the ubiquity and density of typographic expression and the fluctuating sight lines and vantages of its shifting outer fabric, the most inventive typefounders sought new ways to meet the variously posi-tioned, mobile surfaces of the eyes. Illusionistic techniques for letter carving evolved to re-create the experience of Walker's "alignment" from a multitude of angles. Across a great diversity of fonts and styles, these new display types ex-pressed their founders' desire to approximate the effect of imprinting their letter-forms on the surfaces and contours of the inner eye.

As the larger fonts set the scale for commercial job printing, the malleability of wood as a medium allowed the expressive capacities of fat face types to fully flower. Wood allowed for greater size type as well as a greater variety of styles. But it also facilitated more intricate surface elaboration readable from a greater number of visual angles and capable of conveying denser lodes of information. The expansive surfaces of fat faces and wood's supple elasticity invited experimentation and orna-mentation as founders applied the techniques of relief engraving to the articulation of enlarged and enhanced letterforms. Along with distinguishing letterforms from one another, the deployment of parallel lines, known as tints, for shading imbued letters with varying degrees of surface texture, visual weight, or illusionistic depth. These variations lent certain alphabets particular emphasis, or enabled them to convey particular inflections of meaning. Moreover, these letters could make their

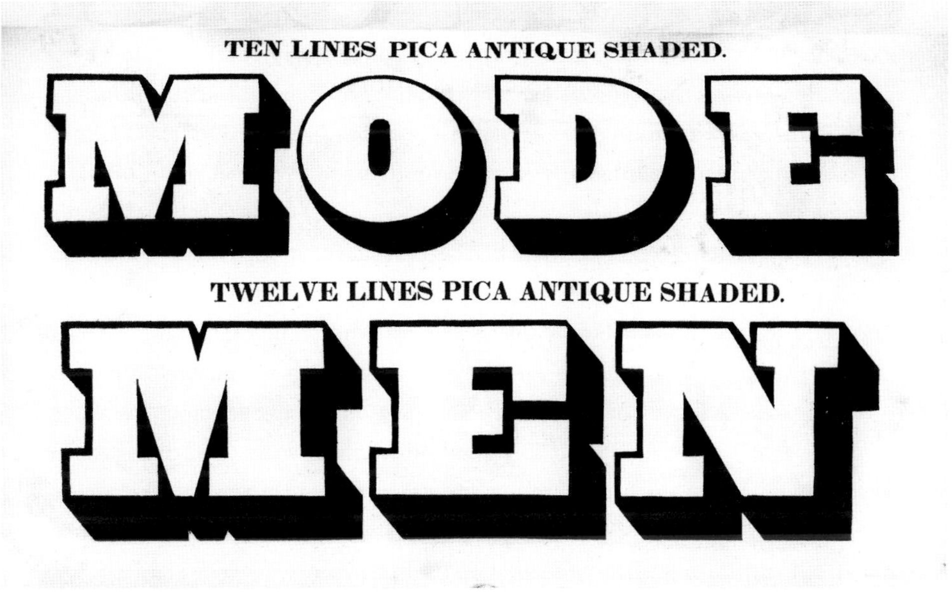

**TEN LINES PICA ANTIQUE SHADED.**

# MODE

**TWELVE LINES PICA ANTIQUE SHADED.**

# MEN

FIGURE 36. Ten and twelve lines pica Antique Shaded, in Alexander Robb, *Specimen of Printing Types and Ornaments Cast by Alexander Robb* (Philadelphia: Alexander Robb, 1844). Library Company of Philadelphia.

appeal in multiple directions simultaneously. But as letter size increased to place stress on a single leading word or line, and as letter design grew more complex, questions of how to employ the empty or negative spaces of the sheet came to figure more prominently in the overall composition process. Indeed, this more elaborated typography increased the need for printers to carefully coordinate typographic forms and other elements such as engraved images or ornmanetal borders as well as the color, brightness, and texture of the paper on which they were printed. Utilizing the positive and negative spaces of the sheet in ever more calculated ways, printers also sought ways to figuratively extend their types beyond the printed surface to meet the roving eyes of passersby.[49] "Shaded" or "perspective" letters formed one intriguing and novel solution to this dilemma (Figure 36). Heavily shaded on one side or another, these letters were crafted in such a way as to give the optical illusion of the letters thrusting outward from the surface in various directions. These letterforms, in particular, bear the imprint of ambulating observers and lend outline to the trajectories of their movement. Often rendered on the slant with shaded or outlined contours, perspective letters were used to emulate the experience of seeing an object in proper perspective from multiple viewing positions. They reflect an optically informed, typographic adjustment to mobile seeing and reading. Just as they represent extended efforts on behalf of job printers and their clients to arrest the eye regardless of visual angle, they may also reflect efforts to momentarily "fix" a particular vantage for moving eyes by sustaining the illusion of a fixed perspective.

Capturing in fixed form the often-fluid experience of street ambulation, Spencer's *Newsboy* (see fig. 23) underscores the importance of a typeface's novelty in a sea of letterforms. The newsboy's casually leaning position before the wall constitutes the painting's "leading line." His outward gaze invites the viewer's approach and analogizes a selection of types adorning the tattered and overlapping remains of various broadsides that appear to extend outward from the wall. But though viewers might be inclined to pause for a moment to scrutinize the boy's scruffy appearance or return his piercing gaze, their eyes are quickly led here and there, from words set in shaded fonts such as "RIOT" to their truncated counterparts, such as the white and black shaded letters reading "DIS/CON," which subtly reference the comings and goings of the newsboy's customers. Indeed, while broadsides suggest the presence of binocular viewing subjects, the dense, palimpsestic layering of typographic sheets in Spencer's depiction accumulates traces of the various sight lines and perspectives of a multitude of roving viewers.

A far cry from the darkened, enclosed space of the monocular camera obscura, which had for centuries emblematized the process of vision, the scene's multiplicity of broadsides, viewers, and viewing positions displaced the camera's static, singular view.[50] Here in the streets of the antebellum metropolis, the camera obscura's fully centered, fixed viewpoint and the "perspective" it provided, was difficult to obtain. Unleashing letterforms into the expanded visual field of public spaces enabled them to be seen and read from varying distances, multiple angles, and moving positions. But doing so undermined their structural correspondence to the human body, destabilizing in the process their appeals to binocular vision. Perspective letters sought to address the roving eye by offering the illusion of a centered vision while also positing a model vision that was continually unfolding, even fleeting. Thus the relatively balanced symmetry of the broadside realized its goal first of attracting and then of momentarily fixing the position of the spectator before it. But the ephemerality of this printed matter now matched the mobility of the observers who consumed it and modeled the fluidity of the perceptual experience it helped to constantly structure and dismantle. Though imprecise and experimental in a vernacular sense, this meeting of eyes and types suggests a more calculated interplay of print and perception. Building on centuries of thought and practice concerning the construction of letterforms and their basis in the human body, antebellum display typography registered a more complex understanding of the eyes' physiological mechanisms. This point was not lost on ophthalmologists and opticians working to standardize and capitalize on measurements for visual acuity and accommodation. But as they found, the use of such letters required their removal from the public sphere, for only by isolating them from the hoi polloi of the antebellum visual field could their effects be precisely measured and exact results obtained.

As evidenced in the cases of Rembrandt and Rubens Peale and opticians John McAllister Jr. and Daniel Widdifield, many took notice of type's utility in determining visual acuity. Their experiences and efforts allude to a growing interest in the development of standardized, measured systems of type to determine acuity with precision. The emergence and evolution of display types during the second quarter of the nineteenth century created the conditions for understanding better the relationship between typefaces and visual acuity, that is the measurability of type and the distance from which one could properly see it. The proliferation of display types and the printed forms that employed them during this period, along with a contemporaneous, and plausibly corresponding, rise in ocular maladies created the conditions for the development of standardized test types. While sourced from the teeming visual field of urban centers, letterforms, in order to assist in the precise determination of focal lengths, had to be extracted from the flux and flow of the streets and returned to the controlled environment of the ophthalmic laboratory. Though experimenters utilized the most "commercial" of the new display types, a more systematic and ordered arrangment of measured letters, one that could enable the precise measurement of visual acuity, required conditions exactly opposite to those found in metropolitan streets and thoroughfares. The utility of these letterforms required the isolation of carefully measured letters and the static position of the observing subject. While methods for the determination of visual acuity remained inexact throughout the first half of the century, the use of type significantly improved upon the largely inaccurate "age" system that had long served as a general guide and relative standard for determining visual acuity. Although approximate, the use of type in the 1840s and '50s signaled the onset of an era of systematization fully realized and implemented in the 1860s and '70s.

Drawing ideas and examples from the vast array of display letters that graced the surfaces of urban centers, a constellation of researchers in Europe developed formulas relating letter size and distance in attempts to calculate visual acuity with a considerable degree of accuracy. Efforts to make visual experience empirically quantifiable relied on a formulation called the "visual angle," which was produced by a calculation of the vertical measurement of the letter and the viewer's distance from it. The convergence of eye, distance, and visual angle formed by the object of vision is figured in the eye charts and test types developed between 1843 and 1862 first by European ophthalmologists and physiologists such as German ophthalmologist Heinrich Küchler (1811–1873), the Austrians Ferdinand Arlt (1812–1887) and Eduard Jaeger (1818–1884), and later perfected by Dutch opthalmologist Herman Snellen (1834–1908).[51] Küchler was the first, in 1843, to describe a uniform and reproducible reading chart composed of Gothic letters of decreasing size for the testing of visual acuity. Arlt is also reputed to have developed a test type system in the 1840s, but there are few if any records of his method. Eduard Jaeger first published his attempts to quantify visual acuity for both near and distant vision in 1854. Jaeger is known as the originator of the *Schrift-Scalen*, a near-vision reading test still in use in innumerable copied or improved forms. Jaeger's test materials consisted of sets of black bars separated by white interspaces of identical width, with which he tried to determine the distance at which the white interspaces in a given group of black bars of known width could be seen and counted by the examined eye.[52] Jaeger's method for measuring visual acuity produced accurate results, especially for testing vision "objectively." But he missed one step on which Utrecht-based ophthalmologist Herman Snellen capitalized, which was to measure and express visual acuity values in terms of visual angle.[53]

In the introductory text of his published findings, *Test-Types for the Determination of the Acuteness of Vision*, first published in 1862, Snellen lists the axioms of his formula for the determination of visual acuity.[54] His nineteen points effectively dissolve the boundary between observing subject and object by inscribing both entities on a single investigative surface. He begins by noting the relationship between objects of known size and form and the size of the image they form on the retina. Through a formula based on the maximum distance at which an object—or letter in this case—of known size can be distinguished at a particular visual angle, Snellen developed a method to determine the acuteness of vision that utilized some of the most commercial display types of his day. With this formula, which worked in conjunction with letterforms whose mathematically devised size corresponded to various distance-to-visual angle ratios, Snellen established as a normative standard the notion of twenty-twenty vision. His was the first system of test objects so arranged that the acuteness of vision could be expressed by a number.[55] Snellen determined that when his No. XX letterform is recognized at a distance of twenty feet, there is normal acuteness of vision. For his test types, Snellen explains, "we have adopted as proper objects square letters, the limbs of which have a diameter equal to one-fifth of the letters' height. Such letters are clearly distinguished by a normal eye at an angle of five minutes." The letters in Snellen's chart are similar to the capital types in the style then known as Egyptian paragon (Figure 37). Later experiments indicated that in comparison with serifed type, of which the Egyptian was one form, Gothic (or sans serif) letters tended to overestimate acuity by 5 to 10 percent.[56] Snellen's experimentation with and conscious choice of an Egyptian typeface, especially when viewed in light of the later discovery concerning Gothic types, offers quantifiable evidence of the varying visual impact of different typefaces. "Subsequent investigations conducted by Snellen and his followers have also shown that words in capitals are read better at a distance than those in lower case and that the determination of visual acuity for distance is in all respects more accurate than that for near."[57] To form his letters, Snellen utilized some of the same geometric formulas devised by writing masters and sign painters in the eighteenth and nineteenth centuries. The precision they encouraged, typically regarded as a sign of personal integrity or commercial prowess, provided geometrically determined standards on which ophthalmology would base its ability to gauge the focal powers of human eyes.[58] Snellen's chart quickly became the institutional standard for a burgeoning field of inquiry that had struggled to achieve professional cohesion and and regulatory precision.[59]

In their singular application, Snellen-type eye test charts eradicated the confusion of overlapping sheets, as well as the overstimulation and ocular exhaustion viewing them caused. The charts pared down the typographic content from phrases and words to rows of letters or similar shapes. Narrowing the viewer's focus to concentrate on these measured black letters, the single white sheets on which they were uniformly arranged were set at predetermined distances from the observer. Often tested within the clinical space of the ophthalmologist or optometrist, subjects were directed to cover one eye while identifying verbally the chart's rows of letterforms. The return to monocular perspective here is interest-

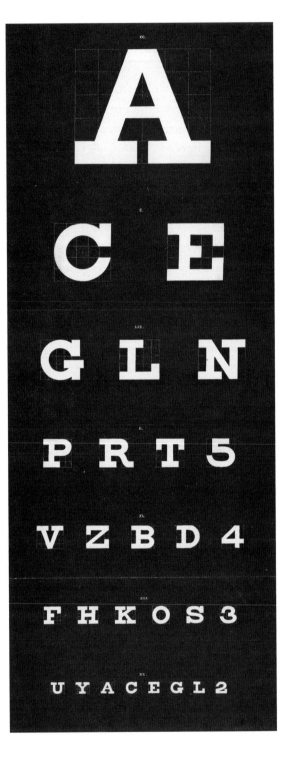

FIGURE 37. Herman Snellen, *Test-Types for the Determination of the Acuteness of Vision*, 4th ed. (London: Williams and Norgate, 1868), 76. Utrecht University Library.

ing. Antebellum eyes now trained on a wide spectrum of letterforms and viewing conditions as a new model of acute, twenty-twenty vision emerged from the intersection of typefounding, commercial job printing, and ophthalmic science. The creation of "perfect and continuous vision" involved both the expressive visuality of the street and the clinical austerity of eye test charts, both of which had disciplinary effects on the emergence and formation of the observer during the mid-nineteenth century.

The letterforms deployed on broadsides to fasten observers' gazes on a particular product, event, or service, expanded the spatial parameters for individual readers already defined by books and newspapers. Even types utilized to test visual acuity defined a clinical space for individual observers premised on the extent of their "normal" vision. These developments involved a thorough sensory immersion in and thus a *bodily integration with* the mechanisms and processes of the marketplace that deployed them. Broadsides presented viewers with a form of print that worked in tandem with the binocular model of vision formulated by physiologists and philosophers in the 1830s and '40s. Along with signboards, the subject of the next chapter, these forms produced, positioned, and interpellated mobile viewers. Public letterforms dismantled the one-to-one, physically fixed relationship of reader and text long established by the behavioral patterns of book and newspaper reading. Instead, they structured new experiences and new market relations—based on physiological and commercial formulations of vision as mobile, transitory, and subjectively linked with desire—between observers and letterforms and between observers and the events, products, and services these letterforms were increasingly used to advertise.

Sign painters and letter carvers created and deployed shaded and perspective letters with increasing frequency and fluency during this period, taking developments in typography to new levels of scale and sophistication. By using such letters they sought to achieve a sense of stability amid flux by meeting the roving eyes of mobile spectators from a variety of angles. This dissolution of single-point perspective and the fixed positions on which this system was based contributed to the chaos of representation that had come to characterize the cultural field of the 1840s and '50s. Even if print enforced a certain ordering of urban spaces and the movement of figures therein, the proliferation of print in those spaces unleashed a profusion of signifiers that assaulted the eyesight of observers, lodging in their minds letterforms and mental images of the products they referenced. Leading buyers to goods, commercially deployed print cultivated a broad set of cultural behaviors related to consumption, which encouraged a state of perception not unlike—in either literal or figurative senses—the ocular condition of myopia.

## CHAPTER FOUR

# Signboards, Vision, and Commerce
# in the Antebellum City

In 1846, William C. Murphy took out a full-page, color advertisement for his sign painting enterprise in Philadelphia's *The Mercantile Register, or Business Man's Guide*. In the bold, outlined capital letters of the latest display types the first lines read: "ECONOMY IS WEALTH. HOUSE, SIGN, AND WALL PAINTING, GRAINING, GLAZING, &C." Just below, the advertisement continues: "The subscriber feeling thankful for the very liberal encouragement he has received from the citizens of Philadelphia and vicinity for the last seven years . . . hopes by strict attention to business to merit a continuance of patronage. He has opened an establishment at No. 47 Chestnut Street, where he is prepared to execute Painting of every description with neatness and dispatch."[1] Capitalizing on the success of his "old established stand" at 82 Spruce Street, Murphy expanded his trade by opening the new shop along a bustling segment of Chestnut Street, just blocks away from the waterfront. Murphy was one of dozens of like professionals who advertised themselves as ornamental, sign, coach, and house painters in Philadelphia that year.

As cities like Philadelphia grew in size and as their business communities expanded, the ranks of sign painters mushroomed in turn.[2] The profession had evolved significantly since 1800, rising to meet the growing demand for commercial advertisement as well as for the ornamentation of private homes and carriages.[3] From the 1840s onward, sign painting firms such as Murphy's became nearly as ubiquitous in the urban landscape as the signs they painted. Deployed on any surface able to hold them, signboards, like broadsides on a smaller scale, proliferated as never before, filling the visual field with letters and words to decipher. In the process, signboards—like broadsides at slightly closer range—instigated a widespread desire to see them clearly. Set at or near eye level, broadsides had expanded the field of vision from the close inspection of a newspaper's fine print to the discernment of mammoth lettered posters from distances measured in feet and yards as opposed to inches. Accordingly, Murphy and his competitors scaled their signboards for maximum visibility and legibility as they were required to accomplish their tasks at even greater distances. Adorned with painted, gilded, or carved letters, signboards simultaneously designated and capitalized on the city's thresholds of visibility, marking both the entrances to shops and stalls while, not uncoincidentally, demarcating the limits of properly functioning vision. As the spirit of exchange came to animate the city's many shops, stores, and general thoroughfares, the navigation of urban centers increasingly involved new forms of visual commerce.

Sign painters often covered their storefronts with signboards featuring the most attractive letters and the boldest colors. Like a typefounder's specimen book or a printer's sample sheet, the façade of a sign painter's shop often testified to his ability to render and deploy eye catching, balanced, well-proportioned letters readable from the street below and from the greatest distances and number of angles allowed by the shifting contours of the built environment. A city directory advertisement for Ackerman's "sign and ornamental painting" shop, located at 101 & 103 Nassau Street in New York, exemplifies this tendency (Figure 38). Associating his artisanal practice with the fine art of easel painting, the advertisement allegorizes the firm's artistic and aesthetic aspirations. Sculpted female figures adorn the second-floor window frames of the shop's façade, while panels featuring allegorical figures alternate with windows on the third. In the vignette on the top floor, a small crowd has gathered before a sign painter, who reveals his latest creation by drawing back the curtain more typical of popular single painting exhibitions.[4] The allegorical figure of a woman and child mediate the sign, which stands between the genteel group on the left and the b-hoys and other street toughs lounging on the right. The flatness of the building's façade, covered by panels that read "Improved Carved Lettters for Signs," and "Gilt/Plain/Signs," is here and there punctuated by orthogonals that facilitate the lithograph's illusion of recessive depth and point to the signboard's capacity to signify in multiple directions. Emerging from the door on the ground floor, two men carry a protruding sign that reads "Sarony & Major," a signature for the famed lithographers responsible for the ad itself. Throughout the building, painters work assiduously at easels set at oblique angles to the viewer, denoting the multitude of angles at which such signs were commonly situated to capitalize on, and thus fashion, new lines of sight. Opening such vistas, signboards plotted a multiplicity of pedestrian pathways and possible perspectives. In a scale that often dwarfed the already inflated size of letters used in the printing of antebellum broadsides and posters,

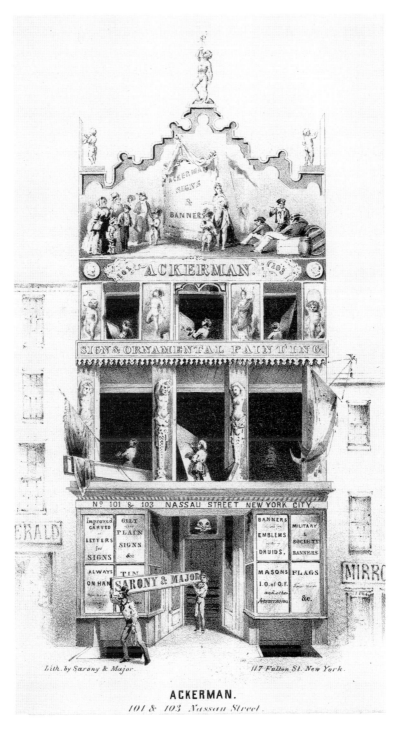

lettered signboards hung over the doorways of commercial establishments and across the sight lines of storefronts and awnings, as seen in the advertisement for Ackerman's. Adorning thresholds of exchange designated by the façades of commercial storefronts, well-positioned signboards also coincided with thresholds of perceptibility. Set within reach of the dispersed and roving gazes of antebellum observers, signs sparked interest in and cultivated desire for the products and services they advertised. But they also aggravated the condition of myopia, or nearsightedness, in those whose eyes were already being tested by typefaces both mammoth and minute set at distances great and small.

Murphy's shop stood just across the street from that of McAllister & Co. John McAllister Jr. had retired from the business in 1836 to pursue his antiquarian interests, but his continued presence at the shop was documented when stationer and amateur Daguerrean William G. Mason made this image in 1843 (Figure 39). It is entirely plausible that the signs adorning the façade of the McAllisters' firm are of Murphy's make. In Chapter 2 we learned about the firm's reputation and longstanding service to a retail and wholesale clientele that included artists and statesmen, as well as countless clerks, copyists, seamstresses, and, of course, general readers. Here, the McAllisters' use of signboards is notably prominent, demonstrating their concern for making their firm *visible* to customers seeking the equipment necessary to improve the quality of their own vision. The daguerreotype's elevated perspective and angle of view suggests that Mason might have perched his camera from the window of Murphy's shop or that of an immediate neighbor. Though Mason deliberately focused on the building's façade, he could not help but to also capture the flux of street traffic below. This blurred parade of ghostly figures along the sidewalk in the lower foreground vivifies the fluidity of movement, the multiple points of view occupied only fleetingly by the signboard's intended audiences.[5]

The antebellum city was, as Edgar Allan Poe wrote in 1844, a place in which "everything wore an aspect of intense life."[6] Writing of New York but equally informed by time spent in Philadelphia and Baltimore, Poe's terse yet vivid phrase locates the city's intensity in the visual fabric of its outer appearances. Some of the most physically intense and therefore visually congested of urban spaces were concentrated in the city's marketplaces and fashionable promenades. Teeming with the intensity that Poe observed, a frenetic intensity that others rejoiced and still others lamented, commercial districts along Broadway and Bowery in New York and along Chestnut and High (later Market) Streets in Philadelphia were marked by tightly packed rows of multistoried buildings, by the increased use of

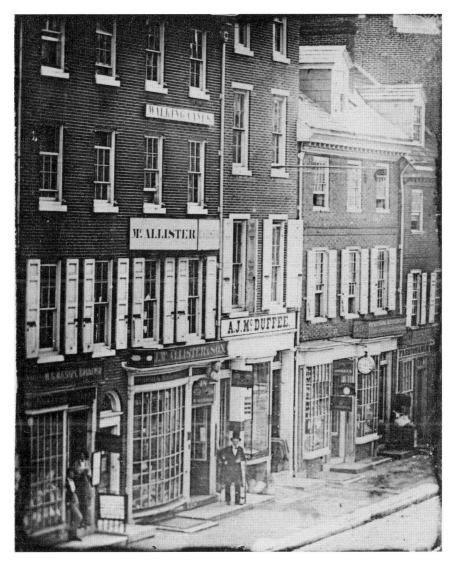

FIGURE 39. William G. Mason, "View of the Houses Nos. 46, 48, 50 and 52, South side of Chestnut above 2nd Street," 1843, albumen print after a sixth-plate daguerreotype. Library Company of Philadelphia.

multipaned or plate-glass shop windows, and by overhanging awnings and canti-levered signs protruding from their façades. Gaslights, crowds, and the kinetic movement of pedestrians and carriages also contributed to this shuffling array of sights, placing new burdens on human vision and challenging the eyes in new ways. In order to "focus" the antebellum city, observers found it necessary to continually adapt their visual aptitudes to the incessantly evolving shapes and structures of the built environment as well as to the bewilderingly complex network of words and images employed to render it navigable.

The city was a work in progress, a city "of perpetual ruin and repair," as a writer for the *New-York Mirror* put it in 1840. "No sooner is a fine building erected than it is torn down to put up a better."[7] Rapid urban growth necessitated the use of broadsides, street signs, and signboards to mediate the city to those attempting to navigate its avenues, streets, and alleyways, its shops, stands, and stalls. Marking the sites for commercial exchange and establishing, in effect, the perimeters of the visible city, signboards also marked points of intersection between the vision of observing subjects and the visuality of commercial forms. Often set at the outer boundaries of the sphere of visibility that comprised "normal" vision, signs tested the limits of visual perception, emphasizing the eyes' ability or inability to obtain proper focus when given the task of discerning and deciphering letters at considerable distances. Already though, the sign had accomplished its task of attracting attention and entreating observers to step closer in order to obtain a clearer view.

Trained on the small print that fueled the penny press revolution of the 1830s and '40s, observers were visually unprepared for the ocular exercises presented by the profusion of broadsides and signage that lent the antebellum city its "intense appearance." Although signs had long been part of the urban landscape, their appearance changed significantly in the decades after 1800 as new typographic letterforms eclipsed the iconographic motifs that had dominated signage for centuries. Often attributed to the spread of literacy, the sign's transformation in the nineteenth century more accurately reflects a confluence of factors, including rising literacy rates as well as the exponential growth of commerce, the influence and adoption of typographic letters created for commercial use, and the emergence of a more sophisticated understanding of the eye's mechanisms and capacities. Calculated to attract attention and designed both for visibility and legibility at the greatest possible distances, letterform signboards illustrate entrepreneurial attempts to capitalize on the lucrative potential of the new "visual literacy" that signs helped to cultivate in observing subjects now positioned in the marketplace as potential *consumers*. But focusing at such great distances tested the eyes' elasticity and tended to emphasize the nearsightedness or myopia that resulted in part from habitual reading and other forms of close work. As myopia became a prominent feature of antebellum visual experience, the condition assumed another life as a metaphor for the shortsightedness encouraged by consumer culture. As objects intended to fashion new relationships between consumers and products, signs effectively cultivated both conditions.[8]

The use of signs among tradesmen and merchants to promote their goods has a history nearly as long as that of commerce itself.[9] The Romans, for example, advertised in a multitude of forms ranging from the roving public crier to signs suspended or painted on walls to inscriptions on tablets or across the façades of official public buildings.[10] Signboards in Western metropolises had become so profuse by the middle of the eighteenth century that the size and placement of signs became regulated by governments in France and England, and in the mid-1800s, in the United States.[11] New rules required that signs be attached to a building's façade, replacing the centuries-old practice of suspending signs on hinged iron rods that extended outward from the façade or that arched over pedestrian walkways.[12] By the time the use of signs elicited the strictures of official regulation, their immense profusion had changed the face of the urban landscape, reconfiguring the outward appearances of urban areas once dotted with the manifestations of a genteel mercantilism into codified yet visually chaotic commercial thoroughfares. From antiquity until the late eighteenth century, image-based signboards dominated the field of public signage. Pictorial signs featuring green dragons, red lions, blue herons, or black and white horses lined the streets of European and American cities.[13] As urban centers swelled with manufacturers, merchants, artisans, and patrons, however, the specialization of trades and manufactures and the variety of their goods had begun to outgrow the older sign system by simply outnumbering the possible images that could effectively advertise their proliferating products and services. The complexity of rapidly growing urban centers required more precise forms of signification. But despite the level of specificity made possible by uniquely lettered signs, the use of typographic lettering in place of emblematic images instilled nineteenth-century marketplaces with a heightened sense of disjunction. Successful competition between tradesmen, manufacturers, and merchants in particular necessitated ever-greater visibility in the marketplace, leading entrepreneurs of all stripes to seek out new ways to advertise their services and map the coordinates of their shops and storerooms.[14]

Sign painters, along with typefounders and job printers, turned to the new display types in answer to this call for greater visibility and for the more efficient circulation of consumers and commodities. Despite widely divergent methods, the letterforms most often deployed by sign painters derived from typefaces that dominated book, newspaper, and especially job printing. As discussed in the previous chapter, type designers and founders enlarged and embellished traditional alphabets to create distinctly "commercial" letterforms—essentially "swollen" versions of traditional letters like the Roman face, or entirely new "fat face" types such as Antique (or Egyptian) and Gothic faces—in efforts to appeal more directly to the eyes of potential customers. Through experimentation and practice, typefounders, sign painters, and ophthalmologists, albeit in loose confederation, concurred that those letterforms in which all the strokes were of equal proportion proved more visually effective from greater physical distances. The sans serif and slab serif letterforms first appeared in typefounders' specimen books during the first two decades of the nineteenth century.[15] The sans serif soon came to be known as Gothic while the slab serif letters came to be designated either as Antique or Egyptian. But typographic historians have suggested that both letterforms almost certainly originated as architectural letters before being taken up by typefounders.[16] As one historian of signage has written: "The Egyptian has been called the letterform of emphasis, its serifs virtually serve as underlining, and provide the greatest possible differentiation from any accompanying matter. The Egyptian slab serif letters sat on the building of the period perfectly, matching the forms of the window sills and string courses." Indeed, it has been considered the most "architectural" of all letterforms for its applicability to the measured surfaces of buildings.[17]

In his 1841 *Treatise on Carriage, Sign, and Ornamental Painting*, Orson Campbell described the more popular and "instantly recognizable" letterforms used for signage, including the Roman, the Antique, and the Gothic. Campbell claimed that Roman letters, "on the account of the elegance of their appearance and distinctness in their lineations are preferred to any others now in use."[18] But visual evidence suggests otherwise. In spite of its dominance in book printing and its instant recognizability, the use of Roman letters in public spaces was actually on the decline. The Roman face, with its combination of thick and thin strokes, was not the most visually effective letterform for use on signboards and buildings. Instead, sign painters turned to other letter styles for the boldness of their chunky forms and for their applicability to the rectilinear features of storefront architecture. Invested with the signature of "official culture," the Roman letter continued to adorn the friezes of government buildings, banks, and churches, as can be seen in a whole plate daguerreotype of Philadelphia's Girard Bank made by William and Frederick Langenheim (Figure 40). At the time of this exposure, the building, situated on the northeast corner of Third and Dock Streets, was occupied by the Military during the anti-Catholic riots of 1844. Frozen in time, the figures in the street, likey nativist protesters, stand sentry before the premises of a cluster of

FIGURE 40. William and Frederick Langenheim, "Northeast Corner of Third and Dock Street, Girard Bank, at the time the latter was occupied by the Military during the riots, 1844," whole plate daguerreotype. Library Company of Philadelphia.

businesses, adorned with numerous signs including one just below the large *Evening Mercury* sign at lower right that reads "Office of the *Irish Citizen*." Taken from a position just outside the Langenheims' studio in Philadelphia's Merchants' Exchange, the optics and point of view of their camera produced a startlingly disjunctive image in which the bank and the building housing the *Sun* directly across the street appear to collide.[19] Here architecture and lettered signs merge. With its collision of vertical elements—the columns of the bank's neoclassical portico, the figures in the street, and the bold, commerical letterforms on the signs

at right, the image is one of sharp contrasts. The camera's collapsing of space between the two structures emphasizes the discontinuity between the bank's neoclassical façade with its chiseled Roman numerals and the squared "modern" style
of the facing commercial row buildings adorned only by a scattershot assortment
of hefty letters set on contrasting dark and light grounds. Signs featuring Gothic
or sans serif letters include those for the *Sun* and *Evening Mercury*. "Letters of
this form of all others now in use," Campbell argued, referring to Gothic letters,
"are most simple in their construction, and rude in their appearance. A variety of
forms, and not elegance of appearance, are sought for in this style of letters."[20]
Generally speaking, the early republican predilection for the neoclassical in politics, painting, and architecture was supplanted in the 1840s and '50s by a growing
taste for a broad range of motifs and aesthetic tendencies associated with the
Gothic revival. Other signs on these façades employ the heavily serifed Antique
or Egyptian faces, including those that read "Card and Job Printing" and "Hair
Seating & Curled Hair." Often deployed without regard for neoclassical linearity
and order, these simple yet substantial letterforms punctuated the surfaces of
storefronts with an irregularity that underscored the uneven, asymmetrical visuality of urban marketplaces. But while shifts in cultural tastes may have bolstered
their popularity, it is more likely that the legibility of these letterforms at great
distances formed the basis for their widespread use.

Alphabets and letter books published for sign painters' use added examples to
the ever-growing source pool of letterforms utilized in newspapers, handbills, and
broadsides. Accurately rendered letterforms in various sizes required a thorough
knowledge, not only of attractive alphabets, but also of methods for calculating
the precise dimensions of letters as well as the spaces between them. A rudimentary grasp of color theory, including the retinal effects of certain color contrasts,
was also necessary. The backgrounds for lettered signage became just as important
as the size, density, and color of the letters themselves. In an 1855 article in *Scientific American* suggesting the use of black paper in newspaper printing, an un-
named author writes:

> You are, doubtless, well aware that a sign board painted with white letters
> on a black ground, can be read at a greater distance, and far more distinctly,
> than when the letters are black upon a white ground, for the simple reason
> that, in the first instance, the letter alone is reflected to the eye, and is a
> positive picture, while the latter instance, the ground is reflected, and the

negative portion, or that which we do not see, serves to form the letter. In one instance the outlines of the letters are distinct and sharp, and in the other indefinite and variable, by the intervening rays of light which emanate from the surrounding surface. Thus while reading a newspaper, we do not see the letters, but only the spaces around them.[21]

Manuals such as Campbell's explained how to prepare paints and grounds and offered formulae for creating correctly proportioned and properly placed letters. Taken en masse, these and other techniques suggest a passing familiarity with and practical understanding of certain optical principles then in circulation.[22] As noted in the previous chapter, the Egyptian letter's retinal appeal extended beyond the field of commercial advertising. Herman Snellen, for instance, used serifed, block letters for his "test types," originally published in 1862.[23] The letters in Snellen's chart are similar to the capital types in the style then known as Egyptian paragon. Signboards like those depicted in the Langenheim Brothers' daguerreotype of the Girard Bank visually bear out the truths of Snellen's claims. But their assemblage attests to the visual confusion that their profusion engendered.

Though the point of advertisement was to rivet the attention of viewing subjects as potential customers, the great proliferation of signs in antebellum cities often had the opposite effect. The great variation of letters and the myriad commercial interests that deployed them encouraged among sign painters and entrepreneurs a syntax premised on distraction. Even if certain fonts were more clearly seen than others, they rarely appeared in isolation outside of their clinical applications. The disjunctive appearance of shop façades crowded with signs set at a number of angles—to be scanned or read laterally across the surface of buildings, or obliquely when hung at angles protruding outward from the surface—signaled a new level of visual saturation as well as ocular sophistication. Capitalizing on available lines of sight in order to captivate the eyes at every turn, signboards, typically consisting of only one to three words, visually boasted an abundance of consumable goods, shops, and skilled tradesmen. A writer for *Mechanic Apprentice* recounted a visit to New York in 1845, describing his walk up Broadway from the Battery to City Hall: "Soon you reach the point where the line of shops commences, and from thence, for about three miles at least, you may journey onward through a pretty wide thoroughfare . . . lined on each side with receptacles for the display of all that the eye can see, the hand can touch, or money can purchase. Stone pavement, instead of brick, predominates, and the sidewalk on either side is bordered by long rows of posts and rails, serving at once for sign-boards and advertisements, and for the support of the over-hanging window-shades." He concludes his description of all there is to see along this popular thoroughfare by noting "the traffic, and hurry, and bustle," as well as "the passing to and fro of coaches and carts," that make attentive focus difficult, static viewpoints nearly unobtainable and frequently unsustainable.[24]

William M. Bobo of South Carolina called New York "one grand kaleidoscope in perpetual motion, with the views passing so swiftly by that one is hardly seen before another is presented."[25] These descriptions attempt to capture the frenetic hustle and flow seen in Thomas Hornor's image *Broadway, New-York: Showing Each Building from the Hygeian Depot Corner of Canal Street to beyond Niblo's Garden*, published in 1836 (Figure 41, Plate 3). Drawn and etched by Thomas Honer, a surveyor and illustrator recently transplanted from London, the busy scene centers on the office of its publisher, Joseph Stanley & Company, and features a broad array of signage that detracts from viewers' singular focus.[26] The raking diagonal instills the entire scene with a sense of hurried movement and guides the viewer's gaze along the avenue as it stretches into the distance at left. Punctuated here and there by promenading pedestrians, hand-drawn carts, horse-drawn wagons, carriages and omnibuses, storefronts and makeshift stalls and stands of various kinds, the view is also framed here and there by the poles and scaffolding of retracted awnings. Plate-glass shop windows also frame views of commodities on display, as well as two women looking out of the second-floor windows of Wright's Hat Warehouse and Hat, Cap, and Fur Store at right. Signs popluate nearly every surface of every building, covering their façades, perpindicularly hung on poles or cantilevered at various angles outward from the structures' outer fabric. Similar to bird's-eye views and maps, images such as this were produced to help viewers untangle and make sense of congested urban spaces. But in the frenzy depicted, such images could only partially succeed. While Hornor's etching momentarily fixes the flux of the everyday, its numerous elements encourage viewers' eyes toward the "constant searching motion" that John Walker described in his *Philosophy of the Eye*. Everything here is in motion, which incites a similar roving motion in the eyes of the engraving's viewers. Kaleidescopic in color, this hand-colored etching embodies the smooth flow of commerce, the confluence of products and people, the animated movement of the marketplace. Viewers' gazes are dispersed laterally across the composition as Broadway sweeps into the distance at left. The signboard

FIGURE 41. John Hill (engraver), after Thomas Hornor (artist), W. Neale
(printer), Joseph Stanley and Company (publisher), *Broadway, New-York,
Showing Each Building from the Hygeian Depot Corner of Canal Street to beyond
Niblo's Garden*, 1836, hand-colored etching. I. N. Phelps Stokes Collection,
Miriam and Ira D. Wallach Division of Art, Prints and Photographs, New
York Public Library, Astor, Lenox and Tilden Foundations. (See Plate 3.)

that reads "BROADWAY HOUSE" designates the limits of visibillity in this particular view. The plume of smoke gestures toward the flag waving atop what is
likely the structure of Niblo's Garden in the distance.[27]

New York–born historian of Philadelphia, John Fanning Watson, captured
the frantic sense of commerce in Hornor's view and corrobated the young mechanic's description of the sign-cluttered thoroughfares of the antebellum city in
a nostalgic footnote to the final edition of his great *Annals of Philadelphia*. In this
compendium of writings describing the city from its origins to the mid-nineteenth

century, Watson contrasted the federal city of the years around 1800 with the city as it appeared to him in the autumn of his life, Watson noted several changes in the city's appearance and in the character of its society. But in more than one instance the antiquarian lamented the encroachment of commerce and trade on the city's once genteel and residential center: "store-keepers are everywhere, buying up and driving out the long planted respectable residences—leaving no place for retired, quiet grandeur;—but turning the whole city into a great city mart of trade,—bustle, display and rivalship." For Watson, signs marked the encroachment of trade on the sanctity of urban and even personal space. As new commercial buildings crowded out residential quarters, signs trumpeted the advance of commerce. Watson expressed his displeasure, indeed his disbelief, in a series of staccato phrases that echo the array of signs seen in Hornor's view of Broadway: "Great signs to houses and some elevated upon roofs for display—and signs to be read perpendicularly—and the formation of new forms of Sign letters—" all of which he considers a new and disturbing "contrivance."[28] Elevated or vertically oriented signs, often set in new letterforms, dispersed viewers' attention in ways that directed their gazes in a variety of directions—up and down and side to side—as well as the left-to-right movement typical of reading.

In his 1853 treatise, *City Architecture; or, Designs for Dwelling Houses, Stores, Hotels*, author Marriot Field extolled the virtues of architecture and explained the lineaments of urban building styles by drawing parallels with another, less tangible form of art. "As Music affects the mind through the ear by measured spaces of time, and intervals of tone, single or combined in harmony," he wrote, "so Architecture affects the eye, by measured spaces of lines and forms, in harmonious contrasts and proportions." Harmony, though, quickly gives way to dissonance as Field turns to excoriate what he sees as the disturbing trend of applying lettered signboards to the façades of buildings. Dismissing signage as so much visual "noise," Field admonishes that "to make our streets nothing but a newspaper column of advertisements is not only the worst of taste, but quackery and puffing, which, when universally adopted, defeats itself, and has no effect upon the passengers but annoyance and distraction."[29] If as Field suggests, architecture pleased the eye through the use of "harmonious contrasts and proportions," then buildings covered with signboards assaulted the eyes and disruptively altered the visual contours of the built environment, replacing architecture's "measured spaces and lines and forms" with disjunctive contrasts and grandiose proportions. As signs redrew the perimeters of visibility, signs were emphatically (and fundamentally) premised on enlargement and even exaggeration. But these features only further underscored the disconnect between sign and referent by introducing the desta-bilizing visual impedance Field deplored. "Exaggeration" writes poet and literary critic Susan Stewart, "is not simply a matter of a change in scale, for the change in scale and quantity is significant only in relation to a corresponding change in quality and complexity."[30] For skeptics of the market's rapid and often reckless expansion, the profusion of signs described above symbolized changes that threat-ened to dismantle the precarious balance of social and economic relationships that had formed the basis for earlier modes of commerce. Opponents of signage feared that aggrandizing the commercial over the aesthetic threatened to disrupt the balance of the architectural city and the rational urban grid on which it was built.[31] Moreover, signs disrupted traditional and more direct forms of market exchange by replacing goods and services available for sale with a cacophony of letters and words positioned above the heads of customers no longer able to meet their sellers "eye-to-eye." As Stewart points out, "in the depiction of the gigantic is a severing of the synechdoche from its referent, or whole."[32] Extricating the part from a whole, signage also extracted exchange from well-established net-works of personal relations and associations, increasingly situating it within the realm of the impersonal. The strong statements of Watson and Field gave voice to a range of concerns extending from the aesthetic to the social to the perceptual. But aside from obscuring or detracting attention from the beauty of architectural ornamentation or marking commerce's encroachment on private life, the prolifer-ation of signboards, to their dismay, also levied a dizzying assault on the senses.

The coordinates of the new commercial city, mapped and marked by sign-boards, can be seen in an engraving published in the the *Illustrated New-York News* in June 1851 (Figure 42). At this bustling intersection of "Nassau and Fulton Streets Viewed from John Street," signs are nearly as populous as the people per-ambulating to and fro. As Nassau Street was the central hub of New York's thriv-ing industries of print, it is not surprising that our view uptown is framed by several key firms. To the left, deployed at an oblique angle, the sign over the shop entrance of Oliver & Brothers, a leading job printing firm, leads the line of sight directly across Fulton Street to the laterally situated signs for James Gordon Ben-nett's *Herald* buildings. The steeple of a church offers the gaze a place to rest momentarily before again sweeping across Nassau Street, where the eyes are met with the vertically arranged word "Printing" set atop the building nearly opposite the church. Other signs, set at oblique angles, continue the circuit of vision by drawing attention to signs for the *Illustrated New-York News* of T. W. Strong, as well as jewellers and Union Hall Clothing. But the eyes are encouraged to con-

NASSAU AND FULTON STREETS, VIEWED FROM JOHN STREET.

**FIGURE 42.** "Nassau and Fulton Streets Viewed from John Street,"
*Illustrated New-York News*, June 1851. Collection of the New-York Historical
Society.

tinue to scan signs for Cook & Lloyd Printers, Arcus, and Andrew M. Shiers Military Goods, which adorn the side of the building at right. A banner with the words "Gold Pens" hangs from a pole protruding from the upper story of a smaller commercial buidling as other signs, cantilevered from the façade, cascade down toward the open stall spilling forth with what look like books. Signs for Fred Smith and J. Clark Engraving & Printing lean outward from the building marked with the stray words "Sherwood," "GOLD," and "PAINT" at lower right. Taking in the sights meant doing so in interrupted intervals, between exchanges of conversation, or while weaving in and out of the pathways of other pedestrians and horse-driven carts and carriages, and amid the caterwall of newsboys hawking their wares—seen running to the left near center—and the ubiquitous sound of the organ grinder entertaining two small children at lower right. Notably, if we turned to our immediate left, we would be standing before Ackerman's elaborated storefront discussed above. Though typefaces are only schematically approximated, their strategic placement, and their prominence in this promotional image, demonstrate the ubiquity and visual effect of letterform signage deployed throughout the commercial city.

In the previous chapter, we learned how John Walker and others assessed and analyzed the movement of the eyes' while reading. But signage further disrupted the typical relationship between beholder and object by replacing the relatively fixed distance and orientation of reader to text with a shifting set of conditions that did not always allow for stable or coherent viewing positions. The visible size and legibility of sign letters fluctuated with the shifting perspectives of observers moving through city streets. Awnings, overhangs, and other impediments to clear and unobstructed views shaped the visual experience of signage as well, potentially further fatiguing eyes already engaged in the roving motions necessary to render signs legible. Walker goes further to explain the eye's actions when viewing its object from oblique angles: "When an impression is made upon the retina, in that unsatisfactory degree which is the effect of its striking any part but the centre, there is an effort made to direct the axis towards it, or, in other words, to receive the rays from it upon the more sensible centre. It is this sensibility," Walker claims, "conjoined with the action of the muscles of the eye-ball, which produces the constant searching motion of the eye."[33] This feature of vision was confirmed in 1878 by French researcher Louis Émile Javal. Javal was the first clinician to observe that the eyes do not move smoothly across the text, but rather in a series of jumps.[34] What Walker designates as a "searching motion" enables the eye to scan the page in order to obtain the proper impression. But the saccadic jumps Javal describes already begin to resemble the processes, which by extension, the eye undergoes when attempting to read sign letters from moving or oblique perspectives. We have already noted that the eye's ability to scan the surface of a distant sign was significantly diminished by a habitual focus on minute and gargantuan letters and objects at close and middle range. Recall that for Walker acuity is further hindered, even diminished, by viewing objects from oblique angles, which, as he argues, initiates a "searching motion" that exerts further strain on eyes attempting to correct the slant in order to render sign letters legible. Both Jules Sichel's description of myopia's causes and Walker's analyses of the ocular experience of reading suggests that the print revolution had ill prepared human eyes to confront the growing number of letterform signs covering the façades and sides of commercial buildings.

As we learned in the case of Edward Tailer, resting the eyes by focusing on objects at great distances, particularly the unadorned horizons of natural settings, was, according to author Johann Franz, particularly restorative. Emerson, who also suffered bouts of ocular ailment, concurred. Favoring the wilderness to the "din and craft of the street," Emerson wrote, "The health of the eye seems to demand a horizon. We are never tired, so long as we can see far enough."[35] This recognition, of course, relied on perceptive and acute vision facilitated by properly functioning eyes with the focal capacity to take the long view. Sailors, in particular, were credited with having the ability to see clearly at great distances.[36] This is precisely the reason that Richard Henry Dana Jr., author of *Two Years Before the Mast* (1840), took a break from coursework at Harvard to enlist as a merchant seaman. Suffering from an attack of measles that temporarily affected his eyesight, the young Dana purposely went to sea to recover his health and his vision.[37] What he saw, both during the voyage and while working on and off shore along the Pacific coast expanded and fueled the minds of literary authors such as Herman Melville, whose seafaring novels from *Typee* to *Moby Dick* were inspired by Dana's book. It also appealed to others interested in the rich commercial potential of California, then part of northern Mexico. However, as Emerson lamented, in the urban visual field of cities back east, buildings adorned with signboards increasingly designated that horizon but gave little relief to eyes continually encouraged to dart this way and that.

Distraction, or a more generalized dispersal of attention, however, represented only one of the many effects of signage on the sensibilities of urban consumers.[38] By the 1840s, the expanded focal distance, the range of acute vision stretching from nearby printed forms—whether minute or monumental—to distant signboards was apparently taking its toll on American eyes. Their combined profusion had pushed human vision beyond what many felt were its "natural" capacities. The roving eyes of individuals walking the streets of the antebellum metropolis had been trained on the fine print of newspapers, pamphlets, and books available in ever-increasing quantities since the middle of the previous century. The ubiquity of printed matter and the expanded presence of signage, combined with the spread of literacy that enabled and encouraged both developments, instigated a widespread demand for visual acuity and for the vision aids and ophthalmic remedies that might help observers achieve and maintain what optician John Thomas Hudson called "perfect and continuous vision."[39] But close reading—an activity often undertaken in the cramped and dimly lit quarters of coffee shops, taverns, countinghouses, lending libraries, and middle-class parlors—disciplined the eyes to focus on objects at close range, a practice that eroded their ability to bring distant objects into sharp focus. An elongation of the eyeball and an irregular convexity of its lens cause this nearsightedness, or myopia, but habitual focusing on objects close at hand exacerbates the condition. In the myopic eye, entering light rays converge anterior to the retina, thus producing only a *confused* or blurry image. The condition had been known since antiquity, but the increasingly *visual* and *textual* culture of the early nineteenth century thrust it to the top of a long list of ocular impairments that plagued Western societies.

"Civilization," wrote Jules Sichel, in his 1850 book, *Spectacles: Their Uses and Abuses in Long and Short Sightedness*, "is myopia's chief cause."[40] In an early chapter, Sichel describes the cultural factors contributing to myopia in civilized societies: "Among those who reside in the country and devote themselves to agricultural employments, short sightedness is rare. When, on the other hand, by inclination or necessity, the sight is assiduously, and from early life, exercised upon small and near objects, as is almost always the case in our state of civilization, the sight, forced to accommodate itself to these distances, becomes, very early, shortened." A worker "habituated continually to adjust his sight to these limited distances . . . finally ends, necessarily, by losing the faculty of accommodation to distant objects, and becomes myopic." As Sichel explains, "when the gaze is suddenly changed from a near object, especially if it is of small dimensions, to a distant one, with an effort to distinguish it as clearly as possible, a painful sensation in the eye is immediately perceived."[41] The complex of muscles, tissues, and lenses responsible for accommodation relied on the elasticity of the eye's component parts, an elasticity maintainable by fixing the eyes alternately on near and distant objects.[42] Consciously exercising the eyes in this manner helped observers to maintain the widest possible range of focal lengths and helped to avoid the extreme limits of sight.[43] Though studies of visual accommodation excited much discussion in the early nineteenth century, the reach of their application appears, at least initially, to have been limited. Extended discussions of myopia and its causes in popular ophthalmic tracts concerning the "use" and "abuse" of spectacles suggest that such exercises to ward off myopia were only just beginning to be embraced and incorporated into daily practice.

Opticians, whose skillful application of spectacles was already integral to the consumption of print, rose to the challenge of equipping observers with eyewear that would enable them to also see distant signs as distinctly as printed materials close at hand. Spectacles, according to Sichel, when properly ground, prescribed, and used were the most efficient means for correcting a wide range of ocular short-comings, including myopia and presbyopia, or farsightedness. Recall that in the myopic eye, the lens is too convex, causing entering rays to converge anterior to the retina. The presbyopic eye loses its elasticity after middle age, making its lens insufficiently convex so that light rays entering the eye are concentrated too far back. Already by the fourteenth century, opticians had the technical skill to grind lenses to correct these conditions: concave lenses corrected myopia, while convex lenses were used to correct presbyopia.[44] By the nineteenth century lenses had become more standardized, but measuring systems, as pointed out in Chapter 2, still varied from country to country. The McAllisters, for instance, refuted the customary applicability of "age" to the proper selection of spectacles and recommended a personal visit to obtain vision aids best suited to correct particular conditions. "Short-sighted persons, who reside at a distance from the place where concave spectacles can be procured, may furnish some idea of the degree that is required, by sending the information how near small print must be held to the eyes in order to read it distinctly—this, however, is only an approximation." Authoritative in their prescriptions, the McAllisters were also quick to admit that "there is a little range to every person's vision."[45] Sichel corroborates this view: "because it is impossible exactly to determine the normal range of vision, the same difficulty must recur when we attempt to establish the precise limits where presbyopia and myopia commence to manifest themselves."[46] Careful examination and prescription, while inevitably imprecise, sought to identify and mark the point of clear vision on this sliding scale between nearsightedness and farsightedness. Spectacles became the outward manifestation of this dividing point, managing the threshold between the perceptible and imperceptible, between the legible and illegible, between near-sightedness and farsightedness. For those who suffered from myopia or other ocular conditions, spectacles defined the perimeters of visibility, the sphere of clear vision that came to define the self, both spatially and socially.

For Watson and others, signs marked the expansion of commerce beyond the customary spaces set aside for trade. Take for instance the long sheds of Philadelphia's New Market or High Street Market, demolished in 1859.[47] Increasingly dispersed throughout the urban landscape, spaces of commerce marked by sign-covered buildings situated along bustling commercial thoroughfares defined the city's often shifting perimeters of visibility. These fluid spaces, established for the movement of people and commodities, comprised what cultural historian Jean-Christophe Agnew has called "thresholds of exchange," a term he uses to describe early modern predecessors to the nineteenth century's stores, shops, and stalls.[48] Over time markets outgrew their traditional boundaries, age-old practices, and calendrical regularity. By the early nineteenth century, spaces of trade had expanded and diversified, spreading into different parts of the urban landscape. "Visibility," however, remained the marketplace's "indispensable quality." To mark and make shops recognizable, to designate them as places of business and trade, entrepreneurs and manufactuers comissioned and displayed signboards. Agnew's term "threshold" is often used to designate an entrance or boundary between two spheres or phases, but the word also defines the point at which a stimulus is just strong enough to be perceived. The signboard adorning the façade of a commercial building, in its material, spatial, and optical properties, combines these definitions, simultaneously marking a store's entrance *and* the physical place at which it begins to be clearly visible to those passing by. Thus, in addition to marking the newly expanded boundaries of commerce and exchange, signboards also came to designate the newly expanded perimeters of visibility.

Along streets now marked by commerce and designated as "places for seeing," the circulation of commodities and impersonal exchange transformed practices of buying and selling as it radically reconfigured related acts of seeing.[49] As early modern "social signs and symbols" continued their metamorphosis into the "detached and manipulable commodities" of the market revolution, mass-produced products, such as the boots and hats for sale in the lower right of Hornor's Broadway scene (see Figure 41, Plate 3), circulated far beyond the once contained and regulated spaces of traditional fairs and market days. Goods once displayed in market stalls receded from view, as opaque broadsides and signboards boasting the name of an artisan or product emerged to mediate relationships between consumers and consumables, relationships formed and fastened by the overlapping experiences of perception and purchase. As word-laden buildings began to reflect the vertical and horizontal arrangements of newspapers and broadsides, the city became, as historian David Henkin has argued, a readable text.[50] But despite the potential clarity that words can bring to processes of representation, their prolixity in antebellum signage tended to impede clear communication by amplifying with painted or carved letters and words products yet procured and services yet rendered. Amid the commercial city's expanded array of visual signifiers, signboards were far from transparent indicators of the character and value of the professionals and products they advertised. As typographic print increasingly supplanted the manuscript-based culture of previous centuries, anxieties stemming from print's inherent duplicity also increased. Whereas handwritten script had been widely regarded in the century prior as a relatively stable indicator of the individual self and conveyer of intended meaning, print, especially when set in typographic forms largely divorced from calligraphic precedents, disrupted communication and obfuscated meaning by obscuring the identity of a text's creator now doubly, even triply removed.[51]

Recall that Roman fonts were formed in accordance with the thick and thin strokes of script rendered by hand with a quill. But Gothic and Egyptian fonts, the two most popular sign letters, had evolved from types developed specifically for use in newspaper headlines, billheads, and broadsheets. Fat face types, used almost exclusively for commercial purposes, expanded print's potential for duplicity, further obscuring the intentions of the text's author while aggrandizing the commodity without regard for veracity or sincerity. Though typically rendered by hand, typographically inspired sign letters illustrate the dilation of print's inherent ambiguities beyond the printed page.

Given their mammoth size and their boisterous method of promoting commercial endeavors and products, lettered signboards extended print's overriding opacity to cloud and confuse the visual fields of public spaces, significantly increasing print's capacities for duplicity and deception in marketplaces purportedly founded on the ideals of fair trade and just price. As visible markers of a process that rapidly rendered the ideal of republican transparency in social, spatial, and commercial relations obsolete, signs implied the detrimental ramifications of these changes for individuals and crowds alike. Publicly available yet privately deployed, words in public spaces irrevocably altered the ways individuals moved through urban spaces and interacted with one another, each increasingly grounded in processes of buying and selling. Signs labeled buildings but did little to showcase products, offering viewers opaque surfaces to be *read* rather than products to be *seen*. Visually available in varying degrees of clarity to the eyes of all, legible to those literate enough to decode the letters and words, and inviting to those with the means to procure the goods or services advertised, letterform signs qualified print culture's "democratic" diffusion of information by targeting *individuals* among the masses and encouraging their desire for particular products and services. Creating a competitive culture based in what Watson termed "rivalship," signage impeded unobstructed urban views and rendered opaque transactions between producers, retailers, and consumers. This opacity provides an evocatively visual metaphor for the convergence of visual, spatial, architectural, and commercial discourses in the formation of subject positions occupied by antebellum consumers.[52]

Signs, in effect, contributed to the visual congestion and mental confusion that by the 1840s had become a defining feature of crowded urban centers. As a proponent for architectural beauty and civic order, Marriott Field criticized the superfluous use of signs as a distracting form of *puffing* that obscured by inflation the true nature of the firm, the character of its owners, and the quality of its products.[53] The duplicity of print clearly expanded the sign's capacity for braggadocio and added further ambiguity to the exaggerated messages they conveyed. As the products not of merchants or tradesmen themselves, but of sign painters on their behalf, signboards conveyed messages at least twice removed from original senders. Moreover, the commodities they advertised were increasingly the products of unknown hands working in manufactories far out of sight. For those skeptical of market development, the signboard's commercial letterforms presented a blank countenance symbolic of the anonymous production of goods and the anonymous modes of impersonal exchange that had increasingly become the market economy's dominant characteristics.

The confused image of commodities mediated by signboards within an increasingly opaque commercial city suggests intriguing conceptual links between the experience of the marketplace and the ocular condition of myopia. In his famous formulation of the commodity fetish, Karl Marx asserts that the appearance of the commodity itself is already blurred because of the way it conceals the labor and the corresponding network of social relations responsible for its production.[54] What Marx calls the "mist" that envelops and obscures the true nature of the commodity extends to the consumer's interaction with the purchased object. By its very nature, the commodity supplies one need as it produces another, offering buyers blurred impressions of a fleeting satisfaction that always manages to elude proper "focus." This sense of delayed or deferred gratification is, of course, the engine that ensures the continuance of consumer culture. The purchase and use of spectacles in the nineteenth century, to take one example, enhanced the observer's view of print and signage, which in turn instigated desires that eventually led to the consumption of other goods. So while a commodity like spectacles helped to diminish the effects of ocular myopia, they actually helped to facilitate the myopic or shortsighted consumption encouraged by the capitalist marketplace. And though they facilitated a clearer view, spectacles could do little to diminish what many considered to be the marketplace's inherent capacity for duplicity, dissemblance, and deception. In the cultural landscape in which these market mechanisms and consumer practices emerged, advertisements that profitably utilized the lines of sight and "democratic" vistas of the urban grid employed new forms of visuality to cultivate desires capable of leading the observer from advertisement to product. Signs and spectacles, exaggerated letterforms, and elaborate signboards helped lend shape to this new kind of observing subject, whose identity was based on ambulating, seeing, purchasing, and owning—all facets of what one historian has aptly called "commercialized personhood."[55] Just as ink-saturated display types suggested surplus and surfeit, myopia provided an apt metaphor for visual relationships that signboards established between consumers and goods. Bombarded by the city's dizzying array of sights, the inability to see beyond one's nose, in a sense, indicated full integration with the market economy.

And so we return to the proximity of sign painter and optician in antebellum Philadelphia whose respective practices outline the ways that consumer subjects were formed by the market through a set of carefully manipulated links fostered between clearly articulated signage and properly gauged and optically assisted eyesight. Under their hands, both *what* antebellum observers saw in the streets of urban marketplaces and *how* they saw it became commodified phenomena simultaneously. Murphy's phrase "economy is wealth," intended to emphasize his ability to paint signs with "neatness and dispatch," resonates equally with the McAllisters' practice and the contributions their spectacles might make to the efficient and sparing use of a valued resource like vision. As opticians and ophthalmologists demonstrated, the eyes had economies of their own, and as such, they were the signboard's most expedient targets for enticing and ensnaring the attention of consumers attempting to navigate their way through the commercially opaque cities of antebellum America. In establishing the boundaries of perception at the thresholds of commerce, market culture situated myopic subjects in an endless pursuit of commodities represented by lavish signboards posted at the thresholds of visibility, points just beyond consumers' grasp. As the 1840s progressed, however, seeing beyond such thresholds, over the horizon, or beyond the range of normal vision became a constituent feature of antebellum visual culture. The vehicle for such longer views: the daily newspaper.

# PART III

## Painting, Print, Perception

## CHAPTER FIVE

# The Optics of Newspaper Vision

From the book to the broadside, the poster to the signboard, antebellum print culture, in all of its myriad forms, continually extended the limits of visibility. At times, it even pointed beyond those limits. Indeed, peering beyond the horizon became something of a national obsession in the 1840s. The microscopes, telescopes, and binoculars marketed by retailers such as Benjamin Pike or McAllister & Co. extended considerably the physical range of normal vision in the antebellum decades. But the cheap, daily newspapers that burst onto the scene in the late 1830s and '40s expanded the conceptual vision of a rapdily expanding nation eager to see the bigger picture. Like optical instruments that made the unseen seen, newspapers both microscopically exposed various facets of urban life and peered telescopically into the distance, across the continent and around the world. Previously, newspapers, particularly daily editions, had been few in number. They were often allied with the interests of the business elite or political faction and tended to be local in coverage and distribution. By the 1840s, however, steam-powered printing presses and recently enhanced modes of distribution to far-flung markets enabled newspapers to proliferate in greater volume and attain broader geographic reach.

By the mid-1840s, the popular press was rapidly changing Americans' perception of their growing country. But it also altered conceptions of perception itself. While ophthalmologists treated vision in ever more physiological or bodily terms, antebellum culture continued to embrace vision's more metaphoric properties, perhaps in an attempt to expand eyesight's reach. Though newspapers did not, could not, actually extend or alter vision—except for weakening it by encouraging the overuse that ophthalmic literature warned against—they did extend and expand conceptions of eyesight's ocular power to augment its figurative reach. This was not lost on newspaper publishers who christened their papers with names like "observer," "telescope," or "spectator" to emphasize their ability to deliver nearly instantaneous news that could be associated with the rapid mechanisms of perception itself. As part of a broader communciations revolution, the periodical press in the 1840s molded itself into a technology of seeing, a combination of vivid text and, increasingly, wood-engraved images, fabricating, to borrow art historian Angela Miller's phrase, a virtual "empire of the eye."[1] While discerning news of distant events involved scrutinizng the newspaper's fine print close at hand, the visual effect it provided was expansive, even dizzying. Facilitated by the steam-powered rotary press and the electromagnetic telegraph, newspapers staged a new way of seeing, extending vision's reach by collapsing time and space via communications sent over great distances.[2]

Like broadsides and signboards, newspapers pointed elsewhere. In spite of their densely packed columns of typographic information, the reach of their reportage, the volume of their output, and the "views" they afforded of local, regional, national, and international events were increasingly expansive. With the introduction of Richard Hoe's rotary press in the 1840s, a steam-powered, multiple-feed printing machine capable of producing thousands of impressions per hour, the publication of cheap newspapers and popular periodicals expanded both rapidly and exponentially.[3] Reporters in the field, express lines for delivering news, and the invention of the electromagnetic telegraph in 1844 all hastened the flow of information from the outer reaches to population centers throughout the steadily expanding nation. Eyewitness reports translated into the dots and dashes of Morse code were relayed electronically over miles of copper wires. These transmissions provided the copy that filled the streams of paper fed into the new steam-powered printing presses. Newspapers were objects to be seen and read, but they functioned as virtual windows onto other worlds. In fact, in many instances, the means through which periodicals like the *New York Herald* and *Niles' National Register* received news from various sources became almost as much a topic of importance as the actual news itself.[4]

Of a number of images made during the 1840s that depict people reading and discussing the news, the modestly scaled but information-packed paintings of the Baltimore-born artist Richard Caton Woodville document the craze for consuming news (Figure 43). Though none of his canvases exceed the size of the average antebellum newspaper, they poignantly demonstrate the centrality of paper to perception in the 1840s, when human vision was newly augmented by its consumption. Centrally placed newspapers form pictorial and narrative fulcrums in a number of the artist's most important and enduring works, all painted within a five-year period that marked the pinnacle of Woodville's remarkably short but meteoric

FIGURE 44. Richard Caton Woodville, *War News from Mexico*, 1848, oil on canvas. Crystal Bridges Museum of American Art, Bentonville, AK, 2010.74, Photography by the Walters Art Museum, Baltimore, Susan Tobin. (See Plate 4.)

BATTLE OF RESACA DE LA PALMA MAY 9TH 1846.
*Capture of Genl. VEGA by the gallant Capt. MAY.*

**FIGURE 45.** Nathaniel Currier, *Battle of Resaca de la Palma, May 9th, 1846. Capture of Genl. Vega by the gallant Capt. May*, c. 1846, lithograph. Library of Congress, Prints & Photographs Division.

Images of the conflict proliferated as never before, making it the first truly mediated war in the United States, a precursor to the Civil War that would erupt with the Confederate firing on Fort Sumter in April 1861. Elaborate chromolithographs depicted raging battles and animated troop movements with an eyewitness realism tempered by heroic romanticization (Figure 45). The new medium of the daguerreotype was enlisted to document the static subjects seen in officer portraits and troop musters in town squares. Other images, such as Emanuel Leutze's ambitiously large composition, *The Storming of the Teocalli by Cortez and His Troops*, which he painted in Düsseldorf in 1848, displaced the action of the war onto the past of Spanish conquest (Figure 46). Strikingly, however, *War News* dispenses with the action of the war altogether, opting instead to telescope past it in response to the dizzying speed of the technological, and thus perceptual, changes that occurred along with it. Preoccupied with the relay and receipt of

FIGURE 46. Emanuel Leutze (American, 1816–1868), *The Storming of the Teocalli by Cortez and His Troops*, 1848, oil on canvas, 84¾ × 98¾ in. Ella Gallup Sumner and Mary Caitlin Sumner Collection Fund, 1985.7, Wadsworth Atheneum Museum of Art, Hartford, CT; Photo credit: Allen Phillips/ Wadsworth Atheneum.

information in its myriad forms, *War News*, too, proliferated in multiple versions. Woodville's painting was purchased by George W. Austen, an auctioneer by trade and treasurer of the American Art-Union from 1847 to 1849. Austen lent the work for exhibition in the American Art-Union's Perpetual Free Gallery the following year. Soon thereafter, the painting was reproduced in two formats. It first appeared as a small etching published as the front plate of the Art-Union's *Bulletin* for April 1851. This was followed by a large folio line engraving by Alfred Jones as a premium for the annual distribution to over sixteen thousand Art-Union members that year, which helped to extend the reach of its popularity.[8] In its various iterations, Woodville's image circulated as widely as the newspaper that forms the painting's main subject.

Reviews of Woodville as fluidly moving expatriate artist also figured prominently in the American Art-Union's *Bulletin*: "Our countryman, Woodville, from Baltimore, who has been for about four years past at Düsseldorf, is one who shows in his works, the advantage of being associated with thorough and careful painters, and surrounded by works of art, of so distinguished an order of merit as to furnish him with a high criterion, and enable him to form a true and just faculty of discrimination. . . . [T]here is no doubt that with moderate application and perseverance, he is destined to occupy a very high place in the list of American painters."[9] A subsequent article tracked the artist's movement: "We learn that Woodville has removed his residence from Düsseldorf to London. We think that this change will be of advantage both in a professional and pecuniary point of view. . . . Whenever he becomes well known, we predict for him great popularity." Woodville's meteoric rise, and the great promise it held, however, ended all too soon when the artist died in Paris of an accidental morphine overdose in 1855. He had completed fewer than twenty-five works and had yet to reach age thirty.

Though modest in size, *War News from Mexico* charts a vast theater of operations that extends from Düsseldorf to New York, from Baltimore to Washington, DC, New Orleans, Texas, Mexico, and California. Woodville's scenes of card players and newspaper readers illustrate a populace on the move, subjected to the flux of mobile perceptions and to the experience of telegraphic simultaneity, a "reality effect" of instantaneous news of firsthand observations telegraphed and printed for daily consumption.[10] To view Woodville's painting is to study this vast network and the artist's shifting position within it.[11] How the painting frames seeing and what it says about the visuality of market revolution and the mediated nature of perception are its most salient features.

Beginning with the publication of Benjamin Day's New York *Sun* on September 3, 1833, a new kind of daily paper appeared in the 1830s. Smaller in format (eight and half by ten as opposed to thirty-five inches by twenty-four) and usually containing fewer pages than its six-penny predecessor, the new daily papers appealed to and capitalized on growing masses of readers gathered in urban centers like New York, Philadelphia, Boston, and Baltimore. No longer sold purely by subscription, the new dailies were hawked in the streets by a growing army of newsboys (see Figure 23) and relied on advertising revenues for their profits. In 1830 there were 65 dailies in the United States with an average circulation of 1,200 copies. In 1840 there were 138 dailies; in 1850, 254. Average daily circulation rose from 1,200 in 1830 to just under 3,000 in 1850. New York alone had 14 dailies that year with a combined circulation running well over 150,000. This, as historian Alexander Saxton has calculated, amounted to one newspaper a day for every four and a half inhabitants, in contrast to one for every sixteen twenty years earlier.[12] Rising literacy rates and rapid urbanization significantly increased the demand for printed matter. In response, new mechanized methods of papermaking and developments in printing machinery made large runs of daily papers technologically feasible and economically profitable.

Powered by steam and fed by what seemed an inexhaustible supply of paper, Richard Hoe's rotary press provided the engine for the penny-press revolution.[13] Like the famed Corliss engine, which debuted at the 1876 Centennial Exposition in Philadelphia, Hoe's printing press was a spectacular feat of engineering that drew much fanfare and reportial coverage. Its vast machinery was the subject of numerous feature articles, occasionally accompanied by elaborate engravings like the one that illustrates an 1851 article in *Scientific American* (Figure 47). Situated in a cavernous space, this multilevel machine dwarfs the individuals who observe, attend to, or facilitate the various processes involved in the hourly printing of thousands of pages of newsprint. Hoe's machinery often summoned bodily metaphors in journalistic descriptions. Describing the printing rooms of the new daily newspapers, George G. Foster, author of *New York by Gaslight* (1850), wrote "The news-carrier issues from the reeking steam-pit, where the ceaseless panting of the city's brain gives forth its myriads of sibylline leaves, to bring pleasure and despair, ruin and recreation to the countless thousands of the city."[14] In the illustration, the press is framed by an archway made of bricks as indicated by a grid overlaid with the lines of engravers' tints to lend them a sense of texture. A series of oculi in the ceiling of this dank space allow cones of light to shower down from above, casting deep, dramatic shadows across the contours of the hulking machine. Its various parts are connected by ladder-like stairways, conveyer belts, and levers. At quick glance, the entire composition—with its lines, shades, and carefully calibrated inter-working parts; with its arched ceilings and bright spots of focused light as in the upper right corner; and with the industrial-sized iris formed by the central cylinder and the squiggly lines that resemble blood vessels and nerves—is in appearance not unlike the scientific diagrams of eyeballs used

## HOE'S MAMMOTH ROTARY PRINTING PRESS.

The Art of Printing consists in having types made of a composite metal, cast into a single piece for every letter that is seen in a book or newspaper. These letters are put together one after another into words and sentences, and punctuated with commas, &c. The words are arranged in lines, the lines in columns, and set up in an iron frame named a *Chase*. The type are all of the same depth, and are wedged up and secured in the chase, when it is then denominated the *Form*. It requires a great deal of labor to set up the type,—the men who do so are termed *Compositors*. The inking of the type in the form, the placing of a sheet of paper on it, then pressing the said sheet down on the type, and afterwards removing it, constitute the art of printing, and these several operations are performed in a more expeditious manner by the press which illustrates this article than by any other in the world. This mammoth press, the largest ever constructed, was designed and built by Messrs. R. Hoe & Co., New York : it is 40 feet in length and 5 wide ; it has a large central drum which revolves like a broad wheel. The *form* (or there may be a number of them) is placed on the periphery of the central drum, but only occupies a portion of it. The *chase* is curved and forms the section of a circle, with the surface of the type forming the outside of the same. The type are secured in the curved chase in a peculiar manner. The column-rules are straight and run parallel with the shaft of the large drum ; the head and dash rules are curved. The column-rules have bottom flanges ; they slide in the grooves in the bed of the chase, and are secured by brass dove-tail wedges. The cross section of a column-rule is

of a wedge shape, being thinner at the bottom than at the top, to wedge in the type at the widest part of a circle which they form with the large drum. This is an essential feature in securing the type, and its application is certainly the result of a very happy thought. The type is firmly screwed up in the chase by set screws.

The surface of the large drum of the press is composed of smooth metal plates, and performs the office of an ink distributor to the small rollers which ink the type. Below the large rotary drum, there is a trough running across the frame, into which the ink is pumped from a reservoir by a force pump, so as to keep the trough always full. Above the ink trough there revolves a large roller, which takes up the ink on its surface, conveys it to another roller, that one to a third, and it to the smooth surface of the revolving drum, distributing the ink on it. The use of the three rollers to convey the ink from the trough, is to work and spread it on the distributing surface. As the type in the chase stands higher than the smooth surface of the rotary drum, the ink-roller below would cover the type with ink when it came round to it, were it not for a contrivance of Messrs. Hoe to obviate this difficulty. The large ink-roller below has its gudgeons worked on springs, which press it up against the smooth surface of the large drum, except at the exact time during the passage of the type ; then a cam forces down the ink-roller below the surface of the type, until the *form* is past the point of contact, when it rises up against the distributing surface with its supply of ink.

Around the fixed frame at different but ex-

act points above the large *drum*, there are eight revolving tympan cylinders, or rollers, which feed in the sheets to the revolving drum, as it revolves, impresses the paper. The attendants push in the sheets, one by one, to the tympans, in each of which is an open section, with fingers worked by a cam, which are open when they come round to receive a sheet, then close upon it, wrapping the said sheet around the smooth surface of the tympan ; at this very period, the type on the large drum has come round, and is acting on the paper. When the type has printed the sheet, the fingers spoken of open like the human hand and the printed sheet is whipped off the tympan and carried away back to the end of the press, there to be taken off and folded neatly down by a vibratory flyer, four of which are placed above one another, (one for each tympan,) at each side of the press. The two outside edges of each sheet of paper are held against a smooth, narrow strap on the tympan at each side. Above each tympan cylinder, it will be observed there are a number of small pulleys, with straps running around them, extending the whole length of each tympan, and running on its surface. The straps of these small pulleys run away back over a like set of pulleys, above the flyers. Whenever the type forms its impression on the sheet, the fingers spoken of let the paper free, and then these small straps whip up the sheet, and carry it along, as on a flying railroad, to be folded by the flyer. After the form makes its impression on the paper which is wrapped around the tympan, it comes in contact with the two small ink rollers,

which ink the surface of the type, and fit it to print the sheet on the next tympan, and so on continually. These small inking rollers have their journals fitted on springs, so as to allow them to be pushed up or down by the type, and then to be forced against the distributing surface, to take up the ink for their next performance.

In this one press, it may be said, " there are eight combined," that is, in respect to its effective power. One, two, three, or more tympan cylinders can be detached, and the rest left free to work. This makes it very convenient, for it requires but a moment's labor to set the press so as to work with any number less than the eight attendants.

Although this machine is so large, strictly speaking it is exceedingly simple in its operation, and it works with a smoothness and regularity that commands admiration. The building of this great press for the New York Sun, was commenced in 1849, and it was completed in 1851.

In the construction of this press Messrs. Hoe & Co. state that there are employed no less than six thousand bolts and screws, one thousand two hundred wheels, two hundred and two wooden rollers, four hundred pulleys, four hundred tape guides, besides an amazing amount of cogged wheel connections, arms, braces, and other connections. There are also required to give motion to various parts of the machine, no less than five hundred yards of belting.

It can print 20,000 copies in one hour. It has been in successful operation printing the New York Sun for the past three months, and it operates with astonishing precision.

FIGURE 47. "Hoe's Mammoth Rotary Printing Press," *Scientific American* 6, no. 36 (May 24, 1851): 283. Collection of the New-York Historical Society.

to illustrate ophthalmic treatises of the period. Moreover, the camera-like aspects of the light-emitting apertures that pierce the darkened shadow areas and the concentration of those rays on the press's platen where impressions are made suggests the interplay of exterior and interior, of stimuli and response that made the camera obscura such a powerful model for demonstrating the anatomy of the eye and the physical processes of vision as a transmission of refracted light.

Stacked in enormous heaps is the cheap paper that Hoe's press consumed in great quanities. Printed with inks that faded or ran, sheets were often folded, stacked, and sent via mail—the substandard materials used in antebellum newspapers accounts for their relative scarcity in extant archives. "Greasy" was the word Charles Dickens used to describe American newspapers during his visit to the country in 1842. Critical of what filled the daily press, Dickens ranted:

> What are the fifty newspapers, which those precocious urchins are bawling down the street, and which are kept filed within, what are they but amusements? Not vapid, waterish amusements, but good strong stuff; dealing in round abuse and blackguard names; pulling off the roofs of private houses, as the Halting Devil did in Spain; pimping and pandering for all degrees of vicious taste, and gorging with coined lies the most voracious maw; imputing to every man in public life the coarsest and the vilest motives; scaring away from the stabbed and prostrate body-politic, every Samaritan of clear conscience and good deeds; and setting on, with yell and whistle and the clapping of foul hands, the vilest vermin and worst birds of prey.[15]

Though Dickens railed against the content of American papers, criticisms often centered on either the "ghastly" or "grotesque" shape of the letters themselves or the ridiculously small amount of space between letters and words. Indeed, the compact type of the midcentury newspaper was as minute as the papers were prolix. Newspapers, even more than the cheapest of books, maximized the space allotted for text by using the smallest and most compact fonts and by condensing the margins around paragraphs and columns. Headlines were set in slightly larger type, sometimes in all capitals, but these, along with the occasional use of stock woodcuts to advertise commodities such as furniture or articles of clothing did little to upset the textual and visual monotony of the typical page of newsprint. The voracious appetite for "copy," already a cause for the editorial piracy that Dickens railed against, led editors to employ an ever-expanding army of reporters to cover local, regional, national, and international events. Of course, original sto-

FIGURE 48. Edwin Forrest Durang and Turner & Fisher, *The Telegraphic Candidates*, 1848, lithograph on wove paper, 31.1 × 44.5 cm. Library of Congress, Prints & Photographs Division.

ries appeared alongside reprints from other publications, a practice common during the period. But increasingly, newsrooms came to rely on a new technology for conveying information with lightning speed over vast distances.

In late May of 1844, the artist and inventor Samuel F. B. Morse, founder and first president of the National Academy of Design, demonstrated his electromagnetic telegraph in the chambers of the United States Supreme Court by sending the message "What Hath God Wrought" over a wire stretched the forty miles between Washington, DC, and Baltimore.[16] Woodville, poised to leave for Europe the following year, could not have missed the news coverage of the event in Baltimore's daily press. Within days of his initial demonstration, Morse employed his device to send up-to-the-minute reports to the Congress in Washington on the activities taking place during the Democratic National Convention held that year in Baltimore. The imperialist Lewis Cass, a general in the War of 1812 and

FIGURE 49. Unidentified Artist, *A War President: Progressive Democracy*, 1848, engraving. Library Company of Philadelphia.

secretary of war under Andrew Jackson eventually lost the party's nomination to James K. Polk, a southern, proslavery expansionist who won the ensuing election and led the country into war.[17] But Cass returned as the Democratic candidate in the 1848 election, lampooned by cartoonist Edwin Forrest Durang in the lithograph *The Telegraphic Candidates* (Figure 48). It presents the election as a race between the telegraph, the vehicle of Cass and his running mate, General William O. Butler, and the railroad, which conveys Whig candidate and Mexican War hero Zachary Taylor and his vice presidential candidate, Millard Filmore. Henry Clay, who lost his party's nomination to Taylor, steers a small boat toward the White House, while Martin Van Buren, candidate for the newly formed Free Soil Party, lags behind on horseback. Cass and Butler skate across an electrified telegraph wire that cuts through the puff of smoke emitted by the locomotive that, according to Taylor, "must be on the wrong track." In another cartoon, the combustible "War President" Lewis Cass is figured as a combative Trojan horse of Manifest Destiny (Figure 49). Brandishing bloody sword and spear, the portly figure of Cass, dubbed "General Gas" in the press, is armed to wage an ocular assault. With eyes, arms, and legs rendered in the form of firing cannon, smoke from all the gas and shot clouds his forward path. With artillery for eyes, the cartoons suggests that Cass's vision for a "progressive democracy" has been replaced by militaristic imperialism. With an eye to expanding the nation into "New Mexico, California, Chihuahua, Zacatecas, MEXICO, Peru, Yucatan, Cuba," Cass, as his critics warned, sought to add a southern trajectory to the well-established east-west axis of national expansion. But how to communicate effectively along these axes? Semophores and other signaling systems had long been in operation, but they relied on the visibility and legibility of their signs and were impeded or disrupted altogether by the atmospheric interference of clouds, fog, or smoke like that emanating from Cass's bodily weaponry. Such signaling systems were regional, at best, stitching local communities together. But they lacked the infra-structural capacity, and consistency, to go the distance.

With the spread of telegraph wires, however, Morse's invention eventually fostered a viable *national* network for the efficient flow of lossless information unreliant on sight. It was Morse's Washington-Baltimore line that conveyed Polk's war message to Congress in May 1846. However, as the conflict began, only 146 miles of telegraph lines existed, none of them south of Richmond, Virginia. But by June of that year, wires connected Washington with Philadelphia, New York, and Boston. "With construction stimulated by the hunger for war news," as one historian has written, the telegraph reached New Orleans and Charleston by the end of the war in early 1848. By 1850, ten thousand miles of wire criss-crossed the United States.[18] Like newly constructed roads and canals, the railroad, and the steamship, the telegraph conquered and collapsed nineteenth-century space. This collapse is registered in *War News from Mexico*'s shallow stage-set composition with its compressed, electromagnetic energy. The interconnectedness of the men on the porch in *War News* even recalls a favorite electrical experiment of the period just prior to the telegraph's invention—the nearly instantaneous passing of a current of electricity through a series of human bodies.[19] As vividly captured in Woodville's painting, telegraphic transmissions were disembodied yet had the capacity to bring together bodies from disparate parts of the country to share in the consumption of transmitted information. This elongation of the lines of com-munication necessarily expanded notions of both individual bodies and the *na-tional* body at large. In his publication, the *Democratic Review*, John L. O'Sulli-van, coiner of the phrase "Manifest Destiny," rejoiced that the American empire now possessed what he called "a vast skeleton framework of railroads, and an infinitely ramified nervous system of magnetic telegraphs" to knit it into an organic whole.[20] A number of voices rang out in chorus extolling the telegraph in similar bodily terms. In "On the Municipal Electric Telegraph; Especially in its Application to Fire Alarms," Boston physician William F. Channing claimed "the Electric telegraph is to constitute the nervous system of organized societies . . . its functions are analogous to the sensitive nerves of the animal system."[21] With the nation as a body, the railroad as its skeleton, and the telegraph as its nervous system, the growing American empire assumed a metaphoric corporeality that unified the nation's disparate regions and diverse populations. Stemming from intense and widespread interest in the body and its various mechanisms, the subject of the emerging field of physiology, such bodily metaphors abounded in antebellum America. From the individual to the masses to the nation, bodies preoccupied antebellum thought, practice, and modes of picturing. Hence the gas of Lewis Cass.

Recall that the discourse of bodily fitness informed ophthalmic practice and undergirded the culture's understanding of the body's anatomy and physiology. The pervasive and overarching concern with embodiment assumed several forms in the 1840s and '50s. One year after Woodville left Saint Mary's College, where he studied from 1836 until 1841, he enrolled as a student in the College of Medicine at the University of Maryland in Baltimore. There, Woodville would have taken core courses in the application of medicine for healing; chemistry; materia medica, or pharmacology; obstetrics; and surgery. The College of Medicine taught anatomy and advertised itself as second only to Paris in the number of corpses available for anatomical study.[22] In place of the copious notes made by other students, Woodville filled the margins of his notebooks with sketches of his instructors, fellow students, and quick renderings of surgical procedures. Though his studies at the college ended after only one year, this experience, and the drawings he made of it, undoubtedly initiated Woodville's ongoing preoccupation with issues of embodiment. He undertook these studies and took his first steps as a practicing artist just as the construction and maintenance of the self became the central focus for reformers and others concerned with the fitness of the body to withstand the new demands placed on it by the market economy. They offered prescriptions for managing physiological processes and impulses that they considered critical to success in navigating the new industrial and urbanizing terrain of a rapidly expanding country. Embodied identity and character became the subject of physiognomic and phrenological investigations of facial features, especially the shapes of the heads, noses, and eyes.[23] The prescriptive literature of William Alcott's *Young Man's Guide* (1834) guided the writing of ophthalmic tracts, the dietary reform physiology of Sylvester Graham, which helped to explain in layman's terms "the science of human life," and the temperance movement's calls for sobriety. All expressed heightened interest in the body and its various functions.[24] Though conceived in these treatises and tracts as susceptible to disease and debilitation, the body was increasingly posited as subject to a disciplinary regime that helped to maintain one's physical and moral health. Temperance, moderation, exercise, and strict diet fitted the body for productive employment as well as consumption of the text-laden visuality of the mid-nineteenth century. The saturation of newspaper media in the visual field raised questions about print's wear and tear on the eyes, as critics wondered aloud about the effect of print on eyesight, focusing in particular on the ocular strain that many felt led to a loss of acuity, fatigue, and even debility.[25] Creating demand (as well stamina) for the consumption of daily news reports, however, required a reshaping of a reader's cognitive expectations and behaviors, which gradually became part and parcel of maintaining a fit, temperate, and healthy body—the goals of reform physiology in all of its manifestations. Nevertheless, the purported threat of ocular strain did little to diminish or dissuade Americans' voracious appetite for digesting the news.

As new daily newspapers proliferated, their consumption became something of a national pastime.[26] A spate of images produced in the 1840s register this phenomenon. Depicting people as they digest and discuss the news, these genre scenes stage the experience of reading the news in bodily, and often communal, terms. Genre painting during this peirod preoccupied itself with figures engaged in the activities of daily life, but it often honed its attention on clashes between easily recognizable character "types" who represented the old and the young of generational conflict, or the contrasting spheres of male and female, urban and rural, rich and poor. They captivated their audiences with their unambiguous yet often unresolved narratives, their meticulous attention to detail, their compositional space, their calculated arrangement of figures, and their depiction of sensory activities—imbibing ale, smelling a roast turkey, or, as was often the case in the 1840s, reading or discussing a newspaper. Grounding conceptions of civil society, citizenship, and selfhood in the consumption of print, such scenes also begin to outline how readers' bodies interacted physically and physiologically with paper and printed forms. The watercolor *Astor House Reading Room*, by the Italian born,

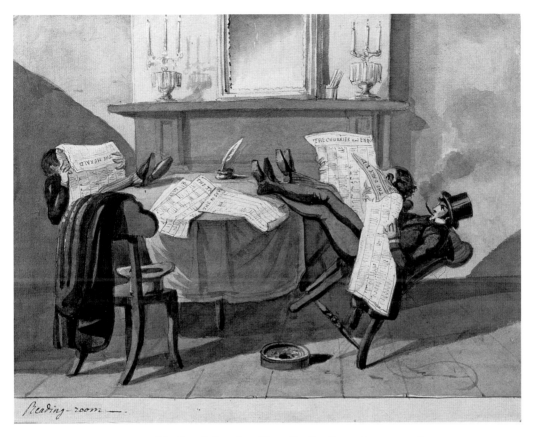

FIGURE 50. Nicolino Calyo, *Astor House Reading Room*, 1840, watercolor on paper, 9⅜ × 12¼ in. © Museum of the City of New York/Bridgeman Images.

Baltimore-based painter Nicolino Calyo (Figure 50), and the daguerreotype titled *California News*, made by Gabriel Harrison in 1851 (Figure 51), picture the embodied nature, the absorptive qualities, and the communal aspects of antebellum reading practices. They illustrate the activity of reading the newspaper with its sheets of thin, ink-stained paper held in the hand or hands at the correct focal length for reading. As a malleable medium, papers were creased, folded, passed around, torn up, or crumpled for disposal as readers handled and exchanged them. Unlike broadsides and signboards, which appealed to without touching the human frame, newspapers engaged the body physically and faciliated a personal, one-to-one relationship with individual readers. Just as spectacles indicated literacy and intellectual or financial engagement, newspaper signaled a similar en-

FIGURE 51. Gabriel Harrison, *California News*, c. 1850, daguerreotype, 14 × 10.5 cm. (5 ½ x 4 ⅛ in.), Horace W. Goldsmith Foundation Gift, through Joyce and Robert Menschel, 2005 (2005. 100.334), Metropolitan Museum of Art, New York, © Metropolitan Museum of Art, Image source: Art Resource, New York.

gagement with current events, literary miscellaney, and, of course, commerce. Harrison's daguerreotype, and the many others like it, signified on behalf of its subjects a certain self-consciousness that conflated the act of seeing with the readerly consumption of printed forms.

But as much as the activity of leafing through and reading a newspaper lent outline to the engaged and literate self, it also convened and engaged makeshift communities of readers and listeners, conveyers of the news and commentators on it. Like *War News*, pictures such as Calyo's *Astor House Reading Room* and Harrison's *California News* demonstrate the communal nature of reading, either silently or aloud. In each, vision—literally in the act of reading and virtually *via* the act of reading—is converted to sound that reverberates, as the pictures suggest, in compressed spaces. In this way, the depiction of newspapers bridges the "sayable and the seeable," coupling word and image and collapsing oral and written communication in the visual representation of textual documents.[27] These images are as much about consuming news in a shared space as they are about *sharing* the physiological experience of imbibing information—whether from reading the news itself or interpreting the reactions of others—via the eyes and bodies of observing subjects. This is more pronounced in Harrison's daguerreotype, in which three young men cluster around a paper being read aloud, while a younger boy, perhaps the newsboy who has just delivered it, stands in the rear. As indicated by the folded paper being consumed as well as the sheaf of papers on the floor in the center foreground, presumably already digested, the presence of the newspaper in paintings and other images indicates that a transfer of information is taking place. The eager reader and his listeners show no signs of satiation, however. While these newspapers remain largely illegible to viewers, the postures, gestures, and reading practices of the figures depicted convey a sense of the information they contain. As responses to the newspaper's import, facial expressions and bodily gestures assume the functions of media; they refract the picture's meanings. This embodied response to the news also extends outward, beyond the surface of these canvases, in their engagement with the paintings' viewers.

But in Calyo's claustraphobic scene, news readers, though precariousy perched, are absorbed entirely; two of the three figures are obscured to the point of having no identity thus blocking the flow of information from reader to viewer in this community. Deeply engrossed, buried in news, the jaunty, fluid figures of Calyo's circle recall the limber alphabetic letters of Carrington Bowles (see Figure 25), each tightly intertwined with the long, wrinkled sheets of greasy newsprint they devour with lackadasical panache. The interwoven convergence of bodies and text enacts the enfolding of the self into the media machinery of the market economy as well as into a much wider, "imagined community," to borrow Benedict Anderson's phrase. Though the transmission of information takes center stage, the readers' absorption in their papers subverts communal exchange, while the unsettling blankness of the picture's many surfaces impedes clear communication. Puffs of cigar smoke waft upward, filtering the radiant light of the gas lamps for which the hotel was known. The mirror above adds another blank surface to scan, echoing the newspapers that engulf and block our view of the figures below.

Consumed in often crowded quarters, newspapers figuratively opened vistas onto expansive spaces. Filled with news from the far West and the settled East, from the Arctic and the Antarctic, from Europe, Asia, Africa, and elsewhere, newspapers figuratively bridged great distances and connected readers with distant events. In *Two Years Before the Mast* (1840), a memoir of his two-year sea voyage from Boston around the Cape of Good Hope to the coast of California, author Richard Henry Dana Jr. wrote of his luck in procuring a trove of Boston *Transcripts* from the month of August 1835 and "about a dozen *Daily Advertisers* and *Couriers*, of different dates." Relishing the immediacy they offered, even after considerable temporal lag, he wrote: "After all, there is nothing in a strange land like a newspaper from home. It takes you back to the spot, better than anything else. It is almost equal to *clairvoyance*." Grounded in the ocular act of reading, the paper stages for Dana a multisensory experience initated, in this case, by signs and advertisements: "The names of the streets, with the things advertised, is almost as good as seeing the signs; and while reading 'Boy lost!' one can almost hear the bell and well-known voice of 'Old Wilson.'"[28] Linking an eager reader off the coast of California with events and activities in distant Boston, newspapers collapsed space even if time had continued to lapse between their publication and their consumption. For those at the greatest distances, time mattered less than the imaginary transcendence of space.

William Sydney Mount's *California News* of 1850, perhaps a source for Harrison's daguerreotype of the same name, performs this connective work in visual form (Figure 52, Plate 5). Mount's painting depicts the antechamber of a post office, but it collapses the distance between New York and California through a clever, contrapuntal pairing of the picture's two most prominent printed texts. The cover of the *New-York Daily Tribune* in the foreground and the large poster advertising passage to San Francisco vie for the beholder's scrutiny, creating a tension that suggests the enticing pull that the discovery of gold in the West had for easterners during the late 1840s. As the central object of attention, the *Daily Tribune* figuratively looks out on a space named in the poster on the facing wall. Again, the gazes of the painting's many figures further direct the viewer's gaze. An eager couple who stand behind the man holding the newspaper avidly discuss what they are hearing and seeing. As the man points toward the paper, the woman rhapsodically clasps her hands together in an acknolwedgment of the West's great promise and potential. Behind her head, a handbill advertises a farm for sale. The man in the right foreground looks to his left as if in response to another figure who remains out of view. His gaze, however, draws attention to the leaflet on the table featuring the word "CALIFORNIA" in all caps, followed by the provocative phrase, "Look Here!" The gazes of the various figures reveal the stakes such travel may have held

FIGURE 52. William Sidney Mount, *California News*, 1850, oil on canvas.
Long Island Museum, Stony Brook, NY, Gift of Mr. and Mrs. Ward Melville,
1955/Bridgeman Images. (See Plate 5.)

for them. Their spatial arrangement, seen most poignantly in the case of the African
American man marginally situated at the far right, also alludes to their proximity
to such potential. Similarly, Woodville's *War News* depicts a constellation of interested parties, figuratively "stitched" together by the paper that rivets the collective
attention. But the generalized location of the scene on the porch of the "American

FIGURE 53. Johann Peter Hasenclever, *Studio Scene (Atelierszene)*, 1836, oil
on canvas, 28⅓ × 34⅔ in. (72 x 88 cm), Museum Kunstpalast, Dusseldorf,
©Museum Kunstpalast-ARTOTHEK.

Hotel," like the "Post Office" of Mount's painting, leaves the viewer with a lingering sense of dislocatedness. Given the titles of these works, it is presumed that we
are not in Mexico or California. But where exactly do these scenes take place?
Given that Mount painted his scene in New York and Woodville painted *War
News* in Düsseldorf, the compressed, congested spaces of these modestly scaled
paintings begins to open up considerably.

Woodville had sailed for Europe a few years earlier, in May 1845, buoyed by
the modest success of the exhibition of his first oil, a humble picture titled *Two
Figures at a Stove* (1845), at the National Academy of Design in New York. Woodville was reintroduced to the issue of embodiment both by the felt experience of
expatriation from his native country and by rigorous study of the body and figure
drawing at the Düsseldorf Academy. Wilhelm Schadow, an adept administrator

FIGURE 54. Johann Peter Hasenclever, *The Reading Room (Das Lesekabinett)*,
1843, oil on canvas, 28 x 39.4 in. Alte Nationalgalerie, Berlin,
© SZ Photo, Scherl/Bridgeman Images.

who became director in 1826, laid the foundation for the academy's success by reorganizing its curriculum to include a two-year course of preparatory classes where studies from models and drawings from plaster casts were augmented by portrait studies. Only those who had proven themselves in portraiture were allowed to paint the figure. Though Woodville officially enrolled at the academy for only one year, he lived and studied in Düsseldorf for six, from 1845 until 1851.[29] Woodville's figures, though occasionally wooden, bulky, or troll-like—evidence arduous study and meticulous handling. More significantly for Woodville's training, Schadow's tolerance in artistic matters allowed for the establishment of classes in landscape and genre painting, the latter of which provided a venue for Johann Peter Hasenclever, with whom Woodville would come to study.[30]

The condensed scale of Woodville's object-filled spaces and the figures that occupy them reveal Hasenclever's influence, as can be seen in the latter's *Studio Scene* of 1836 (Figure 53) and especially in the crowded arrangement of figures in his 1843 painting, titled *The Reading Room* (Figure 54), which Hasenclever painted

FIGURE 55. Richard Caton Woodville, *The Card Players*, 1846, oil on canvas, 18½ × 25 in. Detroit Institute of Arts, Gift of Dexter M. Ferry Jr./Bridgeman Images. (See Plate 6.)

the year before Woodville arrived in Düsseldorf. Woodville's training there, especially under Hasenclever, taught the young artist how to orchestrate multifigured scenes within compact and compressed compositional frameworks. With their emphasis on the close and confined interaction of handily rendered figures, with their interchange of glances and individualized facial expressions, Woodville's paintings are centrally concerned with embodiment, a preoccupation of his practice as an expatriate artist. But so too is movement and transient mobility. His pictures depict the interstitial, ephemeral spaces of train and stagecoach waiting rooms, oyster cellars, and the porches of hotels or taverns that he, like so many other Americans on the move, momentarily occupied and quickly abandoned. The first painting Woodville made in Düsseldorf, titled *The Card Players*, was completed in 1846, but not exhibited in the United States until the following year (Figure 55, Plate 6).[31] Its realism is immediate and striking. Based on a preparatory drawing of a group of card players huddled around a small table, both drawing and painting already showed signs of the Düsseldorf aesthetic, which emphasized "rigorous figure drawing and pictorial construction allied with a strong penchant for narrative."[32] The "super-realism" of the Düsseldorf style, as one historian of the academy has argued, "cannot be understood without the study of contemporary stage properties, and the shallow foreground of the paintings where the *tableau vivant* was placed." These features lend a theatrical quality to Düsseldorf painting that can also be seen in Woodville's most popular and enduring images.[33] The compressed, object-filled spaces of Woodville's interiors illustrate the extent and reach of the market economy in their emphatic delineation of the materiality of daily life. His paintings situate their figures within congested spaces marked by an accumulation of commodified objects to accentuate their sense of compression and to highlight the commercial nature of the exchanges taking place in them.

The shallow space of the room in *The Card Players* was reduced further in *Politics in an Oyster House*, a small painting Woodville made in early 1848 and exhibited briefly at the Art-Union in May of that year (Figure 56). Nestled into the supper box of an oyster cellar, an older gentlemen and younger man converse; the wooden posts that frame their cozy booth also bracket our view of their intercourse, sparked, we are to presume, by the newspaper the younger man clutches in his hand. The horizontality of *The Card Players* is replaced in the latter picture by strong verticals that contain the action and focus the viewer's attention on the exchange taking place therein. The curtain has been pulled back to reveal the discussion underway; the umbrella, spitoon, and especially the newspaper the man at right holds exceed the painting's flatness to protrude outward just slightly, alluding to the viewer's space before the canvas. This feature of the composition is reinforced by the older man's wearied gaze, which indicates that he has been cornered and looks out at the viewer in a plea for help. A smaller format penny paper has been cast onto the floor near the young man's foot and the discarded butt of a cigar. He grips a larger paper that he has been skimming for the bits of news that fuel his conversation with the older man, who apparently has grown weary of the young man's spirited tirade. As an indication that "clear vision" is no longer required, or even possible given the amount of alcohol consumed or the stream of words pouring from the mouth of his companion, the elder has removed his silver spectacles, which he holds gingerly in his right hand. His partially obscured left hand either braces his slightly resting head or cups his ear either to hear his partner's entreaty

FIGURE 56. Richard Caton Woodville, *Politics in an Oyster House*, 1848, oil on fabric, 16¼ × 13 ¹⁄₁₆ in. Walters Art Museum, Baltimore.

more clearly or to dampen its shrill tone. With dark hair and beard, the top-hatted man's appearance is not unlike that of Woodville himself (see Figure 43), which again underscores the artist as newspaper reader (if not also an animated discussant of the latest headlines). Here, the older man's glass is empty, plates of empty oyster shells have been removed. The booth's gaslight is no longer lit; the younger man has extinguished his last cigar as what clearly has been a heated discussion begins to wind down.

In the cluttered room of the 1846 picture *The Card Players* (see Figure 55, Plate 6), however, things are just ramping up. Viewers' gazes are invited to traverse the congested space seeking clues to the painting's narrative in the numerous objects and surfaces that Woodville so ably articulated in the composition—the traveler's bag, the spitoon and cigar butts scattered about the floor, the old stove at left, the small note tacked to the wall, the cuckoo clock, the framed reproductive print near the painting's center, the framed document under which two faded broadsides hang, or the mirror at right. But time and again, viewers' eyes are brought back to the center where the painting's protagonists are locked in a game of cards, another of the composition's many surfaces, which litter the drop-leaf table linking the players' bodies. The two players, however, are visually divided by the presence of the standing man who leans casually on the table and the long scroll of the playbill. These compositional devices mediate the rising tension of the moment in which a friendly game of cards has taken a turn. Their game, at first glance, appears, in historian Ann Fabian's words, to function as a "reciprocal" economy of equals. But on closer inspection, viewers begin to sense that the game is governed "by relations between strangers and designed to end in assymmetrical accumulations."[34] With cards clutched in his right hand, the man at left looks upward to the standing man in a plea for support, while his left hand points emphatically at a card on the table. The card sharp at right peers directly, even scornfully, at his opponent, chews the stub of his cigar, and methodically stirs his toddy as he awaits his next turn. To guarantee his success, he has surreptitiously tucked a card, barely visible, under his left leg. The relay of gazes, from the dupe and his servant at left to the interlocutor between them, and from the card sharp to his victim, directs that of the painting's viewers in a circuit that continually brings their eyes back to the painting's center. Here, elongated playbills for Baltimore's Front Street Theatre nod to theatrical performance and duplicitious fiction, while broadsides for the stagecoach service between Baltimore and Washington invoke transience, transmision, mobility, and movement. With his carpet bag, top hat, umbrella, and African American attendant behind him,

FIGURE 57. Richard Caton Woodville, *The Card Players*, detail, 1846, oil on canvas, 18½ × 25 in. Detroit Institute of Arts, Gift of Dexter M. Ferry Jr./Bridgeman Images.

FIGURE 58. Illustration of refraction in Robert Evans Peterson and John Henry Pepper, *Peterson's Familiar Science: Or The Scientific Explanation Of Common Things*. Revised edition (Philadelphia: Sower, Potts, & Co., 1863), 462. Courtesy of the Smithsonian Libraries, Washington, DC.

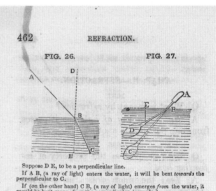

Suppose D E, to be a perpendicular line.

If A B, (a ray of light) enters the water, it will be bent *towards* the perpendicular to C.

If (on the other hand) C B, (a ray of light) emerges *from* the water, it would be bent *away from* the perpendicular towards A.

1690.

Q. Why does an *oar* in water appear bent?

A. Because the part *out* of the water is seen in a different medium to the part *in* the water; and the rays of these two parts, meeting together at the surface of the river, *form an angle*—or in other words, make the oar look as if it were bent.

N. B. As all rays of light are refracted (or bent) more in their passage through *water* than in their passage through *air*, they will tend to cross each other at the surface of the water, and, of course, form an elbow or angle.

1691.

Q. Why does a *spoon* (in a glass of water) always appear *bent*?

A. Because the light (reflected from the

the figure on the left is clearly on the move while the figure at right, with a presumably winning hand in his clutch, is stealthily on the make.

Though the painting's key figures are arranged in the composition on relatively equal footing, viewers are alerted to the asymmetrical exchange taking place. Along with the card secretly tucked under the card sharp's left leg, the drink that he stirs offers another subtle clue that things are out of joint (Figure 57). Frequently called on to demonstrate the optical principle of refraction, the image of a spoon resting in or stirring a glass partially filled with liquid appeared with considerable frequency in scientific primers such as the popular *Boy's Own* books and *Peterson's Familiar Science* (Figure 58). An 1846 article in *Scientific American* explained that "refraction is produced as rays of light are bent from their ordinary direction by passing through an oblique surface of any transparent body."[35] As evidenced earlier in the work of the McAllister and Peale families and vividly illustrated in Rembrandt Peale's *Rubens Peale with a Geranium* (see Figure 15), the science of catoptrics, or the study of reflection and reflective surfaces, had largely been abandoned during the first decades of the nineteenth century in favor of growing attention to dioptrics, or the study of refraction. Refrangibility, a term designating the effect, or degree of light or information passing through bodies, was central to the ground lenses of spectacles, microscopes, and telescopes. The principles of refrangibility and refraction circulated even more widely in metaphoric terms as references to the bending of truth involved in the deception and dissimulation characteristic of the fluid and financially wreckless culture of the 1840s and '50s. In the fluctuating antebellum economy, driven by a "go ahead" ethos of rapid gain, fortunes could be won or lost at the roll of the dice, the flip of a card, the drawing of a lottery ticket, or the exchange of a banknote. Gamesters, gamblers, and crooked salesmen preyed on those eager to get rich quick with underhanded dealings and other speculative ventures, as we will see in the next chapter. The bent spoon reappears in Woodville's 1851 painting *Waiting for the Stage* (Figure 59, Plate 7), which turns the composition of *The Card Players* at an oblique angle to further underscore that things are out of balance. In both images, a toddy awaiting a stir is no longer a toddy but a subtle clue that in these card games between strangers the straight truth has been bent. In *Waiting for the Stage*, the glass and spoon are part of a constellation of ocular and optical motifs that populate the relatively close quarters of the waiting room (Figure 60). With head framed perfectly by the gilded mirror behind him, the man standing at center, nonchalantly holds a newspaper aptly titled *The Spy*. While the paper's masthead features a lurk-

FIGURE 59. Richard Caton Woodville, *Waiting for the Stage*, 1851, oil on canvas, 15 × 18⅛ in. Corcoran Collection, National Gallery of Art, Washington, DC, Museum Purchase, Gallery Fund, William A. Clark Fund, and through gifts of Mr. and Mrs. Lansdell K. Christie and Orme Wilson/ Bridgeman Images. (See Plate 7.)

ing, monocular eye, he sports a pair of four-lens or double-lens eyeglasses. With additional lenses hinged to each side of the temple that rotated behind the first, these were intended, in some cases, to change the optics and in others to add color for therapeutic effect. But for Woodville's dandified grifter they seem mostly likely intended to obfuscate the direction of his gaze. The sagging sheet of newsprint intervenes between the players, while the masthead's monocular eye peers down on the game underway and lurks outwardly, into the space of the painting's beholder. So too do the eyes of the man purportedly reading *The Spy*, who upon

FIGURE 60. Richard Caton Woodville, *Waiting for the Stage*, detail, 1851, oil on canvas, 15 × 18⅛ in. Corcoran Collection, National Gallery of Art, Washington, DC, Museum Purchase, Gallery Fund, William A. Clark Fund, and through gifts of Mr. and Mrs. Lansdell K. Christie and Orme Wilson/ Bridgeman Images.

closer inspection clearly, yet furtively gazes directly and deliberately into the eyes of the painting's beholder, positioned here as an unseen third accomplice in this fraudlent game of cards. Amid this cluttered space of mobile exchange and fluid relations, the regulatory optics of the newspaper's monocular eye no longer held sway. Instead, with vision metaphorically doubled in the man's four-lens eyeglasses and the straight truth bent or refracted, the gazes of the three conspirators—two in the painting and one imagined—triangulate on their unwitting victim. Forever on the move, card sharps, like the daily newspapers and the impressions they left, were there and gone in the blink of an eye.

In *War News from Mexico* (see Figure 44, Plate 4), Woodville reprised a number of elements from earlier pictures. These include the booth's posts from *Politics in an Oyster House*, as well as the printed ephemera, the telling facial gestures of the figures, and the outwardly oriented, theatrical stage-like setting of this picture and *The Card Players*. In *War News'* highly charged composition, however, the newspaper is repositioned; instead of a prompt to conversation, a prop thrust aside within the picture or silent witness to crooked card games, the newspaper is now central. Situated in an upright position, ready for reading, the paper functions as the composition's pivotal centerpiece, its narrative fulcrum, its pictorial center of gravity. Indeed, in *War News from Mexico*, we are confronted with a painting in which the activity of "looking at words" preoccupies both its numerous figures and its viewers. [36] As if to clue us in to this activity, the monocular eye seen on the newspaper's masthead in *Waiting for the Stage* reappears here in the beautifully rendered terminus of the single peacock feather that sticks out from the straw hat in the foreground. Just off center and leaning against the corked jug near the foot of the African American man, its presence might suggest that the clarity of the nation's "vision," forged by the founding fathers and represented by the all-seeing eye of the national seal, had been recklessly trampled under foot, as critics of the conflict suggested. In his 1847 "Speech on the Mexico-American War," Kentucky senator Henry Clay reinforced this bleak view: "The day is dark and gloomy, unsettled and uncertain, like the condition of our country, in regard to the unnatural war with Mexico. The public mind is agitated and anxious, and is filled with serious apprehensions as to its indefinite continuance, and especially as to the consequences which its termination may bring forth, menacing the harmony, if not the existence, of our Union."[37] Though the two-year war's continuance was not "indefinite," as Clay feared, ambiguities remained regarding the war's outcome and its ramifications for the young nation.

The hotel's ramshackle, though classically styled portico frames our view of the central action. A canilevered signboard featuring the bald eagle and "E Pluribus Unum," Latin for "out of many, one" of the national seal, and the words "American Hotel" grace the pediment above while a hand-painted post office sign pointing the way inside and, below it, a handbill calling for volunteers to join the fight punctuate its worn columns (Figure 61). A cluster of small broadsides, indecipherable even under magnification, hangs to the left of the doorway. Another broadside at right advertises horses for sale. The conjunction of so many typefaces—from the Roman faces seen in the signboard for the American Hotel and the post office signs to the thickly serifed Egyptian types of the word "EXTRA" on the front page of the newspaper—recall the visual cacaphony of the broadside cluttered "dead walls" and sign-filled streets examined earlier. Evidence of print's ubiquity in public spaces, these signs and printed forms—a call for volunteers, an advertisement for horses, and other illegible notices—also serve as indicators of a rapidly growing infrastructure for the transfer of information and

FIGURE 61. Richard Caton Woodville, *War News from Mexico*, detail, 1848, oil on canvas. Crystal Bridges Museum of American Art, Bentonville, AK, 2010.74, Photography by Walters Art Museum, Baltimore, Susan Tobin.

the perceptual requirements necessary for discerning, deciphering, and decoding this profusion.

This attention to the delicate rendering and visual scrutiny of paper surfaces in painting, of course, long predates the antebellum era. Svetlana Alpers's reading of the pictorial representation of words, particularly in the form of written letters seen in paintings of the Dutch golden age, is instructive here.[38] As she argues, Dutch paintings from this period devoted themselves to description over narrative, an endeavor that stemmed from the culture's obsession with observation, optics, and "describing the world as seen."[39] The depiction of words, whether on maps, inscriptions, or letters, extends the descriptive project into the representation of the minutiae of daily life, but hardly without significance. Alpers suggests that pictures of figures depicted in the act of reading letters convey information about both reader and sender, about the here and there represented or alluded to. In so doing, as Alpers suggests, letters in pictures function metaphorically in a lens-like capacity, bringing into "focus" persons, events, or things that remain out of view. During the Mexican War, newspapers drew much of their content from letters sent eastward by officers, soldiers, and correspondents at or near the front lines. Such letters provided the bulk of the media's *eyewitness* coverage, often casting personal correspondence as national news. Carried out of Mexico by express riders on horseback or transported by railroad or steamboat, these missives were then translated into the dots and dashes of Morse code for transmission over hundreds of miles of copper wires to cities back East. There are, in fact, a number of epistolary aspects to Woodville's newspaper. Its creased and crumpled look indicates that it has traveled for an extended period of time over great distances, increasing the anticipation with which it has been eagerly unfolded on its arrival.

Dated 1848, the painting likely depicts the receipt of news detailing the war's culminating battle in September 1847, yet outright glee is tempered by a sense of uncertainty (see Figure 44). Indeed, the unifying experience of receiving the news elicts a diverse and varied response. The American Art-Union's 1849 *Bulletin* made this point beautifully. "As an "exhibition of character and feeling," the reviewer wrote, "how admirable is the whole group!"

> How much unity and completeness it possesses! How well the individual peculiarities of each person represented are shown beneath the momentary feeling of common interest which animates them all! The slouching bar-keeper, whom nothing but the recital of something astounding could have drawn from his bottles, is an entirely different sort of person in character and manners, from the free-and-easy, shabby genteel rowdy, who has just taken his cigar from his mouth in order to listen with more intentness. The vacant, unexcited aspect of the aged deaf man, into whose ear a friend is shouting the account of the battle, gives significance to the noisy exultation of the boy who is swinging his cap in the back-ground, and who evidently will be one of the first to volunteer for the war. The old negro sitting upon the step is life itself. [40]

Their varied responses to the news underscores how the figures see the events in their own subjective way.

However "complete" or "unified" the composition, the painting, with its various pairings, remains a study in contrasts. In this depiction of what art historian Elizabeth Johns considered a cross-section of the American populace that invoked the "character of the citizenry," a spectrum of responses from pensive misgiving to cautious optimism animates the scene.[41] Another set of pairings highlight for Woodville the contrasting ways of receiving information that underscores how the various individuals may have seen the highly contentious war with Mexico. Emerging from the doorway, a man, presumably the barkeeper, peers over the

FIGURE 62. Richard Caton Woodville, *War News from Mexico*, detail, 1848, oil on canvas. Crystal Bridges Museum of American Art, Bentonville, AK, 2010.74, Photography by Walters Art Museum, Baltimore, Susan Tobin.

shoulder of the man holding the paper (Figure 62). Resituating his silver-framed spectacles, he gazes intently, though with strained scrutiny. His reliance on the visual, and the view his spectacles afford him, is as pronounced as the "aged deaf man" at right's reliance on the aural. The former is a man of his historical moment, a member of the generation of 1848, or young '48 as Woodville would elsewhere label him; the latter, Old '76, is a representative of the Revolutionary generation, as indicated by his knee breaches and his reluctance to get his news from a printed source rather than by word of mouth. In another of Woodville's Mexican War paintings, titled *Old '76 and Young '48* (1849), an older gentleman (Old '76) listens to news of action at the front from a soldier (Young '48). The competing viewpoints of these two figures in particular, especially their distinct ways of processing and embodying information, bookend these compositions—while the elder man relies on sound and oral transmission, the other clearly relies on eyesight and the consumption of printed information. The seated elder alludes to the perceptual sensibilities of the Revolutionary generation, manifested in the physical immediacy of public proclamations, a largely manuscript-based medium of exchange, and a modest print culture circulated within a limited, relatively transparent public sphere.[42] The energetic gestures of the younger men articulate aspects of an antebellum scopic regime, shaped, as I have been suggesting, by technological, economic, and political forces; by a profusion of popular media, by a new understanding of the body's corporeality and perceptual capacities, and by the way the culture at large confronted and conquered physical space. But during the 1840s and 1850s, racial and ideological divides were the most divisive and difficult to bridge.

The debate over the Mexican War centered on the hotly contested issue of slavery's expansion into newly won territories. In another subtle arrangement of opposites in the painting, Woodville, born and raised in the border state of Maryland, sensitively acknowledges this tension. This pairing involves the two African American figures at right with the rest of the group. The status of their "blackness" is reinforced by the "whiteness," both of the newspaper and the human faces of the figures closest to it. Whether slave or free, the fate of the African American man and that of the child next to him effectively hang in the balance. Both figures watch and listen intently to glean an impression of what for them was to come. Though separated from the main group, the bold red of the man's shirt pulls the viewer's gaze diagonally upward and leftward across the picture to the red of the handkerchief jutting out of the coat pocket of the man rapping on the building's wooden frame and the red sign offering horses for sale. But his gaze actually appears fastened on the facial response of the card sharp at left, who along with his possible accomplice, the hatted man craning his neck at far right, exhibits an eagerness to the make the most of the opportunities that the war provided for shiftless men like him to "get ahead" through gambling or other nefarious enterprises. And while the cramped portico is populated exclusively by enfranchised men, a lone woman looks inquisitively out of the window at right to see what all the fuss is about. Her sideways glance and open mouth suggest how difficult it is to get a clear view of things from an oblique angle. It also seems to suggest that she is always the last one to hear. The centrifigal force of political, economic, and imperialist energies push outward to the composition's edges and beyond the picture frame, while the centripetal gravity of the newspaper's pull continually drags viewers' gazes back to the painting's center, perhaps a result of the eyes' constant effort to center their objects. Neveretheless, these contrasting elements of Woodville's composition are tethered together by the unifying act of witnessing the relay of information. Yet the picture teeters on the brink of bursting at the proverbial seams as each figure subjectively perceives the information in his or her own way.

Gathered around the consumption of what many then regarded as nearly "instantaneous" news—a retelling of actual events refracted through the multilayered prism of eyewitness reporting; transmission via horse and rider, railroad, steamboat, or, increasingly, telegraph; editorial adjustment, typesetting, printing, distribution, and finally, reading—the eleven figures set within Woodville's cramped composition relay to the painting's viewers the import and implications of news they have gathered to read and hear. For again, while the painting's viewers cannot actually read much of the newspapers' text, they are better equipped to "read" figures' facial expressions and gestures. With mouth agape, the central figure, for instance, eagerly scans the paper's fine print, as the barkeeper emerges from the open doorway, peers over his shoulder, and adjusts his spectacles to obtain a clearer view. The card sharp rowdy attentively peers toward the painting's center as does his counterpart at far right, while the other young man raises his hat in patriotic exaltation. The slouching man at left stares more soberly into space as he knocks on the wood of the hotel's rickety exterior. Indeed their varied responses to the newspaper are what capitvate viewers and, more significantly, participate in the newspaper's optic. Here, bodies refract, reflect, and relay the import of the paper's reportage, itself already a derivation of original impressions of events conveyed through a dazzling array of media. As viewers peruse the figures' bodies, costumes, and activities, it is one particular element of their surroundings, namely the optical effect of the painter's delineation of print, that draws and redraws viewers' attention, inviting yet confusing their gazes. Indeed, the painted words in *War News* are visually fleeting, at best. Letters and words oscillate in and out of focus; headlines are prominent but page text generally remains unreadable. As an interesting painterly effect, the blur of the words replicates the experience of catching a glimpse of a headline in passing, the flux of objects moving in space, and the inability of the eye to focus on them. These renderings, and the optical experience of them, continually draw viewers' attention back to the marked surface of Woodville's canvas.[43] Though it circulated as one of numerous images of newspaper readers during the mid to late 1840s, Woodville's painting took a radically different approach in depicting the receipt of news. In so doing, the painting frames a view of embodied perception modified by the mediation of telegraphic newspapers and by an array of refractive bodies that have relevance for the figures in the painting as well as for Woodville himself as he conceived and executed the work.[44] As mentioned earlier, and as the Art-Union's review of the painting suggests, all figures on and off the porch are implicated by the war news. This network of implication is rendered visually in the pictorial interconnectedness of their bodies—all of the figures, including the woman in the window, pictorially overlap—reflecting the interwovenness of their perceptual experiences even as their physical proximity diminished with rapid national expansion from coast to coast. It is this embodied tension, especially in relation to an increasingly elongated visual field, that makes this painting so compelling. Its compressed depth of field references a much wider world.

*War News from Mexico* alludes to this process, the burst of energy at the painting's center suggestive of the nation's sense of itself as increasingly expansive, yet politcally fractious. Each of the painting's figures faces the challenging prospect of achieving a sense of "wholeness" and "unity"—the words used by the Art-Union's *Bulletin* to describe Woodville's composition—amid what Ralph Waldo Emerson called a "world of surfaces," a reference to the pervasively visual world in which artists like he and Woodville lived and worked.[45] Just as newspapers figuratively afforded Americans a longer, broader view, horizons for art and art making expanded in nineteenth-century America, in part, because of peripatetic painters like Woodville. His staged scenes of card players and newspaper readers illustrate a generally informed populace on the move and thus subjected to the flux of mobile perceptions, fleeting glances, and ephemeral impressions. His paintings illustrate how the infrastructure for human perception had been entirely reconstructed to accommodate the telegraphic transmission of instantaneous news and to rewire human bodies in accordance with the impulses, rhythms, and mandates of life in a market-centered, though geographically dispersed, society.

That Woodville's painting seems so interested in addressing these issues gives us reason to pause before his intensive, exquisitely detailed works. His pictures thematize print-oriented visual culture as immersive and posit vision as a multistage process. They collapse entire networks of communication, entire epistemological systems into the compressed pictorial spaces of cabinet paintings. They thematize the fluctuating status of embodied perception in the mid-nineteenth century and elucidate the complex cognitive codes that lent shape to the meanings they held for their original audiences. Like Peale's *Rubens Peale with*

a *Geranium*, Spencer's *Newsboy*, and Charles's *Modern Spectacles Easily Seen Through*, *War News* encodes information about the culturally specific act of seeing, about the fluctuating nature of visual perception and the shifting status of observing subjects, both within and without their compositions. Woodville's paintings delineate aspects of what I have called a culturing of vision, exemplified in the practice of reading typographic lettering on broadsides, maps, and newspapers. Such practices lent shape to antebellum observers' cognitive stock and honed their perceptual skills to visually assess texts and objects near at hand, or to utilize such objects to see, literally as well as figuratively, in greater depth and at greater distances. Created in a historical moment in which ophthalmology and optometry had just begun to gain their footing as institutional practices, and in which urban populations and the images and texts that populated their visual fields multiplied exponentially, Woodville's paintings also demonstrate certain ways in which the period eye of a particular epoch was conceptualized, measured, and tested. They reflect a cultural formation of vision as an embodied phenomenon and foreground the viewing practices encouraged by the very forms of media that helped Americans in the mid-nineteenth century realize the nature and the limits of vision's embodiment.

In spite of antebellum culture's increased economic investment in and medical scrutiny of the body, the acts of reading and viewing its vast proliferation of texts and images both augmented and attenuated selfhood. The practice of reading telegraphic newspaper reports posited a self premised on the embodiment of the dematerialized and disembodied information surging through the telegraph's taut wires. But it metaphorically enacted the process of stringing oneself out, accordion-like, across space and time. This is a fitting analogue for Woodville as an expatriate artist known primarily in his native country as a mediated entity inscribed in the surfaces of the periodicals, prints, and paintings that won him fame. As these forms extended his artistic reputation, the fullness of his embodied subjectivity was attenuated while America's growing empire, an empire of the eye transformed by an expansive and intensive empire of signs, augmented itself through territorial expansion. Undoubtedly, *War News from Mexico*, in its various forms, participated in and, ultimately, helped to facilitate this process.

The newspaper paintings of Woodville (and others) both emblematized and operated within an emerging scopic regime that coalesced across a wide range of institutional spaces, social practices, and perceptual as well as representational techniques. As such, Woodville's paintings enacted what W. J. T. Mitchell calls a "suturing of discourse and representation" that effectively enabled the virtual seeing over the horizon that antebellum Americans eagerly sought.[46] They brought together the concerns of painting with techniques of typecasting and printing, with discourses of reading, and with theories of visual perception—both scientific and vernacular. They are indicative of antebellum visual culture in that they critically reflect on the nature and function of eyesight and mark, in rather bold form, what were subtly felt shifts in the collective understanding of visual perception, a shift that realigned the "noblest of senses" with the demands of life in a rapidly expanding nation animated by the mechanisms of a bustling market society.

## ⇜ CHAPTER SIX ⇝

# Paper Money, Spectral Illusions, and the Limits of Vision

In the decades following the volatile Panic of 1837—an economic breakdown resulting from the expansion and then sudden retraction of the paper currency that facilitated rampant speculation in land—a lively discourse excoriated the perennial instability of paper money, likened banknotes to evanescent traces, even ghosts, of real value, and equated their exchange with gambling and games of chance. The territorial expansion westward alluded to in Richard Caton Woodville's painting *War News from Mexico* was spurred on by speculation in lands fringing the outer limits of settled territory. Facilitated by the use of schematic maps and fraudulent land deeds, speculation typically involved the purchase of properties sight unseen, often paid with banknotes of wildly fluctuating value. Fluid, unstable, evanescent, some would even say ghostlike, the paper money economy that enabled and facilitated rampant speculation was yet another facet of a broader culture of paper goods and printed materials. The shaky and unstable economic system that paper money created, as President Andrew Jackson warned when leaving office in 1838, behooved Americans to become "more watchful," as the "wild spirit of speculation" threatened to "withdraw their attention from the sober pursuits of honest industry."[1] In an atmosphere animated by a "go-ahead" spirit and punctuated by cycles of boom and bust, of prosperity and panic, the scrutiny of banknotes and maps that outlined the boundaries of land parcels beyond the horizon required visual acuity as well as a healthy dose of squint-eyed skepticism.

In 1852, New York banker and painter Francis W. Edmonds completed *The Speculator*, a composition begun over a decade earlier (Figure 63, Plate 8).[2] Edmonds first sketched ideas for this picture in the wake of the 1837 panic (Figure 64), the very turmoil that inspired Ralph Waldo Emerson's mystic declaration of the ocular age in which he lived. The canvas places the viewer in the interior of a small cottage, where a farmer and his wife have momentarily suspended their

FIGURE 63. Francis W. Edmonds, *The Speculator*, 1852, oil on canvas, 25⅛ × 30⅛ in. Smithsonian American Art Museum, Washington, DC, Gift of Ruth C. and Kevin McCann in affectionate memory of Dwight David Eisenhower, 34th President of the United States. (See Plate 8.)

chores at the entreaty of a dandified land speculator, like the newsboy and the card sharp, one of the period's many recognizable character "types."[3] Despite the agent's congenial appearance, the closed door and the slightly congested space of the room underscore the intrusive nature of his visit. Together, farmer and wife inspect the map he has just unfurled. On its surface, the schematic lines forming the boundaries of "1000 Valuable Lots" jut outward, skeleton-like, from the winding spine of "Railroad Ave." The couple's eyes focus on the area of the map indicated by the agent's pointing finger, a gesture that draws the attention of the

FIGURE 64. Francis W. Edmonds, *Untitled Sketch*, n.d., graphite on paper, 3⅜ × 2½ in. William L. Clements Collection, University of Michigan, Ann Arbor.

painting's viewers as well, positioning all beholders as interested parties, as speculators, in the depicted exchange.[4]

Pitting rustic farmer against urbane real estate agent, Edmonds articulated this scene in the terms of an economic debate then raging between proponents of agricultural subsistence and small production and promoters of unbridled commerce and mechanized industry. As traditional cultures of subsistence farming, artisanal labor, and barter gave way to a spreading cash- and wage-based system, a new set of beliefs and behaviors animated production and consumption. Jacksonian rhetoric favored the gradual accumulation of wealth that resulted from honest manual work. But many embraced instead the go-ahead spirit of speculators and other commercial men who sought to grow rich, as critics charged, without labor. Though it framed a skeptical view of land speculation and its allure for hardworking farmers and others eager to get ahead without arduous labor, the true target of the painting's social commentary, given Edmonds's intimate familiarity with its economic and cultural implications, was the circulation of paper money that helped to facilitate, even bolster its practice. Amid this paper econ-

FIGURE 65. Draper, Toppan & Co., Engravers, $2 banknote, Mechanics'
Bank, New York, 1840s, India paper proof on card. Scripophilly.com—
The Gift of History.

omy, currency, credit, and credibility were inscribed in quickly engraved and
widely circulated notes; hence, truth and true value were as fleeting and ephemeral as the paper on which they were printed. The agent's map and sheaths of
paper spilling from his coat pockets make reference to this fluid currency.

"By no means the most polished work of this facetious and fertile painter,"
wrote the *Literary World* of Edmonds's painitng, "it is, however, with this, as with
everything else he does, even to the discounting of a bill, handsomely and unreservedly done."[5] Indeed, in some sense, *The Speculator* echoes the structural logic,
the allegorical import, and even the crisp degree of delineation typical of period
banknotes (Figure 65). As an apprentice engraver who created them early in his
career, and later as a banker who "discounted" them, Edmonds knew the paper
money economy inside and out. In Edmonds's composition and its handling of the
fall of light, all attention is given to the figure of the agent, who points to a map of
land parcels abutting the serpentine curve of Railroad Avenue, a "picture city on
paper," in the words of the Universalist minister Theophilus Fisk, one of paper
money's most vociferous critics.[6] Nestled into a dense shield of white pigment, the
map's graphic is precise, crisp, and linear, yet its schematic is fragmented, its lines
skeletal, its specificity of detail lacking. As the thickness of the scroll in the salesman's hand indicates, there is plenty more. Nevertheless, though rich with potential value, it remains a fictive promise, a ruse written formally and optically in the
map's fugitive details as they oscillate in and out of focus.

By the 1840s, paper was the central medium for exchange across the cultural
landscape, perennially before the eyes of a populace increasingly reliant on the
transmission of printed information in all its myriad forms. In a culture in which

paper stood for specie, land, or other products, paper also served to define individuals—through diaries, wills, land deeds, or bills of sale—and occasionally, for those who produced or conusmed too much of it, facilitated their undoing.[7] Amid such printed profusion, vision was often pushed to its limits. Consumed in great quantities, printed materials provided a source of ocular impairment for those who worked in the clerical trades as well as for readers at large. Like Edward Tailer, the clerk whose faltering vision threatened his professional advancement, Herman Melville's forlorn copyist, Bartleby the Scrivener, first introduced a year after Edmonds's painting, was another such victim. But paper also provided a stage for experimentation in the emerging field of physiological optics, which investigated the eyes' functions and malfunctions as constituent components of "modern" vision. Though it echoed the "self-tests" that involved reading the fine print of a newspaper or sign from various distances as prescribed by Johann Franz, John McAllister Jr., and Daniel Widdifield, as well as the specialized broadsides and standardized eye test charts that evolved from them, the use of paper in clinical experiments took a different turn. Instead of determining precision, they were purposely deployed in clinical settings and makeshift laboratories to document the imprecision and unpredictability that haunted the limits of properly functioning vision. Just as great effort was expended in measuring and delineating what comprised the range of normal vision, the outer thresholds of perception, experienced firsthand by overworked clerical workers, bookkeepers, and authors, were also being explored by physiologists through rigorous experiments. These involved exerting pressure on the eyeballs and staring directly into the sun or obliquely at candles and sheets of white paper. Documenting the "accidental colors," "subjective haloes," and "spectral illusions" resulting from such experiments, proto-physiologists such as Johann Wolfgang von Goethe and Czech specialist Jan Evangelista Purkinje situated these phenomena as crucial components of sight.

For others, such spectral illusions pointed in the direction of the kinds of extrasensory perception that might enable communication with spiritual forces beyond the visible realm.[8] The eyes, as natural philosopher Sir David Brewster wrote, acted as sentinels between the "worlds of matter and spirit," leading some to investigate ocular spectra and other illusions within the context of spiritualism, a highly popular midcentury movement premised on communication with the departed. In fact, the year after Edmonds completed his painting, his brother, the powerful Democratic judge John Worth Edmonds, published a major treatise on the subject. Though *The Speculator* is articulated in the purportedly straightforward manner of antebellum genre painting, it meditates on the subjective nature of eyesight and the ambiguities of vision, a theme that also preoccupies Melville's ill-fated domestic novel, *Pierre*, published the same year. Edmonds's painting in particular discloses the overlapping ways in which paper money economics and subjective visual phenomena came to define modern conceptions of eyesight in a period of rapid, even reckless, economic development.[9]

Born in Hudson, New York, Edmonds demonstrated early on a keen interest in art. Frustrated by a failed attempt to apprentice with master engraver Gideon Fairman, he determined to educate himself in the rudiments of drawing, coloring, and composition as well as the techniques of engraving. Drawing "for the plate" and engraving, especially for the banknotes so prevalent at the time, were profitable pursuits, eventually earning the young artist fifteen dollars a day.[10] His fortunes shifted in 1823, however, when an uncle gave him his first opportunity in banking as an under clerk at the Tradesman's Bank in New York City. For nearly three years, while Edmonds devoted himself to his new employment, he gradually found ways to incorporate artistic study into his busy schedule, devoting spare time to engraving and evening classes at the newly founded National Academy of Design. During this formative period, Edmonds weighed career options. In letters to his older brother, John Worth Edmonds, the young man lamented the instability of banking in an era marked by wild fluctuations in currency and widespread mistrust of banks. In a letter dated January 22, 1829, Edmonds expressed doubt about the permanence of his clerk position and predicted in terms that linked banking with risk-prone games of chance that he would only be able to become a cashier "at some future day *by good luck* (for I am *convinced* it is by nothing else)."[11] At the Academy of Design, he cemented friendships with other engravers including George Hatch, a pupil of Asher B. Durand with whom he shared rooms, and met painters William Sidney Mount and William Page. Perhaps owing to their influence, Edmonds soon began working in oils and exhibited his first painted work at the academy in 1829, when he became an associate member. His star as an artist was beginning to rise, but his star as a banker was rising even faster. The brisk financial winds of the day swept Edmonds into the cashiership of the newly opened Leather Manufacturers' Bank in Wall Street in 1832. Second in command only to the president, the bank's cashier commonly oversaw or had his hand in nearly all aspects of daily

FIGURE 66. Henry R. Robinson, *The Downfall of Mother Bank*, 1833,
lithograph on wove paper, 23.2 × 33.7 cm. Library of Congress,
Prints & Photographs Division.

business. Edmonds balanced the bank's ledgers, extended loans, and discounted notes presented by customers.[12]

As Edmonds assumed his post, American banking was entering one of the most tumultuous periods in its history. That year President Andrew Jackson's removal and redistribution of the federal deposits dealt a crushing blow to the Second Bank of the United States. Note the electrifying effect of Jackson's unscrolled sheet and the placement of his characteristic top hat in the 1833 cartoon, *The Downfall of Mother Bank* published by Henry R. Robinson (Figure 66). Jackson redeposited these funds in seven state or "pet banks," a loose consortium that included the Mechanics' Bank of New York, where Edmonds would later serve as cashier. In the following years hundreds of new state banks opened and issued banknotes for amounts far in excess of the specie held in their vaults. As the ratio of specie in the vault to paper in circulation fluctuated, the value of each bank's

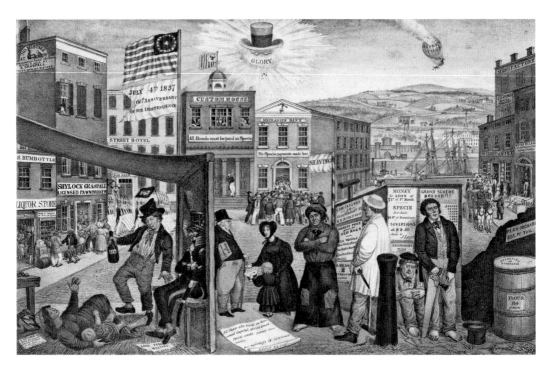

FIGURE 67. Edward Williams Clay (1799–1857) and Henry R. Robinson
(d. 1850), *The Times*, 1837, print, 11.13 × 18.15 in. Museum of the
City of New York.

notes varied according to time, place, and circumstance. Although they pointed
out the problems of an economic system premised on the circulation of paper
notes, Jackson's policies did more to exacerbate economic instability than to relieve or eradicate it. In an attempt to curb the growing mania for speculation,
Jackson issued the Specie Circular in 1836, which required land offices to accept
only gold and silver in payment for public lands. This move placed undue burdens
on overextended banks, contributing to the Panic of 1837 in which the boom and
bust economy finally collapsed.[13]

Edward Clay's lithographic cartoon *The Times*, another Robinson publication,
shows in panoramic breadth and brutal depth the harsh realities of an unstable
paper economy (Figure 67). Our view of this chaotic scene centers on the Mechanics' Bank. The sign across its façade under which a cash-hungry mob has
gathered reads "No Specie Payments Made Here," but as the sign above the entrance to the Custom House next door mockingly stipulates, "All Bonds Must Be
Paid in Specie." Without recourse to paper or specie, the scene's many wage earn-

ers, the ones most susceptible to faulty notes, are clearly the hardest hit.[14] Listless workingmen are scattered throughout Clay's scene. The top-hatted man staggering drunk at left is balanced by the sobering portrait of a barefooted carpenter in the right foreground who holds his saw and hammer idly before him as he looks heavenward in search of relief. Pasted on the wall of the small structure behind him is a broadside advertising a "grand scheme" and other enticements to join the fluctuating paper economy in vain attempts to "get ahead." High above, a corona of sorts emanates from a floating assemblage of Jackson's characteristic top hat, clay pipe, and spectacles, which emblemaized his shortsighted policies. These telling objects emerge from a cloud-like puff of smoke marked "glory." Radiating outward, bands of golden light reminiscent of the specie Jackson treasured shower down over Clay's lithographic city on paper and what has become the legacy of his failed attempts to stabilize a perennially unstable antebellum economy. Though grounded in hard currency, and hard rhetoric, the "ghost" of Jackson's legacy haunted the cultural field of antebellum America.

Jackson's call for vigilance and the anxiety attending his policies find representation in Edmonds's 1838 drawing *The Paper City*, the artist's first fully articulated take on speculation (Figure 68). Here, the "spirit of cold calculation" animates the exchange. The term "paper city" referred to a town that was proposed, not actually extant, at the time of its advertisement or sale. These paper or "lithographic" cities, wrote Theophilus Fisk, "dazzled the eyes of beholders," luring thousands like the man depicted here to leave their farms and workshops "in the vain hope of growing rich in a day."[15] Mirage-like, the scene in *The Paper City* is detached from place and floats in the empty space of the sheet. The tight vignette echoes in slightly expanded form the elliptic register of scenes drafted for antebellum banknotes. Yet the drawing fails to adequately translate into allegory the narrative tension of the scene it depicts. Speculation in land and real estate expanded considerably over the next decade as a result of the proliferation of state-issued banknotes. But the practice also benefited from the circulation of counterfeits, which further qualified and thus undermined confidence in the value of every "legitimate" banknote in circulation. In *A Nation of Counterfeiters: Capitalists, Con Men, and the Making of the United States*, historian Stephen Mimh suggests that the world of banking was paralleled by a "shadow economy" of counterfeiters and fake notes.[16] Every legitimate note in circulation, he argues, had a ghostly double, a point not lost on period economists, writers, and cartoonists who exploited the spectral in withering critiques of the instability and ephemerality of paper money economics. Edmonds's ideas for how to fully expose speculation's threat would continue to gestate over the

FIGURE 68. Francis W. Edmonds, *The Paper City*, 1838, watercolor, black ink, and graphite on paper, 8¼ × 7 in. (21 × 17.8 cm), Collection of the New-York Historical Society.

next decade, becoming infused with the tropes and motifs of an economic discourse that likened paper notes to ghosts.

The financial crises of the late 1830s culminated decades of debate between proponents of hard money and paper over the federal government's role in the production and dissemination of a national currency. No less than the revolutionary agitator Thomas Paine, author of *Common Sense*, critiqued the circulation of paper money in place of specie along these lines. "Gold and silver," Paine wrote, "are the emissions of nature: paper is the emission of art. The value of gold and silver is ascertained by the quantity which nature has made in the earth. . . . Its

PLATE 1. Rembrandt Peale, *Rubens Peale with a Geranium*, 1801, oil on canvas, 28⅛ × 24 in. (See Figure 15.)

PLATE 2. Frederick Spencer, *The Newsboy*, oil on canvas. (See Figure 23.)

PLATE 3. John Hill (engraver), after Thomas Hornor (artist), W. Neale (printer), Joseph Stanley and Company (publisher), *Broadway, New-York, Showing Each Building from the Hygeian Depot Corner of Canal Street to beyond Niblo's Garden*, 1836, hand-colored etching. (See Figure 41.)

**PLATE 4.** Richard Caton Woodville, *War News from Mexico*, 1848, oil on canvas. (See Figure 44.)

PLATE 5. William Sidney Mount, *California News*, 1850, oil on canvas.
(See Figure 52.)

PLATE 6. Richard Caton Woodville, *The Card Players*, 1846, oil on canvas,
18½ × 25 in. (See Figure 55.)

PLATE 7. Richard Caton Woodville, *Waiting for the Stage*, 1851, oil on canvas, 15 × 18⅛ in. (See Figure 59.)

PLATE 8. Francis W. Edmonds, *The Speculator*, 1852, oil on canvas,
25⅛ × 30⅛ in. (See Figure 63.)

being stamped into coin adds considerably to its convenience but nothing to its value."[17] For Paine, the use of paper promissory notes to facilitate transactions between individuals was an acceptable medium of exchange. "Paper, circulating in this manner, and for this purpose," he writes, "continually points to the place and person where, and of whom, the money is to be had, and at last finds its home; and, as it were, unlocks its master's chest and pays the bearer." "But when an assembly undertakes to issue paper *as* money," Paine writes, "the whole system of safety and certainty is overturned, and property set afloat. . . . It is like putting an apparition in the place of a man; it vanishes with looking at, and nothing remains but the air."[18] Like broadsides and newspapers, banknotes pointed elsewhere, often beyond the frame of visibility. When exchanged between individuals, they still pointed to a recognizable source of actual value. However, when dislodged from familiar networks and circulated beyond personal exchanges, their referents seemed to vanish into thin air.

As it turns out, Paine's description of paper money as apparitional had grounding in the vernacular lexicon of the antebellum economy. Along with metaphors of storms, typhoons, and other natural disasters, the association of paper money with spectral illusions and ghostly imagery began early in the nineteenth century.[19] As alluded to in the emblematic rendering of Jackson and his hard money policies, the plume or "puff" of smoke from which his top hat and spectacles emerge in Clay's *The Times* refers to "puffing," that age-old art of inflating the value of something via verbal or printed boast. Posters, signboards, even articles unduly praising artists, writers, or theatrical performances were criticized as "puffs." Banknotes were likewise ridiculed as agents of inflation. As such, smoke, clouds, and mists became motifs common to a broad range of cultural expressions that sought to critique paper money economics and their broader cultural implications. First introduced in 1820 and seen in a later painting by John Quidor (Figure 69), Washington Irving's headless horseman from "The Legend of Sleepy Hollow," for instance, couched critiques of the economic implications of paper in the ghostly and spectral.[20] Other articles equated speculation with "commercial delusions."[21] In the humorous cautionary tale "A Local Record of the Past and Present! Or the Ghost of Wall Street," written by Thaddeus W. Meighan and published in 1847, a ghost representing the Wall Street of old emerges from a thick gloom, warning: "I tell you I am extinct— my ancient glories have departed; my old form is given to the contaminating possession of money-changers and gamesters."[22] Allusions to the ghostly and spectral also assumed visual form in numerous cartoons produced during the first decades of

FIGURE 69. John Quidor, *The Headless Horseman Pursuing Ichabod Crane*,
1858, oil on canvas, 26⅞ × 33⅞ in. Smithsonian American Art Museum,
Washington, DC, Museum purchase made possible in part by the Catherine
Walden Myer Endowment, the Julia D. Strong Endowment, and
the Director's Discretionary Fund.

the nineteenth century, beginning with William Charles's etching, *The Ghost of a
Dollar, or the Bankers' Surprize* in which a coin floats amid a spectral cloud (Figure 70). Charles's etching appeared just two years after his *Modern Spectacles Easily
Seen Through*, suggesting the persistence of the illustrator's preoccupation with the
intertwined issues of vision and commerce. In the wake of the Panic of 1837, Edward Clay followed up *The Times* with a *New Edition of Macbeth. Bank-oh's! Ghost*
(Figure 71). Published by Henry R. Robinson, a Whig lithographer and publisher,
the cartoon pairs Jackson and his successor, Martin Van Buren, as a domesticated
couple haunted by the translucent ghost of commerce who emanates from a cloud.
Commerce has been strangled by the widely unpopular Specie Circular as he holds
forth a sheaf of papers, the most prominent of which calls for its repeal, and notices
of bank failures in New Orleans, Philadelphia, and New York. Van Buren recoils at
the sight of the specter, shifting blame to his predecessor. Strikingly, the ghost's

FIGURE 70. William Charles, *The Ghost of a Dollar or the Bankers Surprize*, c. 1808, etching, plate 37.8 × 26.7 cm. Library of Congress, Prints & Photographs Division.

FIGURE 71. Edward Williams Clay, *New Edition of Macbeth. Bank-oh's! Ghost*, 1837, lithograph on wove paper, 25.2 × 41.5 cm. Library of Congress, Prints & Photographs Division.

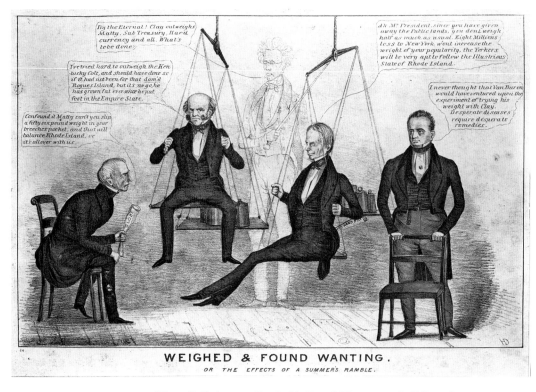

FIGURE 72. Henry R. Robinson, *Weighed & Found Wanting, or the Effects of a Summer's Ramble*, 1844, lithograph with watercolor. Library of Congress, Prints & Photographs Division.

positioning, the paper he holds forth, his pointing gesture, and even the chair on which he sits, set pictorial precedents that would reappear in Edmonds's 1852 painting. In *Weighed & Found Wanting, or the Effects of a Summer's Ramble*, published by Robinson in 1844 (Figure 72), it is the ghost of Andrew Jackson that looms in the background, as the figures of his successor, Martin Van Buren, and Henry Clay, a prominent Whig, hang in the balance.

The ghost imagery in these commerce-related cartoons surely resonated with Edmonds the banker. But a parallel tradition, traceable in a series of ghost-centered paintings made between 1777 and 1828, might have appealed to Edmonds the artist. Just as transparency and elegant refraction had been key to Rembrandt Peale's portrait *Rubens Peale with a Geranium*, integral to these ghostly pictures was the painter's ability to render translucent vapors and apparitions. Depicting scenes from the Old Testament story of Saul and the Witch of Endor, paintings of the subject by Benjamin West (Figure 73) and Washington Allston (Figure 74)

FIGURE 73. Benjamin West (American, 1738–1820), *Saul and the Witch of Endor*, 1777, oil on canvas, 19⅞ × 25⅝ in. Gift of Clara Hinton Gould, 1948.186, Wadsworth Atheneum Museum of Art, Hartford, CT, Photo credit: Allen Phillips/Wadsworth Atheneum.

FIGURE 74. Washington Allston, *Saul and the Witch of Endor*, 1820, oil on canvas, 34⁵⁄₁₆ × 47⅛ in. Mead Art Museum, Amherst College, Amherst, MA/ Bridgeman Images.

must have been to Edmonds instructive for the ways they render the translucent vapor, mists, and clouds that haunt them, both at their centers and their peripheries. Notable, too, across these pictures is the visual gravity exerted by the necromantic spiritualist medium who facilitates the interchange between the living and the departed. In these depictions, King Saul, fearing that he has fallen from God's favor and notwithstanding his own criminalization of witchcraft and necromancy, prompts the Witch of Endor to conjure the spirit of the prophet Samuel for consul as he prepares to confront the formidable Philistine army. Samuel, who can only be seen by the witch, informs Saul of his army's impending defeat and his own death in battle. Taken together, these stories, cartoons, and paintings put "apparitions" in place of men, echoing Paine. But, in evoking vestiges of the past, traces of the present, or prophecies of the future, these apparitional appearances also point to, and beyond, the limits of perceptibility.

In all of these pictures, notable stress is placed on the convincing depiction of paired figures, solid and apparational, with equal emphasis given to rendering fleshy substance and immaterial evanescence. While West and Allston excelled in rendering these surfaces and textures as well as transluscent mists and auras, Edmonds painted objects and figures in a manner more leaden, more earthbound. When Edmonds showed *The Speculator* at the annual exhibition of the National Academy of Design in April 1852, a reviewer for the *Literary World* commented on just this, charging "the painter bestowed more care on the cabbage on the floor or the ham overhead, than on the heads," and suggested that "if Mr. Edmonds would study the drapery of his pictures as carefully as he does the accessories, he would add materially to the value of them, and still more by more delicate rendering of the faces which here are coarse and conventional." In spite of these perceived faults, however, the writer considered *The Speculator* a "clever picture, telling its story with great clearness and mostly well painted."[23] In his solid, squat figures, Edmonds, at the very least, equaled those of Richard Caton Woodville in *War News from Mexico* or George Caleb Bingham in his *Country Politician* of 1849 (Figure 75), both of which Edmonds likely saw in the Art-Union's galleries. Of Bingham's picture, a critic for the *Bulletin of the American Art-Union* wrote, "His figures have some vitality about them, *they look out of their eyes*. They stand upon their legs. They are shrewd or merry or grave or quizzical. They are not mere empty ghosts of figures—mere pictures of jackets and trousers with masks attached to them" (italics mine).[24] In both Bingham's and Edmonds's pictures, two rustics square off against and are seemingly captivated by an urban slick, whose seated position and top hat in both paintings rhyme compositionally and thematically. In *The Speculator*, the resemblance of man

FIGURE 75. George Caleb Bingham, *Country Politician*, 1849, oil on canvas,
20⅜ × 24 in. Fine Arts Museums of San Francisco, Gift of Mr. and Mrs.
John D. Rockefeller 3rd, 1979.7.16.

and woman drew derision from the reviewer for the *Home Journal*, who joked, "a command in the Sanskrit version of the Old Testament that 'a man shall not marry his sister,' was broken."[25] Their proximity, however, emphasizes the discrepancies and conflicts that often arise between competing viewpoints. Indeed, the couple's orb-like heads invoke a pair of eyes, each straining to assimilate slightly different viewing angles. This feature of vision enables binocular disparity, a process in which the eyes amalgamate two lines of sight to produce depth perception. Known since antiquity, binocularity had only recently been addressed by more "modern" formulations of vision grounded in physiological optics. Though Edmonds's three figures are pictorially credible, if a little stiff, and feature the solidity of "real people" who "look out of their eyes" and "stand upon their legs," there nevertheless remains, as I will suggest, an element of the ghostly within their midst.

While the "ghosts" of paper's value fluctuated as wildly as it circulated widely, paper also provided a perceptual, experiential source for the appearance of "ghosts" in the antebellum decades. Indeed, ghosts were everywhere, and not just as traces of specie or the deceased, but as visual experiences incited by the consumption (or overconsumption) of paper. These "ghosts" tended to make their appearance, as specified in the cautionary literature, when one read in insufficient light or for too long a period, without proper diet or exercise out of doors. They appeared during the liminal passages of dawn and dusk, in dim candlelight, and especially when one "looked upon paper." Recall the plight of clerk Edward N. Tailer Jr. whose diary documents his experiences with ocular pain and failure. One Saturday evening he wrote:"this afternoon my eyes felt when the labors of the day were finished as if I was to become blind, *a cloud appeared to hover over them*, which prevented my seeing distinctly those minute objects, which would be presented for admission, to be portrayed upon the retina" (italics mine). Blaming the "miserable light" seeping into the counting room where he labored, Tailer may have more accurately attributed the "cloud" that hovered over his eyes to the sheets of paper upon which he undoubtedly stared as he labored hour after hour. [26] As we know, he sought remedy in the pages of Johann Franz's *The Eye; a Treatise on the Art of Preserving This Organ in a Healthy Condition, and of Improving the Sight.* But as he studied this treatise, Tailer's eyes worsened. To the blank cloud that precluded Tailer's clear sight were added intermittent waves of irritating pain accompanied by equally fleeting sensations of light and dark spots. In May of 1850, he wrote of how his eyes felt at times "as if filled with fine particles of dust" and complained of "sharp, shooting pains through the ball of the eye."[27] Tailer likely identified his malady with what Franz described as "weakness of sight," a condition marked by ocular fatigue, blurred vision, and shooting pain. Its symptoms, according to Franz, often occurred in conjunction with presbyopy, or farsightedness, and with "certain false visual sensations," which are called in "common language motes, and technically muscae volitantes," or, in the terms of physiological optics, subjective visual phenomena. According to Franz,

> These illusions, or muscae volitantes, present the greatest variety as to their form, colour, and duration. Sometimes they are round or angular points or spots, sometimes rings or stripes like those of snakes, sometimes they appear as network or as nebulae; sometimes they are clear and transparent, at other times dark and opaque; at one time they remain stationary, at another they move or disappear, and again appear from time to time. They

are usually most perceptible on looking upon white surfaces, or on very clear days; in the twilight they mostly disappear. They occasion considerable annoyance to the person troubled with them, inasmuch as they often greatly disturb the sight.[28]

Though hindered by this annoyance, Tailer's troubled eyesight, common among those employed in similarly "white collar" trades, recovered to a degree sufficient for him to eventually succeed as a leading man of business. However, others were less fortunate.

In the early 1850s, the literary fame Herman Melville had won as author of *Typee* (1846) and *Omoo* (1847) had begun to wane. As critical indifference to *Moby Dick* (1851), the novel that eventually would become his most famous, set in, the author channeled concerns about the physiological and epistemological shortcomings of his own eyesight into the creation of two characters doomed by writing and the culture of paper. These include the titular character of the failed domestic novel, *Pierre; or, the Ambiguities*, published by Harper & Brothers in July of 1852, and "Bartleby the Scrivener," which appeared in two installments in *Putnam's Monthly* late the following year. Both Pierre and Bartleby experience ocular ailments resulting from the overexertion of their eyes in writing and reviewing copy. And both meet their demise in the Tombs, New York's infamous prison. The plight of Pierre Glendening echoes that of Melville himself, who experienced ocular problems and acute financial anxiety during this period. Pierre is a struggling author under immense pressure to produce the novel that will win him fame and sales sufficient to support his growing family. Confused by the appearance of a mysterious woman who claims to be his long lost sister, Pierre concocts a plan to marry her to ensure that she receives the portion of a family inheritance he is convinced is her due. He abandons his fiancée and flees the comfort of his bucolic family estate for the confines of Lower Manhattan. Joined there by his purported bride, and eventually by his fiancée, Pierre struggles to finish his manuscript. Pressed by financial concerns and confusion stemming from the ambiguities alluded to in the novel's subtitle, Pierre's mental condition quickly devolves. Likewise, the acuity and proper functioning of his vision erode as his eyes fail him as well. Writing some days with the "lids nearly closed," Pierre's "incessant application told upon his eyes. They became so affected, that some days he wrote with the lids nearly closed, fearful of opening them wide to the light. Through the lashes he peered upon the paper, which so seemed fretted with wires. Sometimes he blindly wrote with his eyes turned away from the paper;—thus unconsciously symbolizing the hostile necessity and distaste, the former whereof made of him this most unwilling statesprisoner of letters."[29]

Pierre takes to evening strolls to relieve his eyes, a technique prescribed by Franz and others. On one such stroll, a "sudden, unwonted, and all-pervading sensation seized him . . . he could not see; though instinctively putting his hand to his eyes, he seemed to feel that the lids were open. Then he was sensible of a combined blindness, and vertigo, and staggering; before his eyes a million green meteors danced."[30] A few pages later, Pierre is dead in a dreary prison cell, victimized by his inability to navigate the "ambiguities" of modern life and literally destroyed by the perceptual perils of New York's thriving print culture. The eyes, once considered capable of direct and objective observation and the gathering of unmediated knowledge, were for Pierre prone to slippages of subjectivity, confused by deceptive appearances, and plagued by fits of fatigue.

Melville's forlorn copyist, Bartleby, who first appeared in the November 1853 issue of *Putnam's Monthly*, is like Tailer, another of the city's legion of clerks whose eyes and body are decimated by long hours of copying in low light. Unknown and ultimately unknowable, Bartleby floats like an image through the narrative, lending the story an ethereal, evanescent quality. As the narrator admits early on "What my own astonished eyes saw of Bartleby, *that* is all I know of him. . . . In answer to my advertisement, a motionless young man one morning, stood upon my office threshold, the door being open, for it was summer. I can see that figure now—pallidly neat, pitiably respectable, incurably forlorn! It was Bartleby."[31] The narrator then details the enclosure of the scrivener's workspace within the offices of his Wall Street firm. I quote the passage at length to point out the space's camera obscura–like qualities, for it is this space in which Bartleby, with his prodigious copying, *fixes* his image, at least momentarily:

> I placed his desk close up to a small side-window in that part of the room, a window which originally had afforded a lateral view of certain grimy back-yards and bricks, but which, owing to subsequent erections, commanded at present no view at all, though it gave some light. Within three feet of the panes was a wall, and the light came down from far above, between two lofty buildings, as from a very small opening in a dome. Still further to a satisfactory arrangement, I procured a high green folding screen, which might entirely isolate Bartleby from my sight, though not remove him from my voice. And thus, in a manner, privacy and society were conjoined.[32]

In the narrator's recounting, the figure of Bartleby—from his first impression, formed as the copyist crossed the threshold of his offices, to its consolidation within the disciplinary optics of his camera-like workspace, where Bartleby first copied profusely, then steadfastly refused to copy or, eventually, to abandon his space until he himself was abandoned—functions as an image, a mere trace of a man. However, as the copyist drifts from the space of his initial productivity, he becomes more steadfast in his resistance to his employer's entreaties, while the narrator's image of Bartleby becomes more diffuse, unstable, and fleeting.

The narrator then turns to the copyist's voluminous output: "At first Bartleby did an extraordinary quantity of writing. . . . He ran a day and night line, copying by sun-light and by candle-light. I should have been quite delighted with his application, had he been cheerfully industrious. But he wrote on silently, palely, mechanically."[33] Bartleby evokes in frail human form the day-and-night persistence and steady, mechanical output of Richard Hoe's rotary presses. On the third day, however, Bartleby first expresses his famed "preference not to" review the copy he has just produced, as was custom. Called by the narrator, "like a very ghost, agreeably to the laws of magical invocation, at the third summons, [Bartleby] appeared at the entrance of his hermitage."[34] From here, the situation devolves rapidly. Subsisting entirely on ginger nuts, Bartleby remains lodged within his cloistered space and refuses to take exercise out of doors—a common prescription for maintaining ocular health. Instead, "for long periods he would stand looking out, at pale his window behind the screen, upon the dead brick wall," which, as the narrator puts it, "required no spy-glass to bring out its lurking beauties, but for the benefit of all near-sighted spectators, was pushed up to within ten feet of my window panes."[35] Apparently, the combination of poor light creeping into the copyist's workspace, the poor ventilation, and the lack of exposure to the outdoors brings the copyist's industriousness to a screeching halt. Over the ensuing days, the narrator is repeatedly frustrated by his copyist's continued recalcitrance. Eventually Bartleby ceases work altogether; his manner and appearance devolves from "pallid, neat" and "incurably forlorn" to gaunt and cadaverous. When asked why he did not write, Bartleby replied that he had decided to do no more. When asked the reason for abandoning his trade, Bartleby indifferently replies "do you not see the reason for yourself?" The narrator looked "steadfastly at him" and perceived that "his eyes looked dull and glazed." It occurred to him "instantly" that Bartleby's "unexampled diligence in copying by his dim window for the first few weeks of his stay . . . might have temporarily impaired his vision."[36] From this point on, Bartleby lingers, haunting the premises day and night. Entreating the reader for some solution to this impasse, the narrator implores "What shall I do? . . . what ought I do? What does conscience say I *should* do with this man, or rather ghost?"[37]

Described as a "fixture," a "millstone," an "incubus," and "stationary," a play on his paper-like qualities, Bartleby remains even after the firm relocates.[38] Weeks later, the narrator finally catches up again with Bartleby, now wasting away in the confinement of the Tombs. Here the copyist expires, stooped over with "dim eyes" open, a vestige of his former self. He has been decimated by the culture of paper that employed and eventually consumed him. He is now a ghost, a phantom of the man who had once copied prodigiously and, as such, held great value for his own livelihood as well as that of his employer. As if to emphasize the close tie of Bartleby's clerical output, and his compensation in paper currency, *Putnam's* published an "Inscription for the Back of a Bank-Note" following the end of the story's first installment (Figure 76). The poem's stanzas alternate between praise and critique, a bipolar interplay of point and counterpoint that underscores paper's inherent ambiguities: "Bank-note—foul note! Industry's curse; Ghost of coin, that mocks at toil; Pictured wealth that chance may spoil; Rogues may stamp, and handling soil; Spider weaving credit's coil; Bank-note—foul note! Touch not my purse!" But in alternating stanzas, words of praise replace doubt and distrust: "Bank-note—blest note! Trade's healthy nurse: Key to stores of treasures gold; Making timid business bold. . . . Bank-note—sweet note! Emblem of power; Giving youthful charms to age; Making fools seem strangely sage; Winning, despite critic's rage; Puffs and glory by the page; Bank-notes—sweet notes! Come in a shower!"[39]

Like a banknote, Bartleby, at first, helps to make his employer's "timid" business "bold." But soon, his presence morphs into "industry's curse," a "ghost" of true value (coin) that "mocks at toil." Bartleby's output, comprising his value as an employee, goes from prodigious to nonexistent. To the narrator's chagrin, the value of his recently appointed clerk fluctuates as wildly as the paper economy to which the latter's clerking and copying has contributed. As the narrator quickly learns, Bartleby's presence, like that of the banknotes of the "Inscription," is a blessing *and* a curse, a boon and a burden. Bartleby's worth remains as fluid and ephemeral as paper currency, as his output relies on the persistence of his vision, which ultimately fails him.

At the close of the story's second installment in the December 1853 issue appeared another poem titled "Phantoms." As if extending the coupleted parody of "Inscription" by flashing to paper money's spectral underside, this anonymous

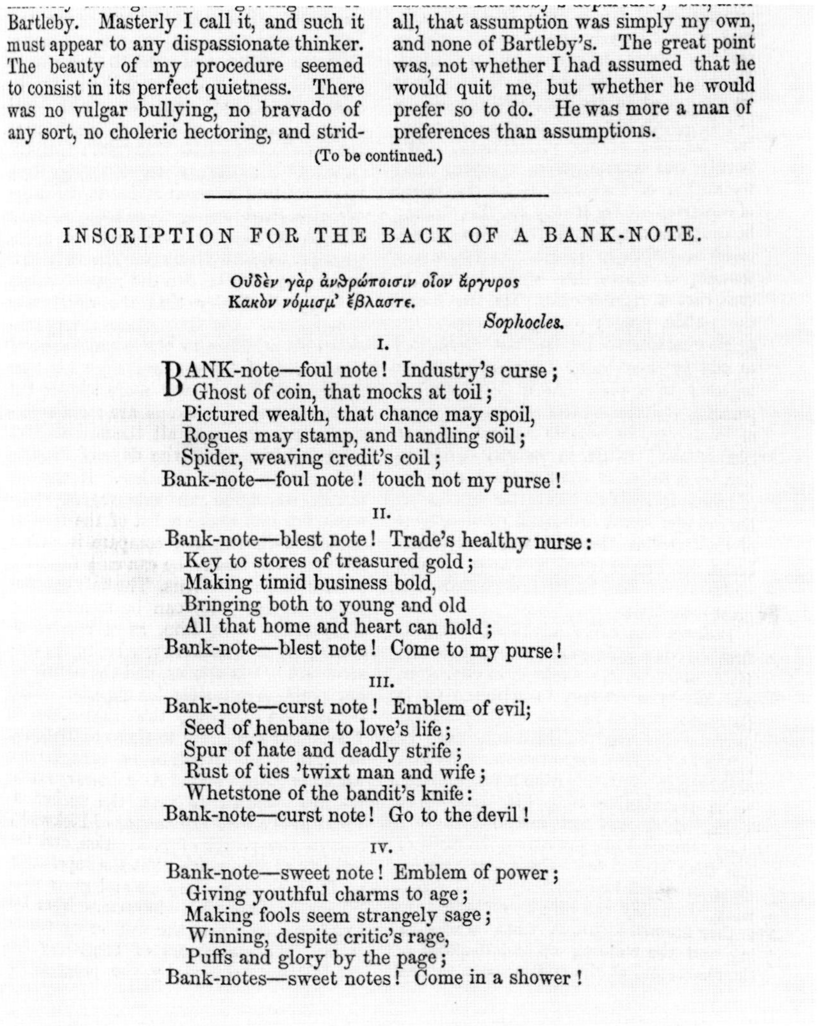

Bartleby. Masterly I call it, and such it must appear to any dispassionate thinker. The beauty of my procedure seemed to consist in its perfect quietness. There was no vulgar bullying, no bravado of any sort, no choleric hectoring, and strid- all, that assumption was simply my own, and none of Bartleby's. The great point was, not whether I had assumed that he would quit me, but whether he would prefer so to do. He was more a man of preferences than assumptions.

(To be continued.)

---

INSCRIPTION FOR THE BACK OF A BANK-NOTE.

Οὐδὲν γὰρ ἀνθρώποισιν οἷον ἄργυρος
Κακὸν νόμισμ' ἔβλαστε.
*Sophocles.*

I.

BANK-note—foul note! Industry's curse;
Ghost of coin, that mocks at toil;
Pictured wealth, that chance may spoil,
Rogues may stamp, and handling soil;
Spider, weaving credit's coil;
Bank-note—foul note! touch not my purse!

II.

Bank-note—blest note! Trade's healthy nurse:
Key to stores of treasured gold;
Making timid business bold,
Bringing both to young and old
All that home and heart can hold;
Bank-note—blest note! Come to my purse!

III.

Bank-note—curst note! Emblem of evil;
Seed of henbane to love's life;
Spur of hate and deadly strife;
Rust of ties 'twixt man and wife;
Whetstone of the bandit's knife:
Bank-note—curst note! Go to the devil!

IV.

Bank-note—sweet note! Emblem of power;
Giving youthful charms to age;
Making fools seem strangely sage;
Winning, despite critic's rage,
Puffs and glory by the page;
Bank-notes—sweet notes! Come in a shower!

FIGURE 76. "Bartleby the Scrivener" and "Inscription for the Back of a Bank-Note," *Putnam's Monthly*, November 1853, 557. Newberry Library, Chicago.

work more ominously bookends the second half of Melville's story in the ghastly feel of its haunting postscript. Relating a "little item of rumor" the narrator gathered in the interim between Bartleby's death and the afterthought of the story's postscript, he shares that prior to Bartleby's employment in his firm, the scrivener had been a "subordinate clerk in the Dead Letter Office at Washington from which he had been suddenly removed by a change in the administration."[40] In a lament leveling men with folded sheets of paper that have failed to reach their recipients, the narrator cries out to the reader: "Dead letters! Does it not sound like dead men?" as he deplores the equation of men and paper, letters and banknotes "sent in swiftest charity." The anonymous poem, "Phantoms," that follows the story's second and final installment, continues the theme of the ghostly, highlighting the pervasive presence of spirits of the departed: "All houses wherein men have lived and died / Are haunted houses. Through the open doors / The harmless phantoms on their errands glide, / With Feet that make no sound upon the floors." Like Bartleby, who haunts the offices of the narrator's firm both day and night, phantoms of the departed float, vaporous and misty, among the living: "The spirit-world around this world of sense; Floats like an atmosphere, and every where Wafts through these earthly mists and vapors dense / A vital breath of more ethereal air."[41] At the outer boundaries of sense perception, but present nonetheless, such phantoms haunted the peripheries of the antebellum imagination, especially in the form of mists and vapors, "stripes," "snakes," or the "million green meteors" occasionally perceived by the eyes in fits of overstimulation and at moments of particular ocular strain. As Franz pointed out, these episodes often involved paper or other brightly lit surfaces. Under the glaring burn of candlelight, or in the bright light of day, paper reflected light as much as its content refracted events, goods, services, or parcels of real estate.

Returning to *The Speculator*, we can read the kind of ocular strain experienced by Edward Tailer, Pierre, or Bartleby in the noticeable squint of both farmer and wife. "Squint" was then and continues to be a vernacular term for strabismus, a disorder in which the muscles of the eyes strain to attain the balance necessary to achieve binocular vision. This condition had become a subject of great interest in medical circles during the early 1840s, an interest that produced several surgical methods for its cure and a spate of treatises that described the condition, its causes, and cures. Illustrations of the condition and its treatment, as in the manual *Observations on the Cure of Strabismus*, published by Alfred C. Post, MD, in 1841 with engravings by Nathaniel Currier (Figure 77), relied on conventions for rendering eyeballs that may have appealed to Edmonds's desire to emphasize the farmer's marked ocular strain. Tailer's cloud and shooting pains, Bartleby's blank stare, Pierre's dancing meteors, Franz's muscae volitantes, even the farmer's squint—each of these demonstrate vision's aberrations and maladies then just beginning to be understood as part of the eye's continually fluctuating physiology. Though seen as indicators of stress and overwork, these phenomena helped to explain the physiological basis of eyesight, including its various lapses and lacu-

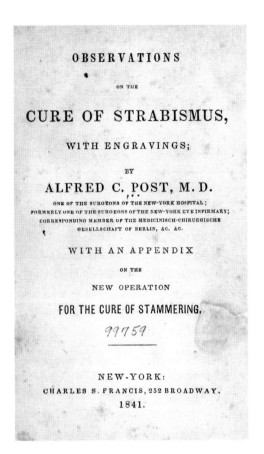

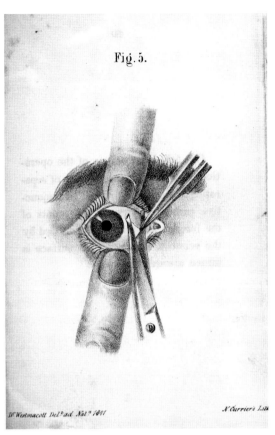

FIGURE 77. Alfred C. Post, *Observations on the Cure of Strabismus, with Engravings* (New York: Charles S. Francis, 1841), title page and illustration of surgical procedure, 65. U.S. National Library of Medicine, Bethesda, MD.

nae, and better defined the parameters of what constituted "normal" vision. The clerk's or writer's malady was the physiologists' test case. Often conducted by candlelight or in the dimmed light or darkness of an enclosed space resembling a camera obscura, experiments also tended to involve sheets of white paper, both marked and unmarked. In his *Farbenlehre* of 1810, Goethe catalogued subjective visual phenomena such as the subjective haloes and blindspots seen in his renderings (Figure 78). These appeared, as Jonathan Crary has explained in detail, when Goethe closed the camera's aperture, noting the colors that undulated seemingly before but actually *within* his eyes in the absence of light projected through the opening. For Crary, Goethe's actions effectively diminished the explanatory power

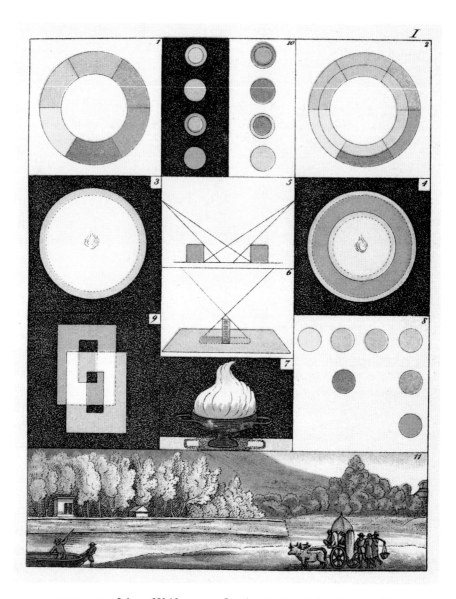

FIGURE 78. Johann Wolfgang von Goethe, *Goethe's Farbenlehre, hrsg. Und eingeleitet von Hans Wohlbold*, 1928, plate 1 (opp. p. 244), illustration. Science, Industry & Business Library, New York Public Library, Astor, Lenox and Tilden Foundations.

of the camera obscura's model of vision premised on the physical transmission of light.[42] Following Goethe, David Brewster, and, especially, Jan Purkinje observed, quantified, qualified, and documented these various subjective responses (Figure 79). Purkinje lent the implications of Goethe's discoveries greater scientific

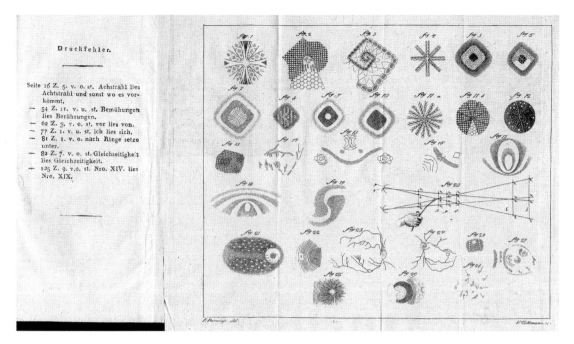

FIGURE 79. Jan Evangelista Purkyne (commonly spelled Purkinje), *Beitrage zur Kenntnis des Sehens in subjectiver Hinsicht* (Contributions to the Knowledge of Vision in terms of Subjective) (Prague: Johann Gottfied Calve, 1819), illustrations of subjective visual phenomena, 188. Max Planck Institute for the History of Science, Berlin.

specificity, even as he amplified the latter's claims: "There are sensations that do not correspond to anything outside the body. Insofar as they imitate the qualities and forms of external things, they thereby often give rise to illusions, phantoms, or appearances with no corresponding reality."[43] In chapters devoted to various experiments involving "Light and Shade Figures," "Scintillating Light Points When Viewing a White Surface," "Afterimages," "Luminous Rings," "The Unity of the Two Fields. Double vision," and "Persisting Images, Imagination, and Visual Memory," to name but a few, Purkinje saw it as the "undeniable" task of the natural scientist "to establish the objective basis" of these phenomena.[44] In so doing, Purkinje traced a model of active, as opposed to purely optical and therefore passive, vision predicated on the amalgamation of exterior stimuli with interior ocular mechanisms.

Though a far cry from the makeshift laboratories of Goethe and Purkinje, the farmer's modest enclosure in Edmonds's painting stages, in visually narrative terms, an episode of subjective vision. The dichotomy of exterior and interior, of seen and unseen, animates *The Speculator* and charges the space it pictures with uncertainty and ambiguity. Edmonds's interiors, like those of Woodville, utlize the stage-box design prevalent among painters seeking to emulate the popular "Düsseldorf style." Others have pointed out how the congested space of the painting increases the pressure of the agent's sales pitch.[45] More notable, however, is the composition's aberration from Edmonds's standard interior formula: like Dutch and British predecessors, he often lighted his domestic scenes with open doors or windows to express continuity, even commerce, between inside and outside spaces. Edmonds's painting *The Image Pedlar* of 1844 best exemplifies this compositional arrangement (Figure 80). In the painting, an effulgence of light pours in from the open window at left and assumes physical form in the billowing sheer curtain that blows into the room on an incoming breeze. Light streaming in from the open window illuminates from multiple angles the pedlar's images and guides the gazes of viewers before the picture as well as of the figure in the painting's background. Edmonds may have painted the windows and doors shut in *The Speculator* to emphasize the disconnect between the possibly fictive negotiations taking place before us and the outer reality to which they refer. Though one may only speculate as to why Edmonds painted the doors and windows shut in this particular picture, that he positioned his figures within an enclosed space is not insignificant. This is especially important in light of the painting's overt concern with the gap between external reality and a subjective vision that emerges in the oscillation between the seen and the unseeable. Like the newspaper in Woodville's *War News*, the real estate agent's map mediates a distant reality to the farmer and his wife and invites the painting's viewers to also inspect their outward facing surfaces. In both paintings, architectural form, both exterior and interior, hinge on a printed document. Both spaces situate their occupants and help to channel their gazes to look upon paper. Though the source of the prominent light that fills the picture remains out of view, the farmer's cottage is similar in nature, if not purpose, to that occupied by Bartleby. Both approximate the chamber of a large camera obscura, the space typically employed in the kinds of physiological experiments that eventually dismantled it as the theoretical and scientific model for vision's mechanisms. Viewers too are enclosed within this shuttered space, left only to ascertain from their impressions, the meaning of the agent's map.

A closer look at *The Speculator* (see Figure 63, Plate 8) reveals just why the farmer's squint is so pronounced. The agent's map's text at first glance seems enticingly legible, yet, on further inspection, below the first line, it remains frustratingly illegible. Scrutiny of the document only reinforces a simple fact: the land, as well as the

FIGURE 80. Francis W. Edmonds, *The Image Pedlar*, c. 1844, oil on canvas, 33¼ × 42¼ in. © Collection of the New-York Historical Society, Gift of the New-York Gallery of the Fine Arts/Bridgeman Images.

value it embodies, remains entirely out of view. Set inside the closed room, without recourse to a view of actual property, the map's observers are forced to supplement its scant perceptual data with their own subjective impressions. In an era marked by a vast increase in the availability of cheap printed materials, the practice of viewing surrogates near at hand for objects that remained out of view became a standard feature of antebellum visuality: broadside and signboard advertisements in place of consumer goods, newspaper stories in place of firsthand observation, banknotes as stand-ins for specie, or real estate maps for parcels of land. Requiring varying degrees of visual acuity and textual literacy, the viewing practices these particular objects inculcated were, in many ways, premised on speculative acts of forming opinions or making decisions on the incomplete data of documents and images close at hand. It is tempting to look for the patterns Purkinje, Franz, and Goethe documented in words and images within Edmonds's painting. If one looks hard enough, such resemblances can be found—the "round or angular points or spots" of the patches on the woman's apron, or the "rings or stripes like those of snakes" echoed in the coils of the farmer's wide basket, or the cracks in the fireplace, which "appear as network or as nebulae."[46] Nevertheless, I do not wish to suggest that the painter intentionally built these into his picture. Nor am I trying to posit Edmonds as an avid reader of physiological tracts, particularly of this stripe. Nevertheless, the figures Purkinje describes were commonly experienced in an era in which readers of print on paper illuminated only by sunlight, candle, and gas lamp and in which the physiological operations of the body were just beginning to be more widely understood. They formed a referent for the painter as well as his audience as both explored the extent to which vision, properly functioning or not, could yield adequate, and accurate, knowledge of the world and beyond. Indeed, as Edmonds painted his canvas to highlight land speculation's enticing lure and inherent risks for subsistence farmers and wage earners, subjective visual phenomena now fell within the quantifying purview of emerging fields of scentific inquiry. But it also attracted the attention of those swept up by the popular movement of Spiritualism with its seances and discourses of spirits and specters.

Preceded by his well-regarded *Treatise on Optics*, published in 1831, Sir David Brewster's *Letters on Natural Magic* (1832) (Figure 81) sought to "imbody the information which history supplies respecting the fables and incantations of the ancient superstitions, and to show how far they can be explained by the scientific knowledge which then prevailed." With a focus on optics, "the most fertile in marvelous expedients," this hybrid text links the clinical detail of Purkinje's recorded observations with the more exploratory and experimental forms of interest in the aberrations of sight, or as Brewster puts it, modern "phantasmagoria."[47] Brewster was probably better known as the inventor of the kaleidoscope in 1815 and later made significant improvments on Sir Charles Wheatstone's stereoscope, which popularized his research on binocular vision. In *Letters*, Brewster likens the eye to a miniature camera obscura, a common trope of the period. Brewster writes, "this wonderful organ may be considered the sentinel which guards the pass between the worlds of matter and spirit, and through which all their communications are interchanged. . . . The eye is consequently the principle seat of the supernatural." Brewster then examines a number of subjective illusions in terms that combine science and the metaphysical. Utilizing candles and sheets of white paper among other implements commonly found in the home—and seen prominently in the paintings of Edmonds and Woodville—he investigates the illusions that occur as a result of the "inability of the eye to preserve a sustained vision of objects seen obliquely" or the "imperfect view" which we obtain of objects seen in

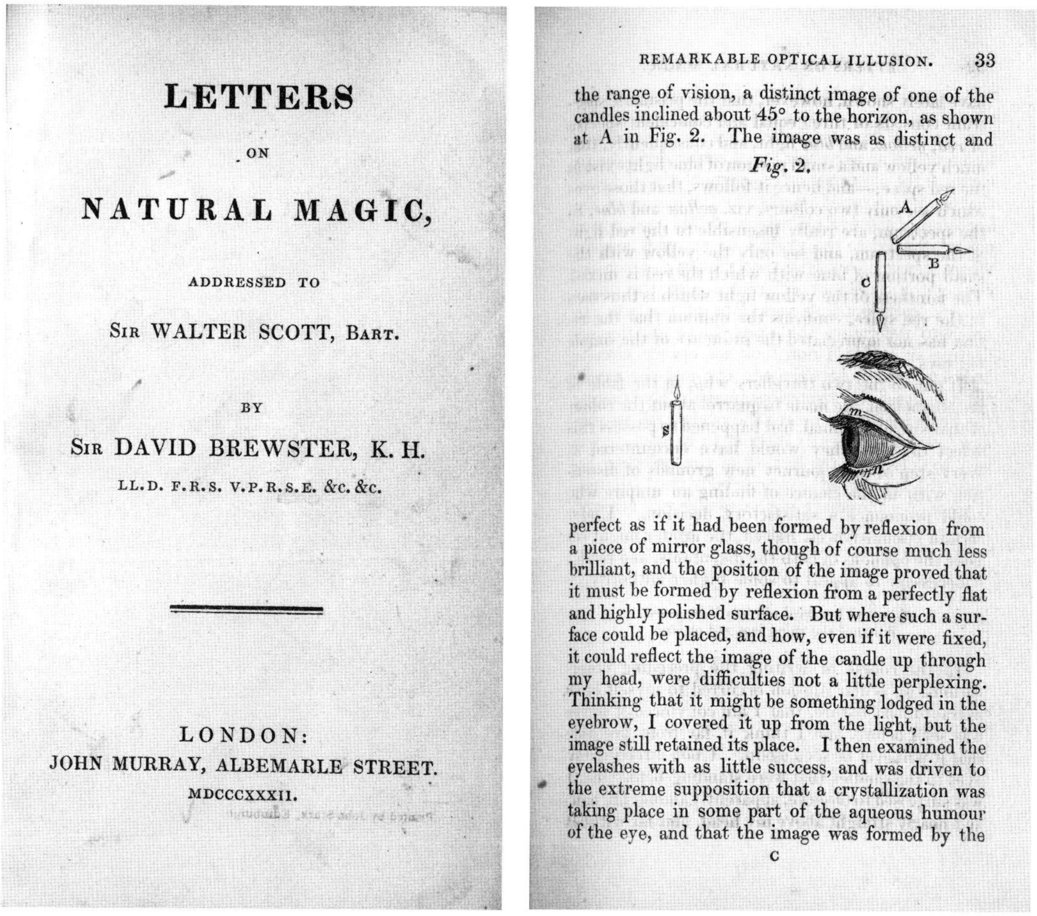

## LETTERS

ON

## NATURAL MAGIC,

ADDRESSED TO

Sir WALTER SCOTT, Bart.

BY

Sir DAVID BREWSTER, K. H.

LL.D. F.R.S. V.P.R.S.E. &c. &c.

LONDON:
JOHN MURRAY, ALBEMARLE STREET.
MDCCCXXXII.

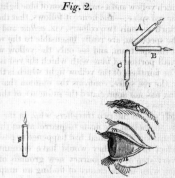

the range of vision, a distinct image of one of the candles inclined about 45° to the horizon, as shown at A in Fig. 2. The image was as distinct and

*Fig. 2.*

perfect as if it had been formed by reflexion from a piece of mirror glass, though of course much less brilliant, and the position of the image proved that it must be formed by reflexion from a perfectly flat and highly polished surface. But where such a surface could be placed, and how, even if it were fixed, it could reflect the image of the candle up through my head, were difficulties not a little perplexing. Thinking that it might be something lodged in the eyebrow, I covered it up from the light, but the image still retained its place. I then examined the eyelashes with as little success, and was driven to the extreme supposition that a crystallization was taking place in some part of the aqueous humour of the eye, and that the image was formed by the

c

FIGURE 81. Illustration of ocular illusion involving eye and candle in David Brewster, *Letters on Natural Magic* (London: John Murray, 1832), 40. Library Company of Philadelphia.

low light, which "forces us to fix the eye more steadily upon them. . . . These affections of the eye are," Brewster continues, "we are persuaded, very frequent causes of a particular class of apparitions which are seen at night by the young and the ignorant." Experienced in light just sufficient to render objects faintly visible, the spectres which are conjured up are always *white*, because no other color can be seen."[48] "From such phenomena," Brewster concludes, "the mind feels it to be no violent transition to pass to those spectral illusions, which, in particular states of health, have haunted the most intelligent individuals, not only in the broad light of day, but in the very heart of the social circle."[49]

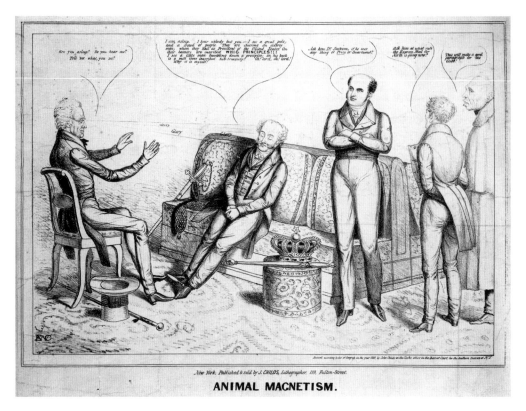

FIGURE 82. John Childs and Edward Williams Clay, *Animal Magnetism*,
1839, lithograph on wove paper, 29.2 × 39.6 cm. Library of Congress,
Prints & Photographs Division.

It could be said that the figures in Edmonds's painting convene a social circle,
of sorts. Set within an enclosed space, the rural couple take an oblique view of the
speculator's map. As they scrutinize its details and squint to discern its finer points,
their gestures recall the experimental activities described by Goethe, Purkinje, and
Brewster. In its conspicuously enclosed space, and its preoccupation with the scrutiny of printed paper, the painting indirectly engages with discourses of physiological optics concerning ocular strain, oblique vision, and strabismus, as well as afterimages, subjective haloes, and other ocular illusions. However, the composition's
arrangement of figures situates the painting within yet another set of related discourses to which I will now turn. As such, *The Speculator* also evokes the kinds of
activities that avocationally occupied Edmonds's own brother during these years.

    Stemming from the religious fervor set into motion by the Second Great
Awakening, the 1840s also witnessed the emergence of Spiritualism, a cluster of

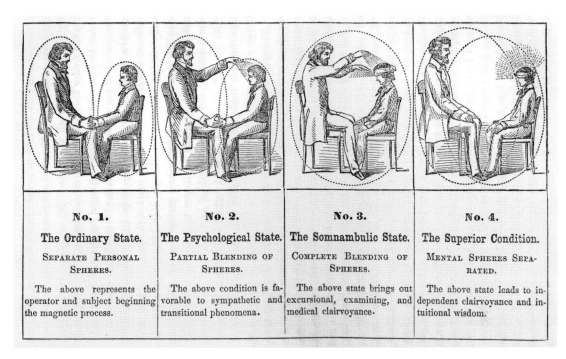

| No. 1. | No. 2. | No. 3. | No. 4. |
|---|---|---|---|
| The Ordinary State. | The Psychological State. | The Somnambulic State. | The Superior Condition. |
| SEPARATE PERSONAL SPHERES. | PARTIAL BLENDING OF SPHERES. | COMPLETE BLENDING OF SPHERES. | MENTAL SPHERES SEPARATED. |
| The above represents the operator and subject beginning the magnetic process. | The above condition is favorable to sympathetic and transitional phenomena. | The above state brings out excursional, examining, and medical clairvoyance. | The above state leads to independent clairvoyance and intuitional wisdom. |

FIGURE 83. Andrew Jackson Davis, *The Magic Staff: An Autobiography* (New York: J. S. Brown & Co., 1857), illustration of "The Ordinary State," "The Psychological State," "The Somnambulic State," "The Superior Condition," 205. Library Company of Philadelphia.

beliefs and practices centered on the communication with the spirits of the departed. As Judge Edmonds described in his 1853 publication, *Spiritualism*, which runs to over five hundred pages, this communication took various forms, often during interviews with clairvoyants, who conveyed messages from beyond the grave. These included sounds known as rappings or tactile sensations initiated by "an unseen power" and other physical manifestations.[50] Premised on the techniques of mesmerism, or "animal magnetism" as spoofed in a political cartoon from 1839 (Figure 82), Spiritualism drew on the eighteenth-century theories of Franz Anton Mesmer. Mesmer held that an ether akin to the "imponderable fluids" such as light, electricity, and magnetism pervaded all space and matter, including the human body. Disease, for instance, resulted when this fluid fell out of balance within the body. The mesmerist's task was to restore this balance by placing the ailing individual in a trance that came to be known as the "superior condition," as illustrated in the engraving from Andrew Jackson Davis's 1857 *The Magic Staff: An Autobiography* (Figure 83). It was Davis who integrated Mesmer's

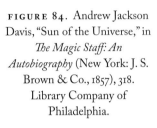

FIGURE 84. Andrew Jackson Davis, "Sun of the Universe," in *The Magic Staff: An Autobiography* (New York: J. S. Brown & Co., 1857), 318. Library Company of Philadelphia.

THE SUN OF THE UNIVERSE.

FIGURE 85. Andrew Jackson Davis, "Diagram of the Spiritual Spheres," in *The Magic Staff: An Autobiography* (New York: J. S. Brown & Co., 1857), 340. Library Company of Philadelphia.

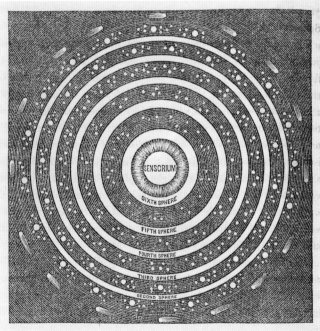

DIAGRAM OF THE SPIRITUAL SPHERES.

notions of magnetic fluid with the idea that through this process one could communicate with the dead whose souls were thought to swim in this cosmic ether. These phenomena, it should be pointed out, occurred outside the realm of the visual sense. But they did have subjectively visual aspects. Davis explains in great detail what a person might experience on entering this trancelike state, first witnessing what he labels "the sun of the universe" (Figure 84) before moving through various rings of the "spiritual spheres" (Figure 85). His diagrams nearly match those of Goethe and Purkinje in their efforts to describe subjective visual phenomena, but Davis emphatically suggests that these effects are undetectable to the human eye and can only be comprehended by what he and others labeled the "mind's eye." Thomas Buckland, writing in 1850, detailed the process of inducing this state, which involved eyesight as a catalyst for its inducment: "Cause your patient to sit down in the easiest position; seat yourself before him if possible, in a seat a little more elevated, so that his knees may be between your's and your feet beside his. . . . Look straight into the pupil of his eye, as if your vision could penetrate to his brain; wink not; be firm and determined, though quiet, and maintain the process and position for fifteen, or even thirty minutes, if necessary."[51] Though attributed to the "mind's eye," the appearance of the visual phenomena that Davis describes and vividly illustrates do bear strong resemblences to the kinds of spectral phenomena that while seeming to dance *before* the eyes, actually occurred within their structures. Though Edmonds's farmer and his wife were roundly criticized for their solidity and stiffness, their inseparability, their nearly identical facial features, they do stage variations on the theme of fascination, a variant of mesmerism current in Spiritualist circles in the late 1840s.[52] Indeed, the entreaty of the speculator positioned as mesmerist and the rapt attention of his listeners bespeaks a certain fascination with the potential for economic gain held forth by his document. But paper, as the antebellum viewer was acutely aware, was ephemeral, even ghostly. Its value relied on confidence, which bolstered its worth in the minds of a skeptical public. Confidence was, as Judge Edmonds argued, a key ingredient in the efficacy of Spiritualism generally and communication with the departed more specifically. Likewise, Spiritualism involved speculation as it sought to connect with and assess the value of that which remained entirely out of view. Just as land speculation mapped the outer edges of settlement in Edmonds's lifetime, the "second sight" and other extrasensory perceptions of Spiritualism articulated the very thresholds of perceptibility, as it attempted to wrest insights and information from the spirits of the departed, to reach beyond the

FIGURE 86. Andrew Jackson Davis, "A Death Scene," in *The Magic Staff: An Autobiography* (New York: J. S. Brown & Co., 1857), 348. Library Company of Philadelphia.

A DEATH SCENE.

FIGURE 87. Henry R. Robinson, "The Explosion," in Junior Junius, *The Vision of Judgment; or, A Present for the Whigs of '76 & '37*, 10 parts (New York: H. R. Robinson, 1838), 31. Library of Congress.

THE EXPLOSION.

visible world into the realm of the invisible, the transitory, the fleeting sphere of spirit as opposed to matter. Indeed, as these spirits departed the body, one cannot help but to associate the ascendancy of their spectral forms (Figure 86), illustrated in Davis's treatise, with graphic and painterly renderings of long, winding sheets of paper, as can be seen in yet another cartoon from the Panic of 1837 (Figure 87). The perception of these "invisibles," however, perenially involved and relied upon the carnal density of embodied vision.

Though a far cry from the subjective visual phenomena elicited by gazing upon white sheets of paper in darkened enclosures or by candlelight, renderings of spectral illusions, including those used to illustrate Davis's treatise, relied on the same pictorial conventions to visualize the fluid values of partial or total invisibility. That such renderings of spirits recalled those of sheets of paper, and that cultural discourse so often equated the two, makes my reading of *The Speculator* plausible, if not entirely probable, for the painting's original audience. The ghosts examined here share certain period formulations of paper: they are at once embodied, disembodied, and disappearing.[53] In *The Speculator*, the itinerant agent points to paper that points to the apparition of land, while the steady gazes of farmer and wife simultaneously designate and test the limits of vision's ability to discern and determine truth in a mobile visual culture of often shifting appearances. It is this complex interplay of visual perception and mental cognition—each shaped by culturally specific habits of inference and analogy and informed in the antebellum era by overlapping discourses of paper money, speculation, and even Spiritualism—that lends the map's schematic a structure and enables its range of meanings.

But the meaning of paper was fluid, its value uncertain, its visual effects mysterious, even alarming. As I have been arguing, distinctly modern formulations of vision had begun, in the 1830s and 1840s, to take into account the eyes' complex physiological functions and their ocular irregularities as crucial components of visual experience. Studies increasingly posited vision as an embodied (and often error-prone) process as opposed to a static and objective phenomenon premised on the passively optical transmission of light. As a picture about seeing, one of several analzyed in this book, Edmonds's painting was part of a broader antebellum discourse concerning the changing character of visual experience, the reformulated status of vision and viewing subjects, and the new perceptual requirements of life in a market economy. Like the broadsides, eye test charts, signboards, and other features of the interwoven print and visual cultures of the antebellum period, *The Speculator* both registers the strains of this new visual culture and muses on the subjective, even spectral, nature of "modern" vision. It meditates on the physiologically determined, subjective experiences of embodied vision even as it points, surreptitiously, in the direction of the disembodied and dematerialized. For just as scientific trends coalesced at midcentury around the specialization of the field and its many new subdisciplines, other discourses sought to explain phenomena, both of this world and the next, that scientific endeavor had yet to identify, quantify, qualify, or explain.

# ~→ NOTES ←~

### INTRODUCTION

1. Ralph Waldo Emerson, "May 14, 1837," Journal C (manuscript pages 70–71) in *Journals and Miscellaneous Notebooks*, ed. William H. Gilman et al., vol. 5, 1835–1838 (Cambridge: Belknap Press of Harvard University Press, 1960–1982), 327–328.

2. On these and other applications of this revolutionary medium, see "Paper," *Friend; a Religious and Literary Journal* 28, no. 23 (February 17, 1855): 178.

3. For a broad and comprehensive view of the economic, social, and cultural developments that historians have recently identified as components of a "market revolution," see Charles Sellers, *The Market Revolution: Jacksonian America, 1815–1846* (New York: Oxford University Press, 1991); Melvyn Stokes and Stephen Conway, eds., *The Market Revolution in America: Social, Political, and Religious Expressions, 1800–1880* (Charlottesville, VA: University of Virginia Press, 1996); and Scott C. Martin, ed., *Cultural Change and the Market Revolution in America, 1789–1860* (Lanham, MD: Rowman & Littlefield Publishers, 2004). Helpful too are David S. Reynolds's *Waking Giant: America in the Age of Jackson* (New York: Harper Collins, 2008); and Sean Wilentz's essay "Society, Politics, and the Market Revolution, 1815–1848," in *The New American History*, ed. Eric Foner (Philadelphia: Temple University Press, 1990), 51–71. On the "communication revolution" as an interrelated counterpart or addendum to the concept of "market" revolution devised and advanced by historians such as Charles Sellers in the 1990s, see Daniel Howe, *What Hath God Wrought: The Transformation of America, 1815–1848* (New York: Oxford University Press, 2007). For a recent historiographic review of these concepts, see Rosanne Currarino, "Toward a History of Cultural Economy," *Journal of the Civil War Era* 2, no. 4 (December 2012): 564–585.

4. Ralph Waldo Emerson, *Nature*, in *Ralph Waldo Emerson: Essays & Poems*, ed. Joel Porte, Harold Bloom, and Paul Kane, Library of America College ed. (1836; New York: Literary Classics of the United States, Inc., 1996), 7–49. For quote, see page 10.

5. The epistemological aspects of Emerson's "transparent eyeball" have been debated by a number of scholars. For the trope's particularly Kantian aspects, see David Van Leer, *Emerson's Epistemology: The Argument of the Essays* (Cambridge: Cambridge University Press, 1986), 51–53. See also Sherman Paul, *Emerson's Angle of Vision: Man and Nature in American Experience* (Cambridge, MA: Harvard University Press, 1952), esp. 71–102.

6. The philosopher's transparent eyeball recalls the solitary, disembodied, all-seeing eye of the Freemasons and the national seal. This "eye of power," to borrow Michel Foucault's phrase, provided the regulatory optics critical to the construction and operation of the panopticon-like Eastern State Penitentiary, a multispoked construction radiating outward from a central tower. Situated just to the north of downtown Philadelphia, it was designed and built by John Haviland for the solitary confinement of its prisoners under centralized surveillance. On Masonic symbolism in the early republic, see

John D. Hamilton, *Material Culture of American Freemasons* (Lexington, MA: Museum of Our National Heritage, 1994). See also David Bjelajac, *Washington Allston, Secret Societies and the Alchemy of Anglo-American Painting* (Cambridge: Cambridge University Press, 1997). In the interview "The Eye of Power," Foucault describes the invention of the prison and its instititionalization of the medical gaze to deal with the "whole problem of the visibility of bodies, individuals and things, under a system of centralized observation." See "The Eye of Power," in *Power/Knowledge: Selected Interviews and Other Writings, 1972–1977*, ed. Colin Gordon (New York: Pantheon Books, 1980), 146–165. See also David J. Rothman, *The Discovery of the Asylum: Social Order and Disorder in the New Republic* (Boston: Little, Brown, 1971). On intersections between panopticism and painting in the antebellum decades, see Alan Wallach, "Making a Picture of the View from Mount Holyoke," in *American Iconology: New Approaches to Nineteenth-Century Art and Literature*, ed. David C. Miller (New Haven, CT: Yale University Press, 1993), 80–91.

7. The camera obscura consists of a box-like device or darkened chamber fitted with a monocular aperture or lens that allows a stream of light to enter its darkened space to project an image, reversed and inverted, of a scene outside onto the surface or wall opposite the aperture. This instrument has been historically called upon in the field of natural philosophy to explain the basic actions of the eye as premised on the physical transmission of light. It functioned as an assemblage of discourse, technology, and practice fundamental to conceptions of vision, visual representation, and philosophy from antiquity to the early nineteenth century. See Jonathan Crary, *Techniques of the Observer: On Vision and Modernity in the Nineteenth Century* (Cambridge, MA: Zone Books, 1990), especially the chapter "Techniques of the Observer." On the historical specificity of vision and visual "regimes," see Michael Baxandall, *Painting and Experience in Fifteenth-Century Italy: A Primer in the Social History of Pictorial Style*, 2nd ed. (Oxford: Oxford University Press, 1988); Svetlana Alpers, *The Art of Describing: Dutch Art in the Seventeenth Century* (Chicago: University of Chicago Press, 1983); and especially Martin Jay, "Scopic Regimes of Modernity," in *Vision and Visuality*, ed. Hal Foster (Seattle: Bay Press for Dia Art Foundation, 1988), 3–23. For an account of the ways that various thinkers from Plato to Lyotard have conceptualized vision, see Jay's *Downcast Eyes: The Denigration of Vision in Twentieth-Century French Thought* (Berkeley: University of California Press, 1993). On the forms "spectacular" consumption assumed in the nineteenth century, see Crary, *Techniques of the Observer*, 19. "Assemblage" is a term central to the rhizomatic analyses of Gilles Deleuze and Felix Guattari in their opus, *A Thousand Plateaus: Capitalism and Schizophrenia*, trans. and foreword by Brian Massumi (Minneapolis: University of Minnesota Press, 1987).

8. This version is one of a number of such sketches illuminating various Emersonian principles. On Cranch, see Nancy Stula, *At Home and Abroad: The Transcendental Landscapes of Christopher Pearse Cranch (1813–1892)* (New London, CT: Lyman Allyn Art Museum, distributed by University Press of New England, 2007).

9. Evelyn Barish, "The Moonless Night: Emerson's Crisis of Health, 1825–1827," in *Emerson Centenary Essays*, ed. Joel Myerson (Carbondale: Southern Illinois University Press, 1982), 1–16. See also her *Emerson: The Roots of Prophecy* (Princeton, NJ: Princeton University Press, 1989), 177–197.

10. Edward Reynolds, *Hints to Students on the Use of the Eyes* (Edinburgh: Thomas Clark, 1835).

11. Barish explains: "Since the cornea has no nerve endings, the operation is painless, and the bacteriostatic quality of human tears acts against infection. The fibers of the eye close up without leaving a scar, and Wardrop and his followers recorded repeating the procedure on a single sufferer as many as seventeen times. The procedure was used widely for many years, but since it treated only the symptoms of the illness and not its cause, it could have no permanent effect, and it fell into disuse by the 1860s." Barish, "Moonless Night," 178.

12. George Lippard, *The Quaker City: or, the Monks of Monk Hall. A Romance of Philadelphia Life, Mystery, and Crime*, ed. and introduction by David S. Reynolds (1845; Amherst: University of Massachusetts Press, 1995), 151.

13. John Walker, *The Philosophy of the Eye: Being a Familiar Exposition of its Mechanism, and the Phenomenon of Vision, with a View to the Evidence of Design* (London: Charles Knight & Co., 1837); Joseph Turnley, *The Language of the Eye* (London: Partridge and Co., 1836).

14. Indeed, the period's "scopic regime," to borrow philosopher Martin Jay's phrase, was a "contested terrain, rather than a harmoniously integrated complex of visual theories and practices." Jay, "Scopic Regimes of Modernity," 3–23.

15. Even in *Nature*, Emerson accords the eye its productive capacities: "The ancient Greeks called the world beauty. Such is the constitution of all things, or such the plastic power of the human eye, that the primary forms, as the sky, the mountain, the tree, the animal, give us delight *in and for themselves*; a pleasure arising from outline, color, motion, and grouping. This seems partly owing to the eye itself. The eye is the best of artists. By the mutual action of its structure and of the laws of light, perspective is produced, which integrates every mass of objects, of what character soever, in a well colored and shaded globe, so that where the particular objects are mean and unaffecting, the landscape which they compose is round and symmetrical. And as the eye is the best composer, so light is the first of painters." Emerson, *Nature*, 14.

16. For quotes, see Ibid., 14.

17. Ralph Waldo Emerson, *Emerson in His Journals*, ed. Joel Porte (Cambridge, MA: Harvard University Press, 1982), 279 (March 20–23, 1842).

18. Emerson, *Nature*, 47.

19. "We've been trained to assume that an observer will always leave visible tracks," Crary writes, "that is, will be identifiable in relation to images. But here it's a question of an observer who also takes shape in other, grayer practices and discourses." Crary, *Techniques of the Observer*, 150.

20. Scholars working in a wide array of disciplines have investigated the human body as a point of departure for explorations of conceptions of identity, subjectivity, and "selfhood." See Janet Moore Lindman and Michele Lise Tarter, eds., *A Centre of Wonders: The Body in Early America* (Ithaca, NY: Cornell University Press, 2001); Ronald Hoffman, Mechal Sobel, and Fredrika J. Teute, eds., *Through a Glass Darkly: Reflections on Personal Identity in Early America* (Chapel Hill: University of North Carolina Press, 1997); Carla Mulford and David S. Shields, eds., *Finding Colonial Americans: Essays Honoring J. A. Leo Lemay* (Newark, DE: University of Delaware Press, 2001). An art historical variant of this scholarly interest can be found in Alexander Nemerov's engaging study, *The Body of Raphaelle Peale: Still Life and Selfhood, 1812–1824* (Berkeley: University of California Press, 2001). On vision's participation in the processes of culture, particularly in Renaissance Italy, see Baxandall, *Painting and Experience in Fifteenth-Century Italy*, 152. On possessive individualism, see C. B. Macpherson, *The Political Theory of Possessive Individualism: Hobbes to Locke* (Oxford: Oxford University Press, 1964).

21. Wendy Bellion, *Citizen Spectator: Art, Illusion & Visual Perception in Early National America* (Chapel Hill: University of North Carolina Press for the Omohundro Institute of Early American History and Culture, 2011).

22. The phrase is the title of William Kitchiner's, *The Economy of the Eyes: Precepts for the Improvement and Preservation of the Sight. Plain Rules which will Enable All to Judge Exactly When, and What Spectacles are Best Calculated for their Eyes, Observations on Opera Glasses and Theaters, and an Account of the Pancratic Magnifier, for Double Stars, and Day Telescopes* (London: Printed for Hurst, Robinson, & Co. Cheapside, 1824).

23. Emerson, *Nature*, 43.

24. See Richard Wollheim, *Painting as an Art*, Bollingen Series XXXV (Washington, DC: National Gallery of Art, in association with Princeton University Press, 1987); and Baxandall, *Painting and Experience in Fifteenth-Century Italy*.

25. See Crary, "The Camera Obscura and Its Subject," in *Techniques of the Observer*, 25–66.

26. Thus, I approach the formation of ideas about vision across cultural, economic, and scientific fields as an assemblage of the kind articulated in *A Thousand Plateaus*, the collaborative work of French

theorists Gilles Deleuze and Felix Guattari. "There is no longer a tripartite division between a field of reality (the world) and a field of representation (the book) and a field of subjectivity (the author)," they argue. "Rather," on the model of the rhizome, "an assemblage establishes connections between certain multiplicities drawn from each of these orders." Deleuze and Guattari, *Thousand Plateaus*, 23.

27. For more on their experiments, see Johann Wolfgang von Goethe, *Theory of Colours*. trans. with notes by Charles Lock Eastlake (1840; Cambridge, MA: MIT Press, 1970); Frederick Burwick, *The Damnation of Newton: Goethe's Color Theory and Romantic Perception* (New York: Walter de Gruyter, 1986), 9–53. On the important work of Czech physiologist Jan Evangelista Purkinje, see Nicholas J. Wade and Josef Brozek in collaboration with Jiri Hoskovec, *Purkinje's Vision: The Dawning of Neuroscience* (Mahwah, NJ: Lawrence Erlbaum Associates, Publishers, 2001); Johannes Müller, *Elements of Physiology*, trans. from the German with notes by William Baly, 2 vols. (London: Printed for Taylor and Walton, Booksellers and Publishers to University College, 1840); Daniel M. Albert and Diane D. Edwards, eds., *The History of Ophthalmology* (Cambridge, MA: Blackwell Science, 1998). For developments in American ophthalmology, see Alvin A. Hubbell, *The Development of Ophthalmology in America, 1800–1870* (Chicago: W. T. Keener & Company, 1908).

28. For an engaging analysis of this transformation in the understanding of vision, see Crary, *Techniques of the Observer*.

### CHAPTER ONE

1. Edward Reynolds, *Hints to Students on the Use of the Eyes* (Edinburgh: Thomas Clark, 1835), 5.

2. James Henry Clark, *Sight and Hearing, How Preserved and How Lost: A Popular Handbook* (New York: C. Scribner, 1856), 23–24. On the increased availability of printed matter and new forms of white-collar work in the antebellum period, see Stuart M. Blumin, *The Emergence of the Middle Class: Social Experience in the American City, 1760–1900* (New York: Cambridge University Press, 1989), 66–107; Richard D. Brown, *Knowledge Is Power: The Diffusion of Information in Early America, 1700–1865* (New York: Oxford University Press, 1989); Ronald J. Zboray, *A Fictive People: Antebellum Economic Development and the American Reading Public* (New York: Oxford University Press, 1993); Isabelle Lehuu, *Carnival on the Page: Popular Print Media in Antebellum America* (Chapel Hill: University of North Carolina Press, 2000); and David M. Henkin, *City Reading: Written Words and Public Spaces in Antebellum New York* (New York: Columbia University Press, 1998).

3. My account of ophthalmology's development in the United States draws on the following works: Alvin A. Hubbell, *The Development of Ophthalmology in America, 1800–1870: A Contribution to Ophthalmologic History and Biography* (Chicago: W. T. Keener & Company, 1908); Daniel M. Albert and Harold G. Scheie, *A History of Ophthalmology at the University of Pennsylvania* (Springfield, IL: Charles C. Thomas, 1965).

4. The "observer" and even more specifically what I am designating as the "optically enabled self" are actually effects of the construction of a new kind of subject or individual in the nineteenth century. As part of a much larger process of modernization coinciding with the Industrial Revolution, the production of manageable subjects through what Michel Foucault calls "a certain policy of the body, a certain way of rendering a group of men docile and useful," the subject is positioned by techniques of "subjection" and "objectification," as well as by "new procedures of individualization." *Discipline and Punish: The Birth of the Prison*, trans. Alan Sheridan (New York: Vintage Books, 1995), 305.

5. For more on medical specialization, see Charles E. Rosenberg, ed., *The Origins of Specialization in American Medicine: An Anthology of Sources* (New York: Garland, 1989). The trial-and-error nature of early American ophthalmic practice retained the character of the wider field of medical practice in the first half of the nineteenth century. See James H. Cassedy, *Medicine in America: A Short History* (Baltimore: Johns Hopkins University Press, 1991), 21–66. On early codification of the field, see Hubbell, *Development of Ophthalmology in America*; Albert and Scheie, *History of Ophthalmology*. For more on the spread of medical licensing and the formation of hospitals, see Joseph F. Kett, *The Formation of*

*the American Medical Profession: The Role of Institutions, 1780–1860* (New Haven, CT: Yale University Press, 1968). For the way the so-called medical gaze delineates the emergence of the clinical sciences at the end of the eighteenth century as reliant on sight and visibilty, see Michel Foucault, *The Birth of the Clinic: An Archaeology of Medical Perception*, trans. A. M. Sheridan Smith (New York: Vintage Books, 1994).

6. James H. Cassedy employs the terms *mainstream* and *sectarian* to differentiate between practitioners working in the early nineteenth century. *Medicine in America*, 25–33.

7. On Philadelphia as a center for surgical training and activity, see Hubbell, *Development of Ophthalmology in America*; and Albert and Scheie, *History of Ophthalmology*. The *American Journal of the Medical Sciences*, published in Philadelphia by the firm of Lea & Carey during the period under consideration, provided ophthalmologists with a stable venue for publication. But even popular magazines such as *Godey's*, *Putnam's*, and *Scientific American* occasionally featured articles on optics, vision, and sight. One such success is touted by ophthalmic surgeon Isaac Hays in his "Report of the Cases Treated in the Wills Hospital for the Blind and Lame during the Months of October, November, and December, 1838, with Observations," *American Journal of the Medical Sciences* 24 (August 1839): 48.

8. Hubbell, *Development of Ophthalmology in America*, 40.

9. Ibid., 43–47.

10. Their relationship may explain the magazine's interest in optical and ocular matters. For more on optical topics in *Littell's Living Age*, particularly as they contributed to Herman Melville's conceptions of eyesight, see my chapter, "Melville's Vision(s), Visual Perception, and the Daguerreotype, 1848–1853," in "'The Economy of the Eyes': Vision and the Cultural Production of Market Revolution, 1800–1860" (PhD diss., George Washington University, 2004), 392–469. On the surgical treatment of strabismus, see Hubbell, *Development of Ophthalmology in America*, 110–112.

11. The period also saw the foundation of a number of hospitals, infirmaries, and dispensaries for the care of both paying patients and those who could not afford treatment. For more on these institutions, see Charles E. Rosenberg, *The Care of Strangers: The Rise of America's Hospital System* (New York: Basic Books, 1987). As Elisha North asserts, "We had attended to eye patients before that time, but it occurred to us then that we might multiply the number of cases of that description and hereby increase our knowledge, advertising the public in regard to an eye institution. This was done, and we succeeded, although not to our wishes in a pecuniary view of the case. Our success or exertions probably hastened in this country the establishment of larger and better eye infirmaries." Elisha North, *Outlines of the Science of Life: Which Treats Physiologically of Both Body and Mind; Designed Only for Philosophers, and other Candid Persons. To Which are Added, Essays on Other Subjects* (New York: Collins and Co., 1829), quoted in Albert and Sheie, *History of Ophthalmology*, 46.

12. For more on the New York Eye Infirmary, see Edward Delafield, "Address Delivered at the Dedication of the New Building of the New York Eye Infirmary, 25 April 1856," quoted in Hubbell, *Development of Ophthalmology in America*, 19. On the Institution for Diseases of the Eye and Ear in Philadelphia, see ibid., 21. For more on other such infirmaries in Philadelphia and elsewhere, see ibid., 25–33.

13. William Campbell Posey and Samuel Horton Brown, *The Wills Hospital of Philadelphia: The Influence of European and British Ophthalmology upon it, and the Part It Played in the Last 100 Years in Developing Ophthalmology in America* (Philadelphia: J. B. Lippincott Company, 1931). The authors also note in one of their reports that in the 1860s the managers deplored the fact that "no provisions had been made in the hospital for people of color." This fact begins to give some outline to the racial makeup of those who successfully received treatment in facilities like the Wills Hospital. Albert and Sheie, *History of Ophthalmology*, 55–58.

14. Joseph R. Ingersoll, *An Address Delivered at the Opening of the Wills Hospital for the Indigent Blind and Lame, March 3, 1834* (Philadelphia: Printed by James Kay, Jr., and Co., 1834), 5–9.

15. These ingredients are listed in recipes for eyewashes written by the following: A. Otis, "Everyman His Own Painter: A Collection of Receipts by A. Otis," 1836; H. N. Pillsbury, "Recipe Book,"

1847; Pratt & Allen, "Daybook" (Boston, 1831–40); and James Bond, "Travel Journal through Part of Pennsylvania," 1822–1831; all in Joseph Downs Collection of Manuscripts and Printed Ephemera, Winterthur Library, Wilmington, DE.

16. Joan Burbick, *Healing the Republic: The Language of Health and the Culture of Nationalism in Nineteenth-Century America* (Cambridge: Cambridge University Press, 1994).

17. For more on Graham and the larger culture of health reform, see Stephen Nissenbaum, *Sex, Diet and Debility in Jacksonian America* (Westport, CT: Greenwood Press, 1980). For an example of popular physiological literature, see Orson S. Fowler, *Physiology, Animal and Mental: Applied to the Preservation and Restoration of Health of Body, and Power of Mind* (New York: Fowler and Wells, 1847); William A. Alcott, *The Young Man's Guide* (Boston: T. R. Marvin, 1834); and Alcott, *Vegetable Diet: As Sanctioned By Medical Men, and by Experience in All Ages* (Boston: Fowlers and Wells, 1838); as well Alcott's children's book, *The House I Live In*, part 1, *The Frame, For the Use of Families and Schools* (Boston: Light & Stearns, 1834).

18. Georg Josef Beer, *The Art of Preserving the Sight Unimpaired to an Extreme Old Age; and of Re-Establishing and Strengthening it when it Becomes Weak: With Instructions how to proceed in accidental cases, which do not require the Assistance of Professional men, and the Mode of Treatment Proper for the Eyes during, and Immediately after, the Small Pox To which are added Observations on the Inconvenience and Dangers arising from the Use of Common Spectacles, &c., &c. By an Experienced Oculist*, 2nd ed. (London: Printed for Henry Colburn, 1815), xiii–xiv.

19. Ibid., 20.

20. Ibid., 34.

21. Ibid., 29.

22. John Harrison Curtis, *A Treatise on the Physiology and Pathology of the Ear: Containing a Comparative View of its Structure, Functions, and Various Diseases* (London: Longman, Bees, Orne and Longman, 1836).

23. John Harrison Curtis, *Curtis on the Preservation of Sight, the Diseases of the Eye, and the USE, ABUSE, and CHOICE of Spectacles, Reading-Glasses, &c. Being Practical Observations for Popular Use*, 1st American ed. from the 2nd London ed. (Philadelphia: G. B. Zieber Co., 1848), 9–15.

24. Comparing the visual field of his own cultural moment with an imagined view of the visual experience of a mythic past, Clark wrote, "It is a wise provision of Providence that the functions of most organs, while in health, are performed without the necessity of care or attention on the part of the individual. The eye, however, is subject, more than any other organ, to man's control, and is peculiarly liable to abuse. In the native state, where the eye of man only met the carpet of green, and foliage of the same grateful color, when occupied with matters of general observation, when letters were not invented, when manufacture was in its rudest state, when men never engraved and women never stitched, and the eye was never taxed, as in a civilized condition of society, there was probably little demand for ophthalmic surgery. In this age of progress, of letters, and of multiform occupations, from the time that education is commenced to that period when active engagement ceases, earnest and practical people are ever taxing the eye to its utmost capabilities." James Henry Clark, *Sight and Hearing, How Preserved and How Lost: A Popular Handbook* (New York: C. Scribner, 1856), 23–24.

25. On clerks in the antebellum era, see Thomas Augst, *The Clerk's Tale: Young Men and Moral Life in Nineteenth-Century America* (Chicago: University of Chicago Press, 2003).

26. For quotes, see Edward N. Tailer Jr., Diary, December 15, 1849, New-York Historical Society, New York. I would like to thank Brian P. Luskey for pointing me to this diary and for generously sharing portions of his transcription. On the plight of clerks in the antebellum period, see his full-length study, *On the Make: Clerks and the Quest for Capital in Nineteenth-Century America* (New York: New York University Press, 2010).

27. Tailer, Diary, May 30, 1850.

28. Ibid.

29. Johann Christoph August Franz, *The Eye; a Treatise on the Art of Preserving This Organ in a Healthy Condition, and of Improving the Sight; to which is Prefixed, a View of the Anatomy and Physiology of the Eye, with Observations on its Expression as Indicative of the Character and Emotions of the Mind* (London: J. Churchill, 1839), 198–199.

30. Tailer, Diary, January 31, 1850.

31. Ibid., August 15, 1850.

32. Franz, *Eye*, 247–248.

33. Ibid., 249, 240.

34. Ibid., 249.

35. Tailer, Diary, August 15, 1850.

36. For more on the Pike firms, see Deborah Jean Warner's "Introduction," *Pike's Illustrated Descriptive Catalogue of Optical, Mathematical, and Philosophical Instruments* (1848; repr., Novato, CA: Norman Publishing, 1993).

37. Tailer, Diary, July 20, 1852.

## CHAPTER TWO

1. J. William Rosenthal, *Spectacles and Other Vision Aids: A History and Guide to Collecting* (San Francisco: Norman Publishing, 1996).

2. Daniel M. Albert and Diane D. Edwards, eds., *The History of Ophthalmology* (Cambridge, MA: Blackwell Science, 1998), 303–304.

3. Ibid., 305.

4. For more on Galen (c. 130 AD–c. 210 AD) and his work on the senses, see R. E. Siegel, *Galen on Sense Perception: His Doctrines, Observations, and Experiments on Vision, Hearing, Smell, Touch and Pain, and Their Historical Sources* (New York: S. Karger, 1970).

5. William Kitchiner, *The Economy of the Eyes: Precepts for the Improvement and Preservation of the Sight. Plain Rules which will Enable All to Judge Exactly When, and What SPECTACLES are Best Calculated for their Eyes, Observations on Opera Glasses and Theaters, and an Account of the Pancratic Magnifier, for Double Stars, and Day Telescopes* (London: Printed for Hurst, Robinson, & Co. Cheapside, 1824).

6. Ibid., 2, 32.

7. Kitchiner claims, "Opera glasses have been one of my favorite hobbies for the last thirty years—and to gain the information contained in these pages, I have carried my experiments to the greatest extent possible, for I think I have tried almost all apertures and all focal lengths," Ibid., 181–182.

8. But their movement required constant adjustment of one's opera glasses, a commodified analog to the faculty of visual accommodation. Kitchiner asserts, "The average distance, at which a common eye can see distinctly, the expression of the human countenance (in a good light) has been calculated to be about 15 feet. The average distance, between the actor and the spectator, in the boxes of a theatre, is about 4 times 15 feet, i.e. about 60 feet—therefore,—to shew distinctly,—an opera glass must magnify 4 times." Ibid., 178.

9. A reviewer for *Littell's Living Age*, writing in 1850, points out the following regarding Kitchiner: "He had the effrontery to request that every reader capable of gratitude would refuse to lend the work, and by tempting commendations seduce friends and acquaintances to buy copies for themselves. There was to be economy of the eyes, and economy to opticians, but economy towards Dr. Kitchiner was 'most intolerable and not to be endured.' When a tradesman is apprehensive that the sale of spectacles will be diminished by the treatise, the doctor chains him to his chariot-wheels, and drags him along in derisive triumph; but every purchaser of the treatise itself was to turn hawker to the doctor, and endeavor to force it unto unnatural circulation. No one, in short, was to be selfish except the author of the *Economy of the Eyes*, who had the weakness to confess his infirmity to the world, and ask their sympathy and assistance." *Littell's Living Age* 26, August 31, 1850, 386.

10. Kitchiner, *Economy of the Eyes*, 3.

11. Edward Hazen, "The Optician," in *The Panorama of Professions and Trades; or, Every Man's Book* (Philadelphia: Uriah Hunt, 1837), 246, 248.

12. From 1789 to 1799, the year he sold his stock to McAllister, Richardson was listed in city directories as "optical instrument maker" or "optician." Deborah Jean Warner, "Introduction," *Pike's Illustrated Descriptive Catalogue of Optical, Mathematical, and Philosophical Instruments* (1848; repr., Novato, CA: Norman Publishing, 1993), 292. For a helpful timeline of the McAllister firm's evolution, visit the Library Company of Philadelphia's website: http://librarycompany.org/mcallister/pdf/McAllister%20family%20business%20timeline.pdf.

13. "Register of Gold Spectacles," McAllister Papers, Hagley Museum and Library, Wilmington, DE, cited in Warner, "Introduction," n15.

14. Warner, "Introduction," 292.

15. The links between the Peale family and the McAllisters' firm are well known. For more on the spectacles in this painting, see Ellen Miles's entry for the work in the National Gallery's *American Paintings of the Eighteenth Century* (Washington, DC: National Gallery of Art, distributed by Oxford University Press, 1995), 48–57; and John Wilmerding, "America's Young Masters: Raphaelle, Rembrandt, and Rubens," in *Raphaelle Peale Still Lifes*, ed. Nicolai Cikovsky Jr. (Washington, DC: National Gallery of Art, in association with Harry N. Abrams, Inc., 1993), 73–93.

16. Rubens Peale, "Memorandum's [*sic*] of Rubens Peale and the Events of His Life &c," circa 1856. vol. 44, Peale-Sellers Family Collection, 1686–1963, American Philosophical Society, Philadelphia, PA.

17. On the Enlightenment and its influence on the Peale family's various endeavors, see Lillian B. Miller, *The Peale Family: Creation of a Legacy, 1770–1870* (New York: Abbeville Press, in association with the Trust for Museum Exhibitions and the National Portrait Gallery, Smithsonian Institution, 1996). See also, David R. Brigham, *Public Culture in the Early Republic: Peale's Museum and Its Audience* (Washington, DC: Smithsonian Institution Press, 1995); and David C. Ward, *Charles Willson Peale: Art and Selfhood in the Early Republic* (Berkeley: University of California Press, 2004).

18. Hazen, "The Optician," 246.

19. Scholars have debated the reasons for the inclusion of two pairs of spectacles in the painting. See Charles E. Letocha, "Rubens Peale and His Spectacles," *Journal of the American Medical Association* 258, no. 4 (July 24, 1987): 476–478; and Billie J. A. Follensbee, "Rubens Peale's Spectacles: An Optical Illusion?" *Survey of Ophthalmology* 41, no. 5 (March/April 1997): 417–424. For quote, see Follensbee, "Rubens Peale's Spectacles," 420.

20. Follensbee, "Rubens Peale's Spectacles," 420–421.

21. On the still-life paintings of Raphaelle Peale, Rembrandt's older brother, see Alexander Nemerov, *The Body of Raphaelle Peale: Still Life and Selfhood, 1812–1824* (Berkeley: University of California Press, 2001). See also Lillian P. Miller, ed., *The Peale Family: Creation of a Legacy, 1770–1870*.

22. For a well-researched "object lesson" probing the intersection of art, science, and commerce in the nineteenth century, see Simon Schaffer's brilliant essay, "A Science Whose Business Is Bursting: Soap Bubbles as Commodities in Classical Physics," in *Things That Talk: Object Lessons from Art and Science*, ed. Lorraine Daston (New York: Zone Books, 2008), 147–192.

23. In a report from Paris, published in *The Port-Folio*, Rembrandt described his technique of painting in encaustic (pigments mixed with hot wax): "I have resumed the task [of painting "heads"] with new vigour and improved materials in encaustic. It is only after nine years' experiments that I have succeeded in vanquishing certain difficulties that stood in the way of the facile execution. . . . I am pleased to assure you that the advantages surpass what I had even wished. No delay from the paint not drying, no cracking, no rotting of the canvas; a rapidity, a facility, a richness, a transparence, that leaves nothing to be desired." Rembrandt Peale, "Original Letters from Paris: Addressed by Rembrandt Peale to C. W. Peale, and Rubens Peale. For *The Port-Folio*," *Port-Folio* 4, no. 3 (September 1810): 275.

24. William Clay Wallace, *The Accommodation of the Eye to Distances* (New York: John Wiley, 1850), 3–4.

25. As Sichel explains, "Whatever may be the compass of vision, it is very important that the faculty of accommodation should be assiduously exercised; but not in a manner too constant, or too long continued in the same direction, that is, not always at short or long distances. It is necessary to exercise the sight alternately upon near and distant objects. The reasons for doing so are easily explained. In the first place, all exercise of the accommodating power is more or less fatiguing, since it is analogous to muscular action, and perhaps even consists in a kind of contraction of the muscles of the eye, as may be readily perceived in one's own person upon looking fixedly at very near or very distant objects. All excessive and irregular muscular action becomes fatiguing and injurious to the organ. On the other hand, an adjustment too long continued to distances always identical, whether at minimum or maximum, deprives the organ of vision of its power of adaptation to less or more considerable ranges, and may prolong or shorten the focal distance beyond due bounds, and permanently." Jules Sichel, *Spectacles: Their Uses and Abuses in Long and Short Sightedness; and the Pathological Conditions Resulting from their Irrational Employment*, trans. from the French by Henry W. Williams (Boston: Phillips, Sampson and Company, 1850), 24–25.

26. Ibid., 14

27. Albert and Edwards, *History of Ophthalmology*, 302.

28. Alvin A. Hubbell, *The Development of Ophthalmology in America, 1800–1870* (Chicago: W. T. Keener & Company, 1908), 122–123.

29. Thomas Hall Shastid, *An Outline History of Ophthalmology* (Southbridge, MA: Published by the American Optical Company, 1927), 580–581.

30. As Sichel points out, "In France and upon all the continent, the numbers of spectacles are regulated according to this rational principle which we have explained [according to a French measuring system]. In England and in America, these numbers [assigned to various lenses] are merely conventional. Thus, for instance, the No. 1, corresponds to our No. 48; the No. 2, to No. 36, etc. Beyond the inherent inconveniences of an arbitrary and irrational scale of numbers, this system has also two other very grave faults, viz: that of starting from too powerful a number, as we shall hereafter see; and that of a too rapid progression," Sichel, *Spectacles*, 20.

31. John Thomas Hudson, *Spectaclaenia; or the Sight Restored, Assisted, and Preserved by the Use of Spectacles; with Suggestions to Spectacle Wearers and Others as to their Choice, and Equitable Prices: Being an Epitome of Practical and Useful Knowledge on this Popular and Important Subject* (London: Printed for the Author, 1833), 29.

32. Ibid., 1.

33. Beals & Homer, printers, *Broadside of Daniel B. Widdifield, No. 141 Washington Street, Boston, Mass.*, circa 1850, Joseph Downs Collection of Manuscripts and Printed Ephemera, Winterthur Library, Wilmington, DE.

34. "The distance at which ordinary print is legible varies from twelve to twenty inches. . . . The shortest distance at which it can be seen with distinctness and without exertion, is from six to eight inches. Any one who habitually brings small objects nearer to the eyes than this may be considered short-sighted. The term myopia (I shut, the eye) has been applied to this condition, because short-sighted persons when looking at distant objects, are in the habit of half closing the lids." William White Cooper, *Practical Remarks on Near Sight, Aged Sight, and Impaired Vision; With Observations Upon the Use of Glasses, and on Artificial Light* (London: J. Churchill, 1847), 39–40.

35. *Poulson's Daily Advertiser*, September 1, 1825, n.p.

36. Kitchiner, *Economy of the Eyes*, 3.

37. Hudson, *Spectaclaenia*, 1.

38. Ibid., 1–2.

39. My phrase "society of spectacles" intentionally plays on that of Guy Debord, whose 1967 *The Society of the Spectacle* claimed: "The spectacle corresponds to the historical moment at which the commodity completes its colonization of social life. It is not just that the relationship to commodities is now plain to see—commodities are now *all* that there is to see; the world we see is the world of the

commodity." Guy Debord, *The Society of the Spectacle*, trans. Donald Nicholson-Smith (New York: Zone Books, 1995), 29.

40. All citations to "The Spectacles" will be to *Complete Stories and Poems* (Garden City, NY: Doubleday, 1966).

41. "The Blunderer. Being a Few Passages in the Life of a Short-Sighted Man. By the Author of the 'The Ordinary Man,'" published in *Knickerbocker Magazine* 9, no. 2 (February 1837): 114–118.

42. Poe, "Spectacles," 462–463.

43. William J. Scheick, "An Intrinsic Luminosity: Poe's Use of Platonic and Newtonian Optics," *Southern Literary Journal* 24, no. 2 (Spring 1992): 90–105.

44. For quote, see Poe, "Spectacles," 463. Johann Kaspar Lavater, *Essays on Physiognomy for the Promotion of the Knowledge and the Love of Mankind*, trans. Thomas Holcraft (London: G. G. J. Robinson, 1789). For more on the significance of the largeness of the eyes, see George Combe's *A System of Phrenology* (New York: Harper, 1849), 44–45; and Combe's *Lectures on Phrenology* (New York: Fowler and Wells, 1851), 107–108. A standard essay treating Poe's interest in phrenology is Edward Hungerford's "Poe and Phrenology," *American Literature* 2 (November 1930): 209–231.

45. Kitchiner, *Economy of the Eyes*, 12.

46. These are precisely the venues in which Jan Purkinje conducted a number of his experiments regarding "vision in its subjective aspects." For more on Purkinje, his experiments, and his findings, see Nicholas J. Wade and Josef Brozek in collaboration with Jiri Hoskovec, *Purkinje's Vision: The Dawning of Neuroscience* (Mahwah, NJ: Lawrence Erlbaum Associates, Publishers, 2001).

47. Poe, "Spectacles," 465.

48. W. J. T. Mitchell has explored the implications of these images in the essay "Metapictures," in his book *Picture Theory: Essays on Verbal and Visual Representation* (Chicago: University of Chicago Press, 1994), 35–82. On the famed duck-rabbit, see Ludwig Wittgenstein, *Philosophical Investigations*, 3rd. ed., trans. G. E. M. Anscombe (New York: Macmillan, 1967), 193–196.

49. Poe, "Spectacles," 470.

50. Ibid., 474–475.

51. Ibid., 475.

52. For quote, see Poe, "Spectacles," 480. Whether or not Poe wore spectacles himself is not known. It is certain, however, that for his numerous portraits, both painted and photographic, he chose never to wear them for the sitting. But Poe was no stranger to subjective vision. As his body of fiction demonstrates, the author's fondness for drink and opium, his predilection for the macabre, and his nervous anxiety surely filled his lived experience with the kinds of visual perceptions we now designate as "subjective."

53. See Leon Jackson, "'The Italics are Mine': Edgar Allan Poe and the Semiotics of Print," *Illuminating Letters: Typography and Literary Interpretation*, ed. Paul C. Gutjahr and Megan L. Benton (Amherst: University of Massachusetts, Amherst, 2001), 139–161.

54. Ralph Waldo Emerson, *Nature*, in *Ralph Waldo Emerson: Essays & Poems*, ed. Joel Porte, Harold Bloom, and Paul Kane, Library of American College (1836; New York: Literary Classics of the United States, Inc., 1996), 47.

55. Martin Jay, "Scopic Regimes of Modernity" in *Vision and Visuality*, ed. Hal Foster (Seattle: Bay Press for Dia Art Foundation, 1988), 3–23.

CHAPTER THREE

1. "Sketches of Life in New York," *Spirit of the Times: A Chronicle of the Turf, Agriculture, Field Sports, Literature and the Stage* 7, no. 23 (July 22, 1837): 182.

2. Ralph Waldo Emerson, "March 20–23, 1842," *Emerson in His Journals*, ed. Joel Porte (Cambridge, MA: Harvard University Press, 1982), 279.

3. "Bill-Sticking," *Albion, A Journal of News, Politics and Literature* 10, no. 15 (April 12, 1851): 170.

4. "Sketches of Life in New York," 182.

5. "Dead Wall Literature," *Eliza Cook's Journal*, *Littell's Living Age* 7, no. 551 (December 16, 1854): 518.

6. Philip B. Meggs, *A History of Graphic Design* (New York: Van Nostrand Reinhold Company, 1983), 156.

7. Philosopher Richard Wollheim calls this elusive figure the "spectator in the picture," which summons period tropes of seeing and visual practice. For more on this figure, see the chapter "The Spectator in the Picture: Friedrich, Manet, Hals," in his *Painting as an Art: The A. W. Mellon Lectures in the Fine Arts, 1984.* Bollingen Series XXXV, 33 (Washington, DC: National Gallery of Art, in association with Princeton University Press, 1987), 101–186. See also Chapters 5 and 6 in this book.

8. Some of these works include Damianus Moyllus's *A Newly Discovered Treatise on Classical Letter Design* (1480), Luca de Pacioli's *De Divina Proportione* (c. 1514), and Geoffroy Tory's *Champ Fleury* (1529).

9. "The Newsboys," *Literary World* 6, no. 160 (February 23, 1850): 169.

10. On the paths and trajectories of individuals moving through urban spaces, see Michel de Certeau, "Walking in the City," in *The Practice of Everyday Life* (Berkeley: University of California Press, 1984), 92–110.

11. For quote see George D. Strong, "Limnings in the Thoroughfares: The News-Man and News-Boy," *Knickerbocker; or New York Monthly Magazine* 15, no. 2 (February 1840): 141–142.

12. Nicolete Gray, *Nineteenth-Century Ornamented Type Faces* (1938; Berkeley: University of California Press, 1976), 11.

13. Elizabeth Harris, *The Fat and the Lean: American Wood Type in the Nineteenth Century* (Washington, DC.: Smithsonian Institution, 1983), 6.

14. W. Turner Berry, A. F. Johnson, and W. P. Jaspert, *The Encyclopedia of Type Faces*, 3rd ed. (New York: Pitman Publishing Corporation, 1963), 16.

15. For more on Caslon's life and work, see Johnson Ball's exhaustive biography, *William Caslon, 1693–1766: The Ancestry, Life and Connections of England's Foremost Letter-Engraver and Type-Founder* (Kineton, UK: Roundwood Press, 1973), especially, 336–374.

16. Daniel Berkeley Updike, *Printing Types: Their History, Forms and Use. A Study in Survivals* (London: Oxford University Press, 1922), 151.

17. Rollo G. Silver, *Typefounding in America, 1787–1825* (Charlottesville, VA: Published for the Bibliographical Society of the University of Virginia by the University Press of Virginia, 1965), 21, 28; Updike, *Printing Types*, 153. See also, *One Hundred Years: MacKellar, Smiths and Jordan Foundry, Philadelphia, PA, 1796–1896* (Philadelphia: MacKellar, Smiths and Jordan Foundry, 1896).

18. Maurice Annenberg, comp., *Type Foundries of America and Their Catalogs* (Baltimore: Maran Printing Services, 1975), 66.

19. A striking number of eighteenth-century printers in England and elsewhere, including Binny & Ronaldson in the United States, used as a text for display the passage from Cicero's Catiline Oration "Quousque tandem abutere, Catilina, patientia nostra," a custom begun by Caslon in 1734. Geoffrey Ashall Glaister, *Encyclopedia of the Book*, 2nd ed. (New Castle, DE: Oak Knoll Press: British Library, 1996), 473.

20. *Specimen of Printing Types from the Foundry of Binny & Ronaldson* (Philadelphia: Fry and Kammerer, Printers, 1812), n.p.

21. Gray, *Nineteenth-Century Ornamented Type Faces*, 13.

22. Although its origins are obscure, print historian A. F. Johnson and others generally concur that the fat face was the product of British founder Robert Thorne at the Fann Street Foundry in Chiswell Street, London. Both William Savage, author of *Practical Hints on Decorative Printing* (1822) and T. C. Hansard, author of *Typographia: An Historical Sketch of the Origin and Progress of Printing* (1824) credit Thorne with its invention. The date of Thorne's invention is also mired in controversy, as he never issued a specimen of his fat face types. His successor, William Thorowgood, showed Thorne's

jobbing types in a specimen of 1820. See A. F. Johnson, "Fat Faces: Their History, Forms and Use," *Alphabet and Image* 5 (September 1947): 43–55.

23. Johnson, "Fat Faces: Their History, Forms and Use," 44.

24. Gray, *Nineteenth-Century Ornamented Type Faces*, 11.

25. Rob Roy Kelly, *American Wood Type, 1828–1900: Notes on the Evolution of Decorated and Large Types and Comments on Related Trades of the Period* (New York: Van Nostrand Reinhold Company, 1969), 33.

26. Quoted in Kelly, *American Wood Type, 1828–1900*, 34. "Born in 1800 in Kingsborough, New York, Wells was apprenticed to William Childs, a printer in Johnstown, New York. By 1822 he had been released from his apprenticeship, married and had moved to Amsterdam, New York where he founded the town's first newspaper, the *Mohawk Herald*. By 1826, Wells had moved to New York City where he established a small printing shop at 194 Greenwich Street. Despite a few failed partnerships, Wells continued to operate a small jobbing shop, and during these years developed an interest in making wooden letters. In 1839, Wells partnered with Ebenezer Russell Webb, an employee of several years to form the company Wells & Webb, and established a plant on Water Street in Paterson, New Jersey. In the preface to his 1840 catalogue, Wells was able to remark on his success and on his role in improving the job printing industry. He notes the scarcity of large-scale types available for printing larger posters prior to his invention and the relative ease with which his wood types finally overcame prejudices against them. Webb oversaw the Paterson mill while Wells operated the New York offices. Wells & Webb moved from 38 Ann Street, in 1842, to the corner of Fulton and Dutch Streets, where they opened the first general printer's warehouse in America. Wells eventually sold his interest to Webb in 1854, but continued to manage the Paterson plant until 1856, when he withdrew from the wood type business altogether. Of historical interest, Abraham Lincoln appointed Darius Wells as postmaster of Paterson in 1861, a post he held for 13 years. Wells died a few years later in 1875." Kelly, *American Wood Type, 1828–1900*, 36–37.

27. Wells collaborated with David Bruce Jr., another typefounder in New York, in an effort to develop the means for mass-producing wood types, but this alliance was short-lived. Kelly, *American Wood Type, 1828–1900*, 36–37.

28. Ibid., 12.

29. Quoted in Ibid., 32. Kelly goes on to explain, "None of the larger types was identified as being wood at the place of specimen showing, but carried the information *only* in small type at the front of the catalogue, usually on the prices list."

30. "Puffing vs. Advertising," *Southern Planter* 19, no. 4 (April 1859): 247.

31. Ibid.

32. Herman Melville, *Pierre; or, the Ambiguities* (1852; Northwestern University Press & The Newberry Library, 1990), 249.

33. Presbyterian, "Moral of Placards," *Weekly Messenger* 9, no. 42 (July 3, 1844): 1836.

34. J. Luther Ringwalt, ed. *American Encyclopedia of Printing* (Philadelphia: Menamin & Ringwalt, J. B. Lippincott & Co., 1871), 143.

35. J. G. Kohl, "Placard-Printing in Vienna," *Illustrated Family Magazine; For the Diffusion of Useful Knowledge* 3, no. 1 (January 1846): 44.

36. Gray, *Nineteenth-Century Ornamented Type Faces*, 133.

37. Rudolf Arnheim, *The Power of the Center: A Study of Composition in the Visual Arts*, rev. ed. (Berkeley: University of California Press, 1982), 12–13.

38. This phenomena echoes what Roland Barthes in his 1980 meditation on photography, *Camera Lucida*, called "the studium," or "an *average effect* of a particular medium within its culture," which, as he suggests, "enacts a certain training" that enables observers to navigate the dense visuality of modern life. "Punctum," Barthes's second term, "will break (or punctuate) the *studium*." He continues, "it is this element which rises from the scene, shoots out of it like an arrow, and pierces me. A Latin word exists to designate this wound, this prick, this mark made by a pointed instrument: the word suits me all the better in that it also refers to the notion of punctuation. . . . This second element which will disturb the *studium*, I shall therefore call *punctum*; for *punctum* is also: sting, speck, cut, little hole—

and also a cast of dice. A photograph's *punctum* is that accident which pricks me (but also bruises me, is poignant to me)." Roland Barthes, *Camera Lucida: Reflections on Photography* (New York: Hill & Wang, 1997), 26–27.

39. In light of the ocular ailments exacerbated by the strain of seeing letters and words at varying distances, Barthes's description of the punctum's "sting," "prick," or "cut" assumes an added charge as this aspect of antebellum visuality threatened to become the new studium. For a useful interrogation of Barthes's formulations of "studium" and "punctum," see Michael Fried, "Barthes' Punctum," *Critical Inquiry* 31 (Spring 2005): 539.

40. J. G. Kohl, *Austria, Vienna, Prague, Etc., Etc.* (Philadelphia: Carey and Hart, 1844), 92.

41. John Walker, *The Philosophy of the Eye: Being a Familiar Exposition of its Mechanism, and the Phenomenon of Vision, with a View to the Evidence of Design* (London: Charles Knight & Co., 1837), 206.

42. "What we now call the visual word form area, or V.W.F.A. is a part of the cortical region of the brain that evolved to recognize basic shapes in nature, but can be redeployed for the recognition of letters or words." Oliver Sacks, "Reading the Fine Print: The Decline of Books for the Visually Impaired Is No Small Loss," *New York Times Book Review*, December 16, 2012, 35.

43. Jonathan Crary argues that one of the "consequences" of the emergence of physiological optics in the early nineteenth century, which "displaced modes of vision that had been predicated on the self presence of the world to an observer and on the instantaneity and atemporal nature of perception," was the "emergence of attention as a model of how a subject maintains a coherent and practical sense of the world." Citing the example of German composer Richard Wagner, whose cultural criticism was "partly framed around issues of attention and distraction," Crary suggests that the composer, who "deplored the "pervasiveness of distracted modes of cultural consumption," prefigured "some early twentieth-century debates about the effects of mass culture which articulated distraction as a term opposed to a self-conscious contemplative perception." *Suspensions of Perception: Attention, Spectacle, and Modern Culture* (Cambridge, MA: MIT Press, 1999), 4, 248.

44. Walker, *Philosophy of the Eye*, 206.

45. Ibid., 207.

46. E. H. Gombrich, "Standards of Truth: The Arrested Image and the Moving Eye." *Critical Inquiry* 7, no. 2 (Winter 1980): 237–273, quote 262.

47. Rudolf Arnheim, *Art and Visual Perception: A Psychology of the Creative Eye*, new version (Berkeley: University of California Press, 2004), 30. Another of Arnheim's concepts relevant to this study is that of "retinal presence": "The center of a circle can be visually present without being marked explicitly by, say, a black dot. The black dot would give the center 'retinal presence.' This means that it would be represented in the physiological pattern of retinal stimulation created by a corresponding pattern in the physical world. A black dot in the center of a circle drawn in ink on a piece of paper will be registered in the retinal projection of any healthy eye focused upon that paper." Rudolf Arnheim, *The Power of the Center: A Study of Composition in the Visual Arts* (Berkeley: University of California Press, 1982), 3.

48. Walker, *Philosophy of the Eye*, 158.

49. For a sense of period thinking on the visual interplay of printed forms and their backgrounds, see "White Printing," *Scientific American* 10, no. 31 (April 14, 1855): 234.

50. See Jonathan Crary, "The Camera Obscura and Its Subject," in *Techniques of the Observer*, 25–66. The monocular aperture of the camera obscura corresponded with the apex of the perspectival pyramid cenral to the formulation of single-point, linear perspective from Alberti to Panosfsky. Leon Battista Alberti, *On Painting*, trans. with introduction and notes by John R. Spencer (New Haven, CT: Yale University Press, 1970). Erwin Panofsky, *Perspective as Symbolic Form*, trans. Christopher Wood (New York: Zone Books, 1991).

51. Arthur Linksz, "The Development of Visual Standards: Snellen, Jaeger, and Giraud-Telon," *Bulletin of the New York Academy of Medicine* 51, no. 2 (February 1975): 278. See also, Paul E. Runge, "Eduard Jaeger's Test-Types (Schrift-Scalen) and the Historical Development of Vision Tests," *Transactions of the American Ophthalmological Society* 98 (2000): 375–438.

52. The narrowest sets, as Arthur Linksz explains, were expected to be discernible by the normal eye at the distance of one Viennese foot, the widest "across the street," at a distance of eighty feet. Using recently published and accepted figures for the position of those so-called cardinal points in a schematic eye, the width of the retinal image of that barely discernable white stripe could be calculated with some confidence. Jaeger included his original publication on visual acuity as an appendix to a book he wrote on cataracts and cataract surgery. This work was titled *Ueber Staar und Staaroperationen nebst aneren Beobachtungen und Erfahrungen* (Vienna: Seidel, 1854). Linksz, "Development of Visual Standards," 278.

53. French ophthalmologist Félix Giraud-Teulon came a bit closer to matching Snellen's invention. In 1862, the same year that Snellen published his monumental work, Giraud-Teulon presented a paper on the measurement of visual acuity by means of letters. Following Robert Hooke, who in 1705 established the critical one-minute visual angle, the angular distance that must, in the average, separate two contours if they are to be seen as two, Giraud-Teulon used not isolated letters but words consisting of lowercase letters the vertical strokes of which were of one-minute thickness and separated by clear spaces of one minute at a specified distance from one to two hundred feet. Ultimately, his system has been lost to history due to its lack of specifications and indeterminate methods for calculating visual acuity. Linksz, "Development of Visual Standards," 280–281.

54. Herman Snellen, *Test-Types for the Determination of the Acuteness of Vision* (Utrecht, Holland: Van de Weyer, 1862). Ironically, outside the field of ophthalmology there is little written on Herman Snellen, the ocular scientist who, with his fellow Dutch ophthalmologist Franciscus Donders, advanced the study of visual acuity that led to the publication of his *Test-types for the Determination of the Acuteness of Vision* in 1862. In spite of numerous proposed modifications since then, the Snellen optotypes are still the generally accepted standard for testing visual acuity. Yet the ophthalmologist responsible for the "Snellen E" that has helped to gauge our vision for over 130 years has gone relatively unnoticed.

55. Linksz, "Development of Visual Standards," 277.

56. James E. Lebensohn, "Snellen on Visual Acuity," *American Journal of Ophthalmology* 53 (January 1962): 153.

57. Ibid., 153–154.

58. On writing instruction and the various meanings conveyed by handwriting in the eighteenth and early nineteenth centuries, see Tamara P. Thornton, *Handwriting in America: A Cultural History* (New Haven, CT: Yale University Press, 1996).

59. American ophthalmologist Ezra Dyer, attending surgeon and member of the Board of Managers at Wills Eye Hospital from 1866 to 1873, is credited with introducing Snellen test types in America. See William Campbell Posey and Samuel Horton Brown, *The Wills Hospital of Philadelphia: The Influence of European and British Ophthalmology upon it, and the Part It Played in the Last 100 Years in Developing Ophthalmology in America* (Philadelphia: J. B. Lippincott Company, 1931), 109.

## CHAPTER FOUR

1. *The Mercantile Register, or Business Man's Guide. Containing the List of the Principal Business Establishments, Including Hotels, and Public Institutions in Philadelphia* (Philadelphia: H. Orr, No. 43 Chestnut Street, 1846), n.p.

2. A number of prominent easel painters, including but not limited to Benjamin West, John Quidor, William Sydney Mount, and Quaker minister Edward Hicks, began their careers in sign painters' shops.

3. In city directories for the years around 1800, few painters designated any sort of specialization. They often listed their trade simply as "painter," as opposed to "portrait" or "miniature" painter, or the more commercial designations of "ornamental," "house," or "sign" painter that became standard in the decades following 1820. For instance, in a Philadelphia city directory for the year 1800, Henry Pealer

of 115 Race Street, Thomas Pearce at the corner of Spruce and Dock Streets, and George Flake of 295 Arch Street uniformly designated their trade "painter and glazier." Cornelius William Stafford. *The Philadelphia Directory for 1800; Containing the Names, Occupations and Places of Abode of the Citizens, Arranged in Alphabetical Order* (Philadelphia: Printed for the Editor by William W. Woodward, 1800).

4. On single-painting exhibitions popular during this period, see Tanya Pohrt's essay "*Gallery of the Louvre* as a Single Painting Exhibition," in *Samuel F. B. Morse's "Gallery of the Louvre" and the Art of Invention*, ed. Peter John Brownlee (Chicago: Terra Foundation for American Art, distributed by Yale University Press, 2014), 77–84.

5. In addition to the firms of Murphy and McAllister, the same block of Chestnut Street also housed a job printing firm as well as that of an engraver. The physical proximity of these enterprises underscores their shared concern with the eye's economic potential, as something to attract with signs or broadsides, to please with prints and fine stationery, or to gauge and correct through optical examinations and spectacles of varying calibration. This cluster of visually oriented trades was echoed in New York City as the shops of opticians, sign painters, engravers, and daguerreotypists lined Broadway in the 1840s. To cite one example, Roach & Warner, manufacturers of optical, mathematical, and philosophical instruments stood at 293 Broadway in 1840, presumably across the street from the firm of Monroe & Derby, house & sign painters at 294 Broadway. A. E. Wright's *Boston, New York, Philadelphia & Baltimore Commercial Directory, and General Advertising Medium* (New York: A. E. Wright, 1840), 197, 212.

6. Edgar Allan Poe, Letter II (May 21, 1844), *Doings of Gotham*, ed. Jacob E. Spannuth with a preface, introduction, and comments by Thomas Ollive Mabbott (1844; Pottsville, PA: Jacob E. Spannuth, Publisher, 1929), 31.

7. "The City of Modern Ruins," *New-York Mirror*, June 13, 1840, 407. Diarist Philip Hone complained that his native New York was difficult to love since the "whole of it [New York] is rebuilt about once in ten years." *The Diary of Philip Hone, 1828–1851*, ed. with an introduction by Bayard Tuckerman (New York: Dodd, Mead & Company, 1910), 360.

8. Extending the so-called duplicity of print into public spaces, letterform signboards exacerbated the slippage between a sign's signfiers and its signifieds, marking crowded urban spaces and marketplaces with an opacity that effectively clouded commercial transactions and the appearances of commodities themselves. See Jean-Christophe Agnew, *World's Apart: The Market and the Theater in Anglo-American Thought, 1550–1770* (New York: Cambridge University Press, 1986). The obfuscation or "clouding" of social relations is, for Karl Marx, inherent to the commodity. See *Capital: A Critique of Political Economy*, vol. 1 (1867; New York: International Publishers, 1992), 76–78.

9. Henry Sampson, *A History of Advertising from the Earliest Times. Illustrated by Anecdotes, Curious Specimens, and Biographical Notes* (London: Chatto and Windus, Piccadilly, 1874); Frank Preserby, *The History and Development of Advertising* (Garden City, NY: Doubleday, Doran & Company, 1929).

10. Jacob Larwood and John Camden Hotten, *The History of Signboards, from the Earliest Times to the Present Day* (London: John Camden Hotten, Piccadilly, 1866), 1–20.

11. Rob Roy Kelly, *American Wood Type, 1828–1900: Notes on the Evolution of Decorated and Large Types and Comments on Related Trades of the Period* (New York: Van Nostrand Reinhold Company, 1969), 171.

12. This was especially true in England in the seventeenth century. Brobdingnagian signs became such a nuisance, that after the great fire in London in 1666, Charles II signed an act restricting their size and placement. Charles L. H. Wagner, *The Story of Signs: An Outline History of the Sign Arts from Earliest Recorded Times to the Present "Atomic Age"* (Boston: Arthur MacGibbon, 1954), 9–10.

13. Ibid., 6.

14. Some wholesale and retail outlets utilized distinct architectural idioms for commercial buildings, drawing inspiration, most notably, from certain elements of Greek revival style. But most shopkeepers, faced with the uniformity in size and appearance that resulted from the compacted spaces available for construction, opted to employ elaborate signs to distinguish their buildings from their neighbors. See Stuart Blumin, *The Emergence of the Middle Class: Social Experience in the American City, 1760–1900* (Cambridge: Cambridge University Press, 1989), 93.

15. Vincent Figgins, *Type Specimens of 1801 and 1815*, ed. with an introduction and notes by Berthold Wolpe (repr.; London: Printing Historical Society, 1967).

16. Ruari McLean, "An Examination of Egyptians," *Alphabet and Image*, no. 1 (1946): 44; Jock Kinneir, *Words and Buildings: The Art and Practice of Public Lettering* (New York: Whitney Library of Design, an Imprint of Watson-Guptill Publications, 1980), 36.

17. Kinneir, *Words and Buildings*, 46–50.

18. "The most fashionable letters for Signs at the present day, are the Roman capitals, in their usual or condensed form, the Antique letter, the Gothic letter, condensed, and the Oblique letter. The Roman capitals in their usual form, either with or without shading, on the account of the elegance of their appearance and distinctness of their lineations, are preferred to any others now in use, for which reason they have been the standing form of capitals in the English language for a great number of years. This form of letters is so common, and even children are so familiar with their construction, that a slight deviation from a correct form would be noticed by them." Orson Campbell, *Treatise on Carriage, Sign, and Ornamental Painting, Containing Directions for Forming the Principal Coloring Substance, Composition of Colors, Varnishing, Polishing, Smalting, Imitation Painting, &c, &c.* (De Ruyter, NY: Russell R. Lewis, Scott, Cortland Co., 1841), 40.

19. On these early pioneers of commercial photography, see George S. Layne, "The Langenheims of Philadelphia," *History of Photography* 11, no. 1 (January–March 1987): 39–52.

20. Campbell, *Treatise on Carriage, Sign, and Ornamental Painting*, 83

21. "White Printing," *Scientific American* 10, no. 31 (April 14, 1855)" 234.

22. Moreover, a painter like William Murphy certainly would have had reason to consult the McAllisters across the street, and it is not at all far-fetched to imagine McAllister directing his customers sampling various lenses to gaze across the street in order to determine which lenses enabled the most distinct view of the letterforms adorning the signs of a facing building.

23. Herman Snellen, *Test-Types for the Determination of the Acuteness of Vision* (Utrecht, Holland: Van de Weyer, 1862).

24. W., "A Trip to New York," *Mechanic Apprentice* 1, no. 7 (November 1845): 51.

25. William M. Bobo, *Glimpses of New-York City by a South Carolinian (Who Had Nothing Else to Do)* (Charleston, SC: J. J. McCarter, 1852), 11.

26. Andrew Gardner, "The Spectacle of Commercial Chaos and Order: Thomas Hornor's View of Broadway and Canal Street, 1836," *Visualizing 19th-Century New York*, 3, accessed October 28, 2016, http://visualizingnyc.org/essays/the-spectacle-of-commercial-chaos-and-order-thomas-hornors-view-of-broadway-and-canal-street-1836/. See also Ralph Hyde, "Thomas Hornor: Pictural Land Surveyor," *Imago Mundi* 29 (1977): 23–34.

27. Gardner, "Spectacle of Commercial Chaos and Order," 3. See also David M. Henkin, *City Reading: Written Words and Public Spaces in Antebellum New York* (New York: Columbia University Press, 1998), 49–68.

28. John Fanning Watson, *Annals of Philadelphia and Pennsylvania, in the Olden Time; Being a Collection of Memoirs, Anecdotes, and Incidents of the City and Its Inhabitants, and of the Earliest Settlements of the Inland Part of Pennsylvania, from the Days of the Founders*, 2 vols. (Philadelphia: J. B. Lippincot & Co., 1870), 591–592, 615.

29. M(arriot) Field, *City Architecture; or, Designs for Dwelling Houses, Stores, Hotels, etc. In 20 Plates, with Descriptions, and an Essay on the Principles of Design* (New York: G. P. Putnam & Company, 1853), 40–41.

30. Susan Stewart, *On Longing: Narratives of the Miniature, the Gigantic, the Souvenir, the Collection* (Durham, NC: Duke University Press, 1993), 89.

31. On the grid, see Dell Upton, especially chapters 5 and 6, "The Grid and the Republican Spatial Imagination" and "Gridding Consumption," in *Another City: Urban Life and Urban Spaces in the New American Republic* (New Haven, CT: Yale University Press, 2008), 113–179.

32. Stewart, *On Longing*, 89.

33. John Walker, *The Philosophy of the Eye: Being a Familiar Exposition of its Mechanism, and the Phenomenon of Vision, with a View to the Evidence of Design* (London: Charles Knight & Co., 1837), 206–207.

34. John M. Findlay and Iain D. Gilchrist, *Active Vision: The Psychology of Looking and Seeing* (Oxford: Oxford University Press, 2003), 83.

35. Ralph Waldo Emerson, *Nature*, in *Ralph Waldo Emerson: Essays & Poems*, ed. Joel Porte, Harold Bloom, and Paul Kane, Library of American College ed. (1836; New York: Literary Classics of the United States, Inc., 1996), 14–15.

36. On the vision of sailors, see "A Long-Sighted Subject," *Eclectic Magazine of Foregin Literature* 59, no. 4 (August 1863): 505.

37. Richard Henry Dana Jr., *Two Years Before the Mast: A Personal Narrative of Life at Sea* (1840; New York: Modern Library Paperback Edition, 2001).

38. On the oscillation between states of attention and distraction, see Jonathan Crary, *Suspensions of Perception: Attention, Spectacle and Modern Culture* (Cambridge, MA: M.I.T. Press, 1999).

39. John Thomas Hudson, *Spectaclaenia; or the Sight Restored, Assisted, and Preserved by the use of Spectacles; with Suggestions to Spectacle Wearers and Others as to their Choice, and Equitable Prices: Being an Epitome of Practical and Useful Knowledge on this Popular and Important Subject* (London: Printed for the Author, 1833), 1

40. Jules Sichel, *Spectacles: Their Uses and Abuses in Long and Short Sightedness; and the Pathological Conditions Resulting from their Irrational Employment*, trans. from the French by Henry W. Williams (Boston: Phillips, Sampson and Company, 1850), 10–13. Other titles include, in chronological order: William Kitchiner, *The Economy of the Eyes: Precepts for the Improvement and Preservation of the Sight* (London: Printed for Hurst, Robinson, & Co., 1824); John Harrison Curtis, *Curtis on the Preservation of Sight, the Diseases of the Eye, and the Use, Abuse and Choice of Spectacles, Reading-Glasses, &c. Being Practical Observations for Popular Use*, 1st American from the 2nd London ed. (Philadelphia: G. B. Zieber & Co, 1848); James Henry Clark, *Sight and Hearing, How Preserved and How Lost: A Popular Handbook* (New York: C. Scribner, 1856).

41. Sichel, *Spectacles*, 9–12.

42. William Clay Wallace, *The Accommodation of the Eye to Distances* (New York: John Wiley, 1850), 1–4.

43. Sichel explains, "Whatever may be the compass of vision, it is very important that the faculty of accommodation should be assiduously exercised; but not in a manner too constant, or too long continued in the same direction, that is, not always at short or long distances. It is necessary to exercise the sight alternately upon near and distant objects. The reasons for doing so are easily explained. In the first place, all exercise of the accommodating power is more or less fatiguing, since it is analogous to muscular action, and perhaps even consists in a kind of contraction of the muscles of the eye, as may be readily perceived in one's own person upon looking fixedly at very near or very distant objects. All excessive and irregular muscular action becomes fatiguing and injurious to the organ. On the other hand, an adjustment too long continued to distances always identical, whether at minimum or maximum, deprives the organ of vision of its power of adaptation to less or more considerable ranges, and may prolong or shorten the focal distance beyond due bounds, and permanently." *Spectacles*, 24–25.

44. Thomas Hall Shastid, *An Outline History of Ophthalmology* (Southbridge, MA: Published by the American Optical Company, 1927), 580–581.

45. *Illustrated Catalogue of Optical, Mathematical and Philosophical Instruments, for Sale by McAllister & Brother* (Philadelphia: William S. Young, Printer, 1855), 5–6.

46. Sichel, *Spectacles*, 14.

47. Helen Tangires, *Public Markets and Civic Culture in Nineteenth-Century America* (Baltimore: Johns Hopkins University Press, 2003), 95.

48. In his important study of the signifying aspects of marketplaces in early modern England, historian Jean-Christophe Agnew posits them as "places for seeing" defined by the movement of what

he calls "artificial" persons and commodities. Such traffic instigated certain "crises" of representation that Agnew traces in period theatrical productions. Jean-Christophe Agnew, *World's Apart: The Market and the Theater in Anglo-American Thought, 1550–1770* (New York: Cambridge University Press, 1986), 17–56.

49. Agnew, *World's Apart*, 40–41, 149–194.

50. David Henkin, *City Reading: Written Words and Public Spaces in Antebellum New York* (New York: Columbia University Press, 1998), passim.

51. "With respect to the author," writes literary historian Tamara Thornton, "type presented a blank countenance behind which the authorial presence was impossible to detect. The impersonal, mechanical aesthetics of the new typeface designs presented the visual counterpart of that unsettling blankness. In both cases, the opacity of print opened up the possibility of its duplicity, for who knew what lay behind the expressionless face of type?" Tamara Thornton, *Handwriting in America: A Cultural History* (New Haven, CT: Yale University Press, 1996), 31.

52. On the spatial and architectural manifestations of republican ideals of social and political transparency in the early United States, see Dell Upton, *Another City: Urban Life and Urban Spaces in the New American Republic* (New Haven: Yale University Press, 2008), particularly 113–179.

53. M(arriot) Field, *City Architecture; or, Designs for Dwelling Houses, Stores, Hotels, etc. In 20 Plates, with Descriptions, and an Essay on the Principles of Design* (New York: G. P. Putnam & Compmany, 1853).

54. Karl Marx, *Capital: A Critique of Political Economy*, vol. 1 (1867; New York: International Publishers, 1992), 76–87.

55. Upton, *Another City*, 16.

CHAPTER FIVE

1. On the "communication" revolution as an interrelated counterpart or addendum to the concept of "market" revolution advanced by historians such as Charles Sellers in the 1990s, see Daniel Walker Howe, *What Hath God Wrought: The Transformation of America, 1815–1848* (New York: Oxford University Press, 2007). See also, Angela Miller, *The Empire of the Eye: Landscape Representation and American Cultural Politics, 1825–1875* (Ithaca, NY: Cornell University Press, 1993).

2. The literature on these two technologies is vast and growing. For recent studies, see Aileen Fyfe, *Steam-Powered Knowledge: William Chambers and the Business of Publishing, 1820–1860* (Chicago: University of Chicago Press, 2012); and Jennifer L. Roberts, *Transporting Visions: The Movement of Images in Early America* (Berkeley: University of California Press, 2014). See also Richard Menke, *Telegraphic Realism: Victorian Fiction and Other Information Systems* (Stanford, CA: Stanford University Press, 2008); and Paul Gilmore, *Aesthetic Materialism: Electricity and American Romanticism* (Stanford, CA: Stanford University Press, 2009).

3. Allen Hutt, *The Changing Newspaper: Typographic Trends in Britain and America, 1622–1972* (London: Gordon Fraser, 1973), 45–46.

4. For instance, from the October 2, 1847, issue of *Niles' National Register* we get the following passage in which the "news" becomes a sort of metacommentary on receiving the news itself: "The painful suspense which pervaded all community last week in relation to the state of affairs in Mexico, left by previous accounts in so delicate a posture, has been increased from day to day during the present week. Until the morning of the 1st inst. *nothing whatever could be relied upon, was received. The reports got up meantime were numerous and contradictory* [emphasis added][gives report].... Since placing the above in type the southern mail has arrived with N. Orleans papers to the 24th and Mobile to the 25th. At New Orleans they had no late intelligence from the army—and the above contains all that the Mobile papers afford, except a verbal report that there had been a revolt at Puebla and that Gen. Scott's loss since leaving Puebla was about three thousand men." *Niles' National Register*, October 2, 1847, 65.

5. On Woodville's career and significance, see Francis S. Grubar, *Richard Caton Woodville: An Early American Genre Painter* (Washington, DC: Corcoran Gallery of Art, 1967); Elizabeth Johns,

*American Genre Painting: The Politics of Everyday Life* (New Haven, CT: Yale University Press, 1993); Justin Wolff, *Richard Caton Woodville: American Painter, Artful Dodger* (Princeton, NJ: Princeton University Press, 2002); and Joy Peterson Heyrman, ed., *New Eyes on America: The Genius of Richard Caton Woodville* (Baltimore: Walters Art Museum, distributed by Yale University Press, 2012).

6. On the mediation of the conflict, see Martha Sandweiss, Rick Stewart, and Ben W. Huseman, *Eyewitness to War: Prints and Daguerreotypes of the Mexican War, 1846–1848* (Fort Worth, TX: Amon Carter Museum and Smithsonian Institution Press, 1989); on the war as a source for sensationalist fiction, see Shelley Streeby, *American Sensations: Class, Empire, and the Production of Popular Culture* (Berkeley: University of California Press, 2002). On Woodville's techniques, materials, and changes made during the composition of *War News* and other paintings, see Eric Gordon, "Woodville's Technique," in Heyrman, *New Eyes on America*, 65–81.

7. President James K. Polk had asked Congress not for a declaration of war, but for authorization to bring the war to a "speedy and successful termination." Quoted in Heyrman, *New Eyes on America*, 99.

8. Mary Bartlett Cowdrey, *American Academy of Fine Arts and American Art-Union*, vol. 1. (New York: New-York Historical Society, 1953), 261.

9. Ibid., 5.

10. Roland Barthes, "The Reality Effect," in *The Rustle of Language* (New York: Hill & Wang, 1984), 141–148.

11. In his groundbreaking article, "All the World's a Code: Art and Ideology in Nineteenth-Century American Painting," art historian Bryan J. Wolf situates Woodville's arrangement of figures in *War News* at the center of the penny-press revolution that put inexpensive newspapers in the hands of the masses. Citing the convergence of economic imperatives and cognitive codes that bear on these figures and animate this charged space, Wolf leaves aside the perceptual actions of the bodies in the painting as well as the issue of their interconnectedness. Brian J. Wolf, "All the World's a Code: Art and Ideology in Nineteenth-Century American Painting," *Art Journal* 44, no. 4 (Winter 1984): 328–337.

12. Alexander Saxton, *The Rise and Fall of the White Republic: Class Politics and Mass Culture in Nineteenth-Century America* (London: Verso, 1990), 96.

13. Allen Hutt, *The Changing Newspaper: Typographic Trends in Britain and America, 1622–1972* (London: Gordon Fraser, 1973), 45–46.

14. George G. Foster, *New York by Gas-Light and Other Urban Sketches*, ed. with an introduction by Stuart M. Blumin (1850; Berkeley: University of California Press, 1990), 195.

15. Charles Dickens, *American Notes for General Circulation*, in *Works of Charles Dickens*, Library Ed. vol. 17 (1842; London: Chapman and Hall, 1866), 229, 271.

16. For astute analyses of the development of Morse's telegraph, the code that bears his name, and their implications for art and communication, see Lisa Gitelman, "Modes and Codes: Samuel F. B. Morse and the Question of Electronic Writing," in *This Is Enlightenment*, ed. Clifford Siskin and William Warner (Chicago: University of Chicago Press, 2010), 120–138; Roberts, *Transporting Visions*, 140–160; Jean-Philippe Antoine, "Inscribing Information, Inscribing Memories: Morse, *Gallery of the Louvre*, and the Electromagnetic Telegraph," and Richard Read, "Painting and Technology: Morse and the Transmission of Visual Intelligence," in *Samuel F. B. Morse's "Gallery of the Louvre" and the Art of Invention*, ed. Peter John Brownlee (Chicago: Terra Foundation for American Art, distributed by Yale University Press, 2014), 111–129, 131–147.

17. Howe, *What Hath God Wrought*, 2.

18. Ibid., 696.

19. On the telegraph and the role of electricity in the formation of aesthetic thought in the United States, see Paul Gilmore, *Aesthetic Materialism: Electricity and American Romanticism* (Stanford, CA: Stanford University Press, 2009), 29.

20. Quoted in Daniel Walker Howe, *What Hath God Wrought*, 697, and in William Earl Weeks, *Building the Continental Empire: American Expansion from the Revolution to the Civil War* (Chicago: Ivan R. Dee, 1997), 85.

21. William F. Channing, "On the Municipal Electric Telegraph; Especially in its Application to Fire Alarms," *American Journal of Science and Arts* 2nd ser., 13 (January 1852): 58–59, quoted in Gilmore, *Aesthetic Materialism*, 54.

22. Wolff, *Richard Caton Woodville*, 28.

23. Orson Squire Fowler and Lorenzo Niles Fowler, *The Illustrated Self-Instructor in Phrenology and Physiology with One Hundred Engravings, and a Chart of the Character* (New York: Fowler and Wells, 1849).

24. Quote taken from the title of Graham's 1839 opus, *Lectures on the Science of Human Life* (Boston: Marsh, Capen, Lyon, and Webb, 1839).

25. Two outstanding examples of this cautionary literature are John Harrison Curtis, *Curtis on the Preservation of Sight, the Diseases of the Eye, and the Use, Abuse, and Choice of Spectacles, Reading-Glasses, &c. Being Practical Observations for Popular Use*, 1st American from the 2nd London ed. (Philadelphia: G. B. Zieber & Co., 1848); and James Henry Clark, *Sight and Hearing, How Preserved, and How Lost: A Popular Handbook* (New York: C. Scribner, 1856).

26. For a particularly "textual" analysis of this trend, see David M. Henkin, "Print in Public, Public in Print: The Rise of the Daily Paper," in *City Reading: Written Words and Public Spaces in Antebellum New York* (New York: Columbia University Press, 1998), 101–136.

27. W. J. T. Mitchell, "Metapictures," in *Picture Theory: Essays on Verbal and Visual Representation* (Chicago: University of Chicago Press, 1994), 69–70.

28. Richard Henry Dana Jr., *Two Years Before the Mast: A Personal Narrative of Life at Sea* (1840; New York: Modern Library Paperback Edition, 2001), 274.

29. Wolff, *Richard Caton Woodville*, 55.

30. Wend Von Kalnein, "The Düsseldorf Academy," in *The Düsseldorf Academy and the Americans: An Exhibition of Drawings and Watercolors*, ed. Donelson F. Hoopes (Atlanta, GA: High Museum of Art, 1972), 13–14. An enormously important recent resource on the Düsseldorf Academy is Bettina Baumgärtel, ed., *The Düsseldorf School of Painting and Its International Influence, 1819–1918* (Düsseldorf: Museum Kunstpalast, Michael Imhof Verlag, 2011). See also Jochen Wierich's insightful essay, "Woodville and the Düsseldorf School," in Heyrman, *New Eyes on America*, 39–50.

31. Wolff, *Richard Caton Woodville*, 61.

32. William Gerdts, "Die Düsseldorf Gallery," in *Vice Versa: Deutsche Maler in Amerika, amerikanische Maler in Deutschland, 1813–1913*, ed. Katharina Bott and Gerhard Bott (Munich: Hirmer, 1996), 51.

33. Kalnein, "Düsseldorf Academy," 17.

34. Ann Fabian, *Card Sharps and Bucket Shops: Gambling in the Nineteenth Century* (New York: Routledge, 1999), 3–4. On confidence men, swindlers, gamblers, and their unwitting victims, see Karen Halttunen, *Confidence Men and Painted Women: A Study of Middle-Class Culture in America, 1830–1870* (New Haven, CT: Yale University Press, 1982). On deception in art, see James W. Cook's *The Arts of Deception: Playing with Fraud in the Age of Barnum* (Cambridge, MA: Harvard University Press, 2001), which engages with issues of visuality, first in regard to some of P. T. Barnum's illusionist spectacles and especially in his chapter "Queer Art Illusions," which examines late-nineteenth-century trompe l'oeil paintings. Another important book that deals more directly with visuality in the socalled Age of Barnum is Michael Leja, *Looking Askance: Skepticism and American Art from Eakins to Duchamp* (Berkeley: University of California Press, 2004).

35. "The Philosophy of Illumination," *Scientific American* 2, no. 7 (November 6, 1846): 51.

36. Svetlana Alpers, *The Art of Describing: Dutch Art in the Seventeenth Century* (Chicago: University of Chicago Press, 1983), 196.

37. For quote, see Henry Clay, "Speech on the Mexican-American War," TeachingAmericanHistory.org, accessed December 10, 2015, http://teachingamericanhistory.org/library/document/speech-on-the-mexican-american-war/.

38. Svetlana Alpers, "Looking at Words," in *Art of Describing*, 169–200, especially 192–207.

39. Alpers, *Art of Describing*, xxv.

40. American Art-Union, *Bulletin* 2, no. 2 (May 1849): 9–10.

41. Johns, *American Genre Painting*, 1.

42. Michael Warner, *The Letters of the Republic: Publication and the Public Sphere in Eighteenth-Century America* (Cambridge, MA: Harvard University Press, 1992).

43. In *Painting as an Art*, philosopher Richard Wollheim delineates a distinct kind of perception premised in the phenomenological experience of a painting's "twofoldness." The first and most fundamental operation of what he calls "seeing-in" involves the way our experience of a painting oscillates between an awareness of the marked surface and discerning something in the marked surface, or what Wollheim calls the painting's "recognitional aspect." In *War News*, commercial typography, commonly used to test visual acuity in the early to mid nineteenth century, conveys much of the painting's meaning and serves as a pictorial device for the thematization of vision's processes of accommodation and the limits of its acuity. Richard Wollheim, *Painting as an Art: The A. W. Mellon Lectures in the Fine Arts, 1984* (Washington, DC: National Gallery of Art, in association with Princeton University Press, 1987), 46.

44. The "space of the beholder," which Wollheim associates with the spectator of the picture, is pronounced and shaped by the outward orientation of several of Woodville's paintings, from the floorboards in the tightly compressed spaces of *The Card Players*, *Politics in an Oyster House*, and *Waiting for the Stage* to the outward-facing newspapers in this painting and in *War News* held forth for the inspection of spectators inside and outside the painting. To be a spectator, Wollheim suggests, "is not to be a certain kind of person: it is to fill a certain role." The space of the painting's viewer-reader is one also simultaneously occupied by its painter: a figure the art historian Michael Fried has called the "artist-beholder" positioned before his canvas. See Wollheim, *Painting as an Art*, in particular chapter 3, "The Spectator in the Picture: Friedrich, Manet, Hals," 101–186. The figure of the artist-beholder is pivotal to Michael Fried's reading of certain paintings by Gustave Courbet. See his *Courbet's Realism* (Chicago: University of Chicago Press, 1992).

45. Ralph Waldo Emerson, *Emerson in His Journals*, ed. Joel Porte (Cambridge, MA: Harvard University Press, 1982), 279 (March 20–23, 1842).

46. Mitchell, "Metapictures," 69–70.

### CHAPTER SIX

1. Andrew Jackson, "Farewell Address (A Political Testament), May 4, 1837," in *American Presidents: Farewell Messages to the Nation, 1796–2001*, ed. Gleaves Whitney (Lanham, MD: Lexington Books, 2003), 76.

2. On Edmonds's career as banker and artist, see Nichols B. Clark, *Francis W. Edmonds: American Master in the Dutch Tradition* (Washington, DC: Smithsonian Institution Press for the Amon Carter Museum of American Art, 1988). On issues of labor, paper money, and speculation in Edmonds's painting, see Peter John Brownlee, "Francis Edmonds and the Speculative Economy of Painting," *American Art* 21, no. 3 (Fall 2007): 30–53.

3. On the formation and circulation of antebellum character "types," see Elizabeth Johns, *American Genre Painting: The Politics of Everyday Life* (New Haven, CT: Yale University Press, 1993).

4. "Some seem to suppose that it is peculiar to Wall-street, or at most, that it is indulged in to a limited extent by the dealers in pork, cotton, and dry-goods . . . . Had we time and space we might show how this principle enters into all the ramifications of life—that those seeking the gain of money are not the only speculators: but that men, women, and children, are all endeavoring to acquire something of which they are not now possessed—in fact, that we are *all speculators*." "Speculation," *Merchants' Magazine and Commercial Review* 24, no. 6 (June 1851): 781.

5. "Exhibition of the National Academy of Design—No. II," *Literary World*, May 1, 1852, 316.

6. Theophilus Fisk, *Labor the Only True Source of Wealth; or, the Rottenness of the Paper Money Banking System Exposed, Its Sandy Foundations Shaken, Its Crumbling Pillars Overthrown. An Oration*

*Delivered at the Queen-Street Theatre, in the City of Charleston, S.C. July 4, 1837* (Charleston, SC: Office of the *Examiner*, 1837), 32.

7. In a late interview, philosopher Jacques Derrida called attention to paper as a bodily experience while underscoring its evanescence in the face of digital technology. "Paper is utilized in an experience involving the body, beginning with hands, eyes, voice, ears," Derrida said; "it mobilizes both time and space." With its history "tangled up with the invention of the human body," the "body of paper has a bodily hold on us." As it is written into the structures of political, economic, and cultural fields, something akin to what Derrida termed the "graphosphere," the body shares with paper a "sense of corporeality, extension in space, and the capacity to receive impressions." Calling it a "self or ego," Derrida equated the page with the person. Yet elsewhere in the interview he asked "Isn't paper always in the process of 'disappearing'—dying out—and hasn't it always been?" For all their distance from Edmonds's moment, Derrida's comments propose a structure for attending to the medium of paper, often overlooked in our singular attention to the information it conveys. Jacques Derrida, "Paper or Me, You Know . . . (New Speculations on a Luxury of the Poor)," in *Paper Machine,* trans. Rachel Bowlby (Stanford, CA: Stanford University Press, 2005), 44–50.

8. The period literature on apparitions and spectral illusions was profuse. See for example, Samuel Hibbert, *Sketches of the Philosophy of Apparitions; or, an Attempt to Trace Such Illusions to Their Physical Causes* (Edinburgh: Oliver & Boyd, 1824); David Brewster, "Spectral Illusions," *Spirit of the Times,* November 3, 1832, 3; "Optical Magic of Our Age," *Albion, A Journal of News, Politics and Literature,* May 19, 1849, 232; "Visions and Phantoms," from Reverend P. C. Baldwin's *Redemption of Sinners by the Free Grace of God* (Philadelphia, 1849), printed in *Christian Observer,* March 31, 1849, 49; "Optical Magic of Our Age," *Chambers' Journal, Littell's Living Age,* November 17, 1849, 319; and Reverend E. Pond, "Spectral Illusions: Their Causes and Laws," *Christian Review,* October 1, 1852, 594, among several others. For a recent study of spiritualism and the fine arts in the United States, see Charles Colbert, *Haunted Visions: Spiritualism and American Art* (Philadelphia: University of Pennsylvania Press, 2011).

9. The overlapping discourses of paper money, physiological optics, and spiritualism also contributed to what literary historian David Anthony has provocatively called the "radical imateriality" of the antebellum paper economy. David Anthony, "Banking on Emotion: Financial Panic and the Logic of Male Submission in the Jacksonian Gothic," *American Literature* 76, no. 4 (December 2004): 725.

10. On this emerging profession, see Maybelle Mann, "The Arts in Banknote Engraving, 1836–1864," *Imprint: Publication of the American Historical Print Collectors Society, Inc.* 4 (April 1979): 29–30, 35–36.

11. Francis W. Edmonds to John Worth Edmonds, January 22, 1829, Francis W. Edmonds Papers, William L. Clements Library, University of Michigan, Ann Arbor. On Edmonds's strong Democratic political connections, see Clark, *Francis W. Edmonds,* 19–35.

12. On the responsibilities of bank cashiers in the antebellum era, see J. S. Gibbons, *The Banks of New-York, Their Dealers, the Clearing House, and the Panic of 1837. With a Financial Chart* (New York: D. Appleton & Co., 1859), 70–104. Edmonds managed the daily affairs of the Leather Manufacturers' Bank (1832–1839) and the Mechanics' Bank of New York (1839–1855) and eventually served on the board of directors for the New York and Erie Railroad.

13. For quotes, see Jackson, "Farewell Address (A Political Testament), May 4, 1837," 76. A useful synthesis of "Jacksonian" history relevant to antebellum banking and commerce can be found in Harry L. Watson, *Liberty and Power: The Politics of Jacksonian America,* 2nd ed. (New York: Hill and Wang, 2006), 132–171. On Jackson's policies, including the ill-fated Specie Circular, and their effects, see Bray Hammond, *Banks and Politics in America: From the Revolution to the Civil War* (Princeton, NJ: Princeton University Press, 1957); Edward Pessen, *Jacksonian America: Society, Personality, and Politics* (Homewood, IL: Dorsey Press, 1969); and Howard Bodenhorn, *A History of Banking in Antebellum America: Financial Markets and Economic Development in an Era of Nation-Building* (New York: Cambridge University Press, 2000).

14. Francis W. Edmonds, *Defence of Francis W. Edmonds, Late Cashier of the Mechanics' Bank, Against the Charges Preferred Against Him by Its President and Assistant Cashier* (New York: McSpedon & Baker, 1855), 14–15.

15. Fisk, *Labor the Only True Source of Wealth*, 8.

16. Stephen Mimh, *A Nation of Counterfeiters: Capitalists, Con Men, and the Making of the United States* (Cambridge, MA: Harvard University Press, 2007), 13, 65.

17. Thomas Paine, *Dissertations on Government, the Affairs of the Bank, and Paper-Money: By the Author of Common Sense* (Philadelphia: Charles Cist, 1786), 45.

18. Ibid., 45.

19. On these and other metaphors for fluctuations in the antebellum economy, see Ann Fabian, "Speculation on Distress: The Popular Discourse of the Panics of 1837 and 1857," *Yale Journal of Criticism* 3, no. 1 (1989): 137.

20. On the economic subtext of Washington Irving's "The Legend of Sleepy Hollow," see Anthony, "Banking on Emotion."

21. "'Commercial Delusions'—Speculations," *American Review: A Whig Journal of Politics, Literature, Art, and Science* 2, no. 4 (October 1845): 341–357.

22. Thaddeus W. Meighan, "A Local Record of the Past and Present! Or the Ghost of Wall Street," *New York Illustrated Magazine of Literature and Art* 3 (January 1, 1847): 265.

23. "Exhibition of the National Academy of Design—No. II," *Literary World*, May 1, 1852, 316.

24. For quotes, see *St. Louis Daily Missouri Republican*, April 17, 1849; Andrew Warner, *Bulletin of the American Art Union* 2, no. 5 (August 1849): 10. Both reprinted in *The Rockefeller Collection of American Art at The Fine Arts Museums of San Francisco*, ed. Marc Simpson and Patricia A. Junker (San Francisco: The Fine Arts Museums of San Francisco, in association with Harry N. Abrams, Inc., Publishers, 1994), 125–126.

25. "The Fine Arts, National Academy of Design—The Pictures," *Home Journal*, May 8, 1852, 2–3.

26. For quotes, see Edward N. Tailer Jr. Diary, December 15, 1849, New-York Historical Society, New York.

27. Ibid., May 30, 1850.

28. Johann Christoph August Franz, *The Eye; a Treatise on the Art of Preserving This Organ in a Healthy Condition, and of Improving the Sight; to which is Prefixed, a View of the Anatomy and Physiology of the Eye, with Observations on its Expression as Indicative of the Character and Emotions of the Mind* (London: J. Churchill, 1839), 196–197.

29. Herman Melville, *Pierre, or The Ambiguities* (1852), The Writings of Herman Melville: The Northwestern-Newberry Edition, vol. 7, ed. Harrison Hayford, Hershel Parker, and G. Thomas Tanselle (Evanston, IL: Northwestern University Press and Newberry Library, 1990), 340.

30. Ibid., 341.

31. Herman Melville, "Bartleby the Scrivener: A Story of Wall Street" (1853), in *The Piazza Tales and Other Prose Pieces, 1839–1860*, The Writings of Herman Melville: The Northwestern-Newberry Edition, vol. 9, 13.

32. Ibid., 13, 19.

33. Ibid., 19-20.

34. Ibid., 25.

35. Ibid., 31, 28, 14.

36. Ibid., 32.

37. Ibid., 38.

38. Ibid., 32, 38, 41.

39. "Inscription for the Back of a Bank-Note," *Putnam's Monthly* , November 1853, 557.

40. This "sudden change in administration" may refer to the election of Franklin Pierce, who succeeded Millard Filmore.

41. "Phantoms," *Putnam's Monthly* , December 1853, 615.

42. See Jonathan Crary, *Techniques of the Observer: On Vision and Modernity in the Nineteenth Century* (Cambridge, MA: Zone Books, 1990), especially the chapter, "Subjective Vision and the Separation of the Senses," 67–96.

43. Jan Purkinje, *Observations and Experiments on the Physiology of the Senses. By J. Purkinje. Contributions to the Knowledge of Vision in its Subjective Aspect* (1825), in *Purkinje's Vision: The Dawning of Neuroscience*, Nicholas J. Wade and Joesf Brozek in collaboration with Jirí Hoskovec (Mahwah, NJ: Lawrence Erlbaum Associates, 2001), 67.

44. Ibid., 67.

45. On Edmonds's career and the painting's claustrophobic space, see Clark, *Francis W. Edmonds*, 102.

46. Franz, *Eye*, 196–197.

47. Sir David Brewster, *Letters on Natural Magic, Addressed to Sir Walter Scott, Bart* (London: John Murray, 1834), 5–6.

48. For quotes see Ibid., 15–16.

49. Ibid., 38.

50. John W. Edmonds and George T. Dexter, *Spiritualism, with an Appendix by Nathaniel P. Tallmadge*, 8th ed. (New York: Partridge and Brittan, 1853), 18–19.

51. Thomas Buckland, *The Hand-Book of Mesmerism, for the Guidance and Instruction of all Persons Who Desire to Practise Mesmerism for the Cure of Diseases and to Alleviate the Sufferings of their Fellow Creatures*, 3rd ed. (London: Bailliere, 1851), 16.

52. See John B. Newman, *Fascination; or the Philosophy of Charming: Illustrating the Principles of Life in Connection with Spirit and Matter* (New York: Fowlers and Wells, 1847), 17.

53. Jacques Derrida, "Paper or Me, You Know . . . (New Speculations on a Luxury of the Poor)," in *Paper Machine*, trans. Rachel Bowlby (Stanford, CA: Stanford University Press, 2005), 45–50.

# ~ INDEX ~

type: Antique, 86–87, 118 n.18, 120; display, 2, 60, 73, 78, 80, 81, 82, 84, 86, 87, 89, 92, 95, 97, 101, 102, 105, 106, 111, 117, 134; Egyptian letters, 96, 107, 118, 120–21, 132, 168; Egyptian paragon, 107, 121; fat face letters, 81, 86–88, 95, 96, 102, 118, 132; Gothic letters: 86–87, 96, 106–7, 118, 120–21, 132; modern, 83, 86–88, 96; ornamented letters, 95, 97; perspective letters, 96, 103–4; printers' type specimens, 6, 43, 61, 83–86, 88, 99–100, 112, 118; Roman letters, 83, 86–87, 89, 118, 120, 132, 168; sans serif letters, 107, 118, 120–21; "shaded" letters, 96, 103; "shadow" letters, 96; slab serif letters, 87, 118; type casting techniques: metal, 78, 83, 87–88; sand, 87; wood types, 78, 88, 89, 97, 99, 102

typefounders: artisans, 40; display types, 117–18; emerging field of, 8; Fry, Edmond, 87–88; foundry, 83; inventive, 102; Robb, Alexander, *Specimen of Printing Types and Ornaments*, 61; specimen books, 6, 43, 112, 118; typefounding, 109; Wells, Darius, 78, 89

United States Supreme Court, 24, 148

Van Buren, Martin, 149, 188, 190

vapor, 190, 192, 200

vision, 2, 4; ambulatory, 3; binocular, 6; Emerson, Ralph Waldo; 3; mechanics of, 4; model of, 4; objects of, 6; philosopher's, 3; physiological, 3; problems of, 4; properly functioning, 6; transcendent, 3

visual acuity: absence of visual standards, 73; accuracy, 73; commodity of, 61; cultural, 18; degree of, 41, 205; determination of, 55, 105–7; Gothic letters, 107; Jaeger, Eduard, 106; maps, 177; market economy, 38; measurement of, 41, 60, 67, 72, 105–6; Melville, Herman, "Bartleby the Scrivener," 195; ocular health, 11, 152; Peale, Rembrandt, 52, 55; Peale, Rubens, 53; production of, 45; Purkinje, Jan Evangelsta, 57; Snellen, Herman, 106; spectacles, 41; typefaces, 105; types, 109; Widdifield, Daniel B., 58–60, 72; widespread demand for, 128; widest possible range of, 2

von Goethe, Johann Wolfgang, 13, 181, 201, 205, 211; *Goethe's Farbenlehre*, 78, 202–3, 208

von Helmholtz, Herman, 23

Wallace, William Clay, 19; *The Accommodation of the Eye to Distances*, 56 n.24

Walker, John, *The Philosophy of the Eye*, 99, 101–2, 122, 127

Walton, H. H., *Treatise on Operative Ophthalmic Surgery*, 23

War of 1812, 63, 148

*A War President: Progressive Democracy*, **49**, 149

Washington, DC, 148, 150, 163, 199

Watson, John Fanning, *Annals of Philadelphia*, 123–25, 130, 132

*Weekly Messenger*, 93

Wells, Darius, 78, 88; with Webb, Ebenezer Russell, *Ten line Pica Roman, Antique, and Gothic fat face types*, **29**, 86–88

West, Benjamin, *Saul and the Witch of Endor*, **73**, 190–92

Wheatstone, Sir Charles, 206

White, Hagar & Co., 89

Widdifield, Daniel B., 58–60, 71–72, 105, 181; broadside for No. 141 Washington Street, Boston, 59

William H. Page Wood Type Co.: *Forty Line Clarendon, Ornamented, No. 4*, **34**, 98–99; *Various twelve-line shade letters*, **35**, 100; 89, 99, 182

Williams, Henry W., 129

Wills Eye Hospital (Philadelphia), 23, 25–26, 48, 57; *Wills Eye Hospital*, **6**, 26. See also Hays, Isaac; Ingersoll, Joseph; Littell, Squier

Wilson, Alexander, *American Ornithology*, 83

Wittgenstein, Ludwig, 69 n.48

Woodville, Richard Caton, 138–41, 144, 151, 158–59, 170–75, 206; Works: *The Card Players*, **55**, **57**, 160–61, 163–65, 167; *Old '76 and Young '48*, 171; *Politics in an Oyster House*, **56**, 161–63, 167; *Self-Portrait with Flowered Wallpaper*, **43**, 138–39; *Two Figures at a Stove*, 158; *Waiting for the Stage*, **59**, **60**, 165–68; *War News from Mexico*, **44**, **62**, 139–44, 150, 157–59, 167–68, 170–75, 177, 192, 204

Young, Thomas, 57

# ⇥ ACKNOWLEDGMENTS ⇤

All books accrue debts, and this one, stretched over many years, has accrued its fair share. My thanks begin with Rip Lhamon, who long ago offered advice, encouragement, and friendship. At The George Washington University, where this book began its life, I would like to thank David Bjelajac and Teresa Murphy, along with Melanie McAllister, Chris Sten, and John Michael Vlach for their guidance of this project in its infant stages and for their helpful criticisms of early drafts. Thanks also go to Barney Mergen for introducing me to American genre painting, to Melanie McAllister for being the first to suggest I read Jonathan Crary's *Techniques of the Observer*, and Jeffery Cohen, who assigned students in his critical theory seminar the task of analyzing Herman Melville's "Bartleby the Scrivener." During formative years in Washington, DC, Stephanie Batiste, Jim Deutsch, Brian Finnegan, Paul Gardullo, Frank Goodyear, Stephen Kidd, Denise Meringolo, Laura Schiavo, Margaret Whitehead, Betsy Wiley, and Sandy Zipp rounded out extensive seminar reading and discussion with great intelligence and good cheer. A big shout out to the Dang Gang, who over the years asked and heard about this project on numerous occasions and always cheered me on. And thanks to Peter Pachano for helping to track down images in New York archives, and for everything else.

Research for this project was generously funded by a Reese Fellowship in American Bibliography at the Library Company of Philadelphia; by a Patricia and Philip Frost Fellowship at the Smithsonian American Art Museum; a one-month research fellowship at the New-York Historical Society; a Barra Fellowship at Winterthur Museum, Garden & Library; and a Barra Foundation Fellowship at the McNeil Center for Early American Studies at the University of Pennsylvania. At the Library Company, thanks go to Jim Green, Cornelia King, Wendy Woloson, and Sarah Weatherwax for sharing their deep knowledge of and enthusiasm for printing history, printed ephemera, and photographs. An advanced-level internship, research assistanceship, and a Patricia and Philip Frost Fellowship in American Art and Visual Culture at the Smithsonian American Art Museum and the National Museum of American History provided the fertile ground and key financial support that helped to bring this project into existence. At the Smithsonian Institution, I thank former and current staff Lynda Roscoe Hartigan, George Gurney, Bill Truettner, Merry Foresta, Helena Wright, the late Richard Murray, Charlie McGovern, and Stan Nelson for their support and encouragement. At Winterthur Museum, Garden & Library, my fellow fellows in residence were collegial, smart, and fun: Ellen Avits, Michael Murphy, Melissa Duffes, and Stephanie Foote. My very productive and memorable semester of research there was graciously facilitated by Gretchen Buggeln, Neville Thompson, and Jeanne Solensky. Of the thriving early Americanist community in and around Philadelphia, I would like to thank in particular Daniel J. Richter, Martha Schoolman, Josh Greenberg, Cathy Kelly, Brian Luskey, and Roderick McDonald for good conversations and the avidity of their interests. For their encouragement, suggestions, questions, and help along the way, and for the example of their probing and articulate work in American art history and visual studies, I thank Ross Barrett, Wendy Bellion, David Bjelajac, Alan Braddock, Sarah Burns, Maggie Cao, David Peters Corbett, John Davis, Meredith Davis, Rachael DeLue, Ellery Foutch, Jennifer Greenhill, Patricia Hills, Michael Leja, Jennifer Marshall, Leo Mazow, Chris McAuliffe, Richard Read, Jennifer L. Roberts, Emily Shapiro, Joshua Shannon, Karen Sherry, Alan Wallach, Jason Weems, and Jochen Wierich.

I would also like to express my thanks to all those who invited and attended lectures drawn from this project at its various stages. I thank the audience for their questions and suggestions following talks in/at the Department of Fine Arts and Art History, The George Washington University; the Smithsonian American Art Museum; Winterthur Museum, Garden & Library; the McNeil Center for Early American Studies, University of Pennsylvania; the Department of American Studies, University of Massachusetts Boston; the Fine Arts Department at Syracuse University; the History of Art Department, University of California, Riverside; the Department of Art History and Archaeology, Washington University, St. Louis; and the Department of Art History, University of Minnesota, where I especially would like to thank Jennifer Marshall who provided just the occasion I needed to draft Chapter 6. At the University of Pennsylvania Press, I would like to thank Bob Lockhart, whose stalwart support, positive encouragement, pragmatic guidance, and, most of all, patience kept the project moving forward, slowly but surely. Over the years spent writing this book, the Terra Foundation for American Art provided an exceptionally interesting place to bring it to completion.

Portions of Chapter 1 appeared in the article "Ophthalmology, Popular Physiology, and the Market Revolution in Vision," published in the *Journal of the Early Republic* (Winter 2008). Portions of Chapter 6 were published in the article "Francis Edmonds and the Speculative Economy of Painting," *American Art* (Fall 2007). I thank the editors of those publications for generously allowing me to reprint that material here.

Most of all, I have my family to thank. To my mother and father, Jerry and Stevie, and to my grandmothers, Christine and Evelyn, and grandfathers, Erwin Franco and Andrew Jackson Brownlee, who told me stories and sparked my interest in things, who expanded my world, pushed me to work hard and play hard, and laid the groundwork for my career as a scholar, my gratitude and appreciation are immeasurable. Thanks to my brother, Jonathan, and my sister, Crissie, for always looking up to me. To my wife, Sandy Levinson, who patiently listened to my ideas while I conceptualized the first germs of this project around the turn of the last century and gracefully and persistently orchestrated the image permissions and index for this publication in the final stretch sixteen years later, I owe too much for words, for this and everything else she has done over the years to make this book possible. To her and our beautiful daughters, Sari Ava and Isla Jane, I lovingly dedicate this book.